AF520032

Library Without Walls

Ajay Pratap Singh
T.A.V. Murthy

Ess Ess Publications

4837/24, Ansari Road
Darya Ganj
New Delhi-110 002
Phone: 51563444
Fax: 51563334
E-mail: info@essessreference.com
url: http://www.essessreference.com

First Published 2005

ISBN: 81-7000-422-5

Rs.750/-

Published by:
Ess Ess Publications
4837/24, Ansari Road, Darya Ganj,
New Delhi-110 002.
Phone: 51563444
Fax: 51563334
E-mail: info@essessreference.com
url: http://www.essessreference.com

Printed in India at:
Printline, New Delhi

Contents

PREFACE

The human society is undergoing a transformation due to the rapid development and diffusion of Information and Communication Technology (ICT) in all walks of life. Large scale computerization enormous growth of electronic information and its worldwide access are the key factors of the present change. The Internet has added a new dimension to information technology, giving birth to the rich concept of Digital Libraries, Knowledge Management, and archiving of indigenous culture and heritage. Digital libraries have emerged as a crucial component of global information infrastructure. The impact of digital library is now considered so widespread and general that all subject periodicals have featured articles and majority of national/international conferences are focusing on various aspects of digital librarianship. The objective of this text is to provide a source suitable not only for university based library and information science courses on digital librarianship but one useful for library professionals in the field as well.

Few days back, after an intense analysis, Curriculum Development Committee of University Grants Commission suggested a number of changes in the course curriculum of library and information science courses and thereafter added several aspects of digital librarianship as part of the bachelor and master degree LIS courses. While adopting these recommendations most of the Indian library schools/departments have adopted all of these recommendation partially or fully.

Presently most of the Indian text on digital library is just focusing on the definition or exploring the applications of digital library. These are covering procurement and maintenance aspects of digital documents and therefore guide an information officer for maintaining a parallel library of digital objects along with the paper based library. While developing a digital library it is equally essential to convert the paper based worthwhile collection into the digital/digitized collection for easy and wider access. This book is designed to offer not only a basic understanding of the issues and elements involved in creating and maintaining an ideal digital li-

applications and libraries and nine chapters.

Chapter 1 provides an introduction to the field of digital library and some of the relevant issues like Indian digital initiatives, etc.

Chapter 2 deals with a discussion on all of the related aspects of digitisation technology and covers process of digitisation, establishment of digitisation laboratory and variety of file formats for specified purposes.

Chapter 3 continues the discussion of chapter 2 and provides an extensive note on various tools which are essential for digitizing documents. It covers both software as well as hardware aspects of digitisation process.

Chapter 4 introduces a topic, world wide web, which is relatively very popular among library community, a lot of information may be collected easily. Here the thrust area of coverage is the problem being faced by the world wide web users. It also discusses the development and maintenance of www.

Chapter 5 addresses the topic of designing and development of world wide web. It covers a number of technologies for the creation of an ideal multimedia based library portal over web. It also provides a list of application tools along with their features and availability.

Chapter 6 discusses a topic which is of prime importance for any information professional, it is Metadata. Digitisation of documents and making them available over a well developed library portal is not the only goal. The next step is to make the information searchable and thus provide an easy access to the user. Here various metadata standards have been discussed along with their full description.

Chapter 7 discusses the background and historical development of Artificial Intelligence and its application tool, Expert System. The main area of interest is the applicability of these concepts in the information profession for the refinement of its services.

Chapter 8 provides a background to Data Mining. It begins with a discussion of general purpose data mining techniques and then discusses the application of data mining to information profession. It further discusses OLAP and OLTP in terms of their usage.

then discusses the application of data mining to information profession. It further discusses OLAP and OLTP in terms of their usage.

Chapter 9 is the last part of this text and provides a brief explanation on the Data Warehousing concept. It presents various characteristics and process of data warehousing. Some of the models of data warehousing are also addressed.

Finally, we close the text with a glossary of technical terms and a list of suggested/consulted web sites, bibliography.

Ajay Pratap Singh
T. A. V. Murthy

PART I : DIGITAL LIBRARY

1
DIGITAL LIBRARY

Introduction:

Doorways to libraries are becoming gateways to the world as digital content, through new and constantly changing technology, becomes available. Organizational innovations are challenges that libraries face with digital complementing print, on site challenging remote access and recognition of the inter relatedness of the library function with scholarly communication. Coupled with technological innovations we need to establish a framework that is deeply tied to the core mission of our libraries, universities, archives and museums to enable quality and value added solutions to be addressed to ensure the long term progress towards our vision. The term digital library is now widely accepted to mean the use of digital technology in the provision of library services and operations, which include acquisition, organization, storage, conservation and dissemination of information to users.

Definition:

Digital libraries are still evolving and taking shape. At times the term digital is used interchangeably with electronic and virtual. Definitions of a digital library range from broad to narrow, with some disagreement on its actual function. Some prominent definitions of Digital Library are:

According to Lynch digital library is "an electronic information access system that offers the user a coherent view of an organised, selected, and managed body of information", This definition recognizes the more traditional role of a library or archive in the digital world, at the very least offering services, along with information.

The *Digital Library Federation* defines a digital library as "Organizations that provide the resources, including the specialized staff, to select, structure, offer intellectual access to, interpret, distribute, preserve the integrity of, and ensure the persistence over time of collections of digital works so that they are readily and economically available for use by a defined community or set of communities".

T.B. Rajashekhar defines the digital library as "a managed collection of information, with associated services, where the information is stored in digital formats and accessible over a network".

John Milard defines digital libraries as "libraries that are distinguished from information retrieval systems because they include more types of media, provide additional functionality and services, and include other stages of the information life cycle, from creation through use. Digital libraries can be viewed as a new form of information institution or as an extension of the services libraries currently provide."

Ian Witten, et a1 defines a Digital Library as "a collection of digital objects, including text, video, and audio, along with method of access and retrieval, and for selection, organization and maintenance of the collection".

According to *Williams Arms* "An informal definition of a digital library is a managed collection of information, with associated services, where the information is stored in digital formats and accessible over a network." A crucial part of this definition is that the information is managed. A stream of data sent to earth from a satellite is not a library. The same data, when organized systematically, becomes a digital library collection.

From the above definitions some of the important factors regarding Digital Libraries are:

* Digital libraries are organizations that provide digital information to users.
* The digital library comprise a managed collection of

electronic resources that is shared within a network which therefore means that anybody anywhere and at any time can have access to the information resources.

* Functions involved in the digital library are selection, structure, offer access, interpret, distribute information to users.
* Digital libraries are special forms of information retrieval systems.
* The digital library consists of a critical mass of digital information in different formats such as words, still images, moving images, sound and combinations either online or offline of all these made available on demand within an organized and ordered service framework to any user at anytime and anywhere in the world.

Access to Information in Digital Libraries:

Digital library resources can be accessed in a variety of ways, for example through:

* The web site of institute or library.
* The web site of specific digital libraries such as NDLTD, NCSTRL, NZDL, ACM digital library, PubMed, etc.
* Subject Gateways, such as SOSIG, Biz/ed, OMNI, etc.
* Search service providing agencies, such as Dialog, Ovid online, Proquest, etc.
* Web search tools: search engines including meta search engines and speciality search engines like Google, AskJeeves, Kartoo, Vivisimo, etc. and directories like Yahoo.

Access to information in digital libraries is influenced by a number of factors. Several researchers have studied human information behaviour on the web, and the findings of such studies are quite relevant to digital libraries.

Building Effective Digital Library Community:

It is necessary to realize the principles set up for Digital

Library Initiatives through more concrete action plans. In order to establish and develop a significant corpus of digital collections that are relevant to the target community, several activities are essential for keeping in mind, some of them are:

* Developing guidelines for the selection of analog collections to be converted and existing digital resources;
* Educating community on DLI standards and best practices;
* Establishing management structure based on broad community participation with active links to state and national efforts,
* Removing barriers of policy and practice that may inhibit full citizen access to and use of the digital library.
* A collaborative management approach that encourages broad contribution to and use of the DLs will be the key to the success of the whole digital library enterprise. For which stringent actions needs to be taken such as:
    * Develop a resource strategy that addresses the need for support from both public and private sources to provide the means to build and maintain an infrastructure and to launch new initiatives.
    * Long term planning, collaboration and ongoing assessment will be key principles for ensuring success.
    * Fund raising for building the infrastructure and for starting digitizing projects.
    * Manpower development in a holistic way.
    * Adopt and promote common standards and best practices to create interoperability within cooperating entities and outside other digital libraries to:

- Ensure universal accessibility and protection of user rights,
- Optimize retrieval and navigation for a diverse spectrum of users while maximizing the amount and quality of the information that is captured in the system; and

- Assure archiving and enduring access.
- Attention to both current functionality and long-term sustainability in the selection of standards and practices will be critical to the success of the library.
- Monitor the digital library community for emerging and stabilizing standards and practices, and induce new standards as appropriate.
- Establish a comprehensive assessment program that involves ongoing feedback and wide dissemination of key findings.

POLICY AND STRATEGIC ISSUES ON DIGITAL LIBRARIES:

The digital library is basically a computer-based system for acquiring, storing, organizing, searching and distributing information in digital format to end-users. The growth and development of digital library involves digitization of library materials held at the traditional library, connecting users to the online and offline, integrating the networks and making materials on the World Wide Web available to users. The transformation of the traditional library system to digital will then depend on library policies, strategies and planning geared towards the digital libraries. The formulation of library policy and strategic planning is meant to guide libraries to successfully integrate traditional and digital formats.

The following are some of the crucial policy and strategic issues that need sincere attention for the successful implementation of the digital library.

Legal Issues:

The concept behind the development of the internet was that information was to flow freely among professionals and community members. With time authors and other information generators started publishing and posting information on the internet to have access to these materials, one must pay for the same. This calls for appropriate legal framework to address serious issues such as copyright, obscenity, intellectual property, communication laws etc. The *American Library Association* states that "Copyright issues are among the most hotly contested issues in the legal and legislative world; billions of dollars are at stake. Legal principles and technological capabilities are constantly challenging each other and every outcome can directly affect the future of libraries."

Indeed digitization is creating serious problems and strains on the traditional copyright issues. With digitization it is not easy to recognize a work of authorship posted on the internet. One may download an entire book from the internet, print it, and even make several copies and distribute them without being noticed. The policy should therefore address issues such as downloading and printing information from the internet.

Collection Development:

Now that the electronic initiatives are first sweeping the globe, libraries are also moving from the traditional library to the e-library. There is therefore need to either review the current collection development policy or formulate new ones based on digital collections. Some of the crucial issues to be addressed here include:

* Define the digital materials to be acquired i.e. online or offline materials such as CDs, DVs, video tapes, audio tapes etc.
* Determine whether it is necessary to retain the traditional library while developing the digital library.

Infrastructure:

This refers to the various infrastructure and equipment to be used for digitization, storage and access of information. The policy should address issues such as storage, space, and server capacity, networking hardware/software etc.

Access:

Once information has been generated it must be

disseminated to users. The policy should therefore address issues such as what should be posted on the Internet either full text or abstract. The policy may also address other issues such as:

* Who should have access to the information?
* Should there be subscription fee to access the resources etc?
* How will the disadvantaged members of the community e.g. the visually impaired get access to the resources?

Capacity Building:

The policy should lay emphasis on training and retraining of both end users and library staff in the use of IT based resources and services such as use of search engines, subject gateways, application software, online information resources, digitization etc. With the introduction of the digital library the roles of the librarian will be required to play the following roles:

* Multi-media user who are comfortable with a wide rage of electronic media and data formats.
* Connecting users with information and information systems.
* Evaluators shifting free and paid for resources on behalf of users.
* Metadata producers creating records of information sources in a variety of schemes.
* Negotiators dealing with publishers and suppliers particularly on software. Data and information licensing and collaborative sharing of ICT resources.

The library and information science curriculum will have to be revised and updated to include changes in the digital library environment.

Funding:

A digital library is an expensive undertaking. Funding is required to:

* Purchase the high quality digitization equipments to facilitate the digitization of current traditional library holdings.
* To train both staff and end users on the use of modern technology.
* Purchase of other machines such as servers, workstations etc.
* For the subscription of online and offline information resources.
* Purchase of appropriate software.
* Maintenance of the systems etc.

The policy should therefore identify the sources of funding.

Partnerships and Collaboration:

Digitization being an expensive initiative, there is need to collaborate with other libraries. The collaborating libraries may for example decide to contribute and acquire digitization equipments or pay for the subscription of digital information, of staff training, exchanging ideas, sharing digital information etc.

Awareness of Digital Resources:

There is little awareness in the developing countries on the value and importance of digital resources. Most people still prefer the print based information resources. The policy should then address issues of creating public awareness on the importance cf digital resources.

Bibliographic Control:

Traditional libraries have been compiling bibliographic details of information materials produced i.e. each country complies and publishes it national bibliography. Information materials in the digital library are massive and dynamic hence compiling bibliographic details is not possible. The policy should therefore address such issues.

Preservation:

There is serious problem in the preservation of digital

materials caused by the fact that digital information is very dynamic. The databases are always being updated. What one gets on the web site today now may not be there in the next few seconds. The digital media are fragile with a limited shelf life. Further still, the digital information on the storage devices with time will be rendered unreadable by obsolescence of technology, this is due to the fact that information technology evolves very fast and the old systems are no longer in use.

To preserve the digital information, libraries will keep on migrating information from one digital hardware and software configuration. The policy should address these issues. If preservation of digital resources will not be in place then future generations will look back at this time as a digital dark age- a time when, somehow, the records of human knowledge went missing.

Current Digital Library Scenario:

Recognizing the importance of e-resources in education, learning and research, the academic and research organizations in India have undertaken some initiatives to facilitate access to e-resources on the Internet some are as follows:

* *Indian Digital Library of Engineering, Science and Technology (INDEST)* sponsored by Ministry of Human Resources Development (MHRD), Govt. of India, offering consortium access to important full text journals published by major international publishers.
* *CSIR Consortium* sponsored by CSIR for providing access to Elsevier Science journals.
* *UGC-INFONET* for providing access to e-journals from selected publishers.
* *Forum for Resource Sharing in Astronomy and Astrophysics (FORSA).* A cooperative venture by a group of libraries for providing access to selected number of journals in the field of astronomy and astrophysics.

* *IIMs Consortium*. A cooperative venture for providing access to selected number of journals in the field of management.
* The National Informatics Centre in Delhi is maintaining a portal of Govt of India website. It contains full text resources on various activities of the government of India and of several institutions funded or approved by it. It has plans for e-granthalya up to district levels.
* The Central Secretariat Library, Department of Culture is creating a digital library of Gazette of India and Annual Reports of departments and ministries under the Govt. of India.
* Indian Academy of Sciences, Bangalore is publishing its journals in electronic form and offering open access to these journals via Internet.
* Indian National Science Academy, New Delhi has started publishing its journals in electronic form and offering open access to them via Internet.
* National Library, Kolkata: Digitization of rare and brittle books and other documents-English books and documents published before 1900 and Indian publications of pre 1920.
* C-DAC operates a mobile digital library *DDGS* (*Dware Dware Gyan Sampada*)
* The web portals, newspapers, and institutional websites contain lot of digital information and evolve as prototypes of digital libraries, though they lack many of the functionalities of the same.

Digital Library projects in India:

There are several examples of innovative applications of Digital Libraries in India. These range from capturing traditional knowledge to a digital library of doctoral level thesis and dissertations. Some of the most prominent initiatives are :

The Digital Library of India is an ambitious project of the Indian Institute of Science and the Ministry of Communications and Information Technology of the Government of India. The partners to this project include the Carnegie Mellon University USA and the National Science Foundation. This library has made available around 27,000 books on the Internet. The plans are to have around 500,000 books on the Internet by end 2004 and around 1 Million books on the Internet by end 2005.These books would be in Indian language interfaces and would be available to the remote rural parts of India. The Digital Library of India will be a great step forward in enabling the bridging of the knowledge divide between urban and rural peoples of India.

Honeybee experiment of the National Innovation Foundation and the Indian Institute of Management, Ahmedabad is a project by which innovations made by villagers to solve their problems are captured on video and stored in a PC in a multimedia database. This is then showed to other villagers of other villages and they are then encouraged to think of ways by which the idea being presented to them could also be implemented by them in their conditions. Examples include a tilting bullock cart to new ways of storing grain. This is an off-line digital library of innovations used to capture and disseminate knowledge to villagers in multimedia form.

BAIF Development Research Foundation, Pune in collaboration with IDRC Canada has set up a GIS based knowledge base of traditional knowledge of groundwater in districts of Maharashtra in India. Tribal folk in the Deccan region of India have the knowledge that the existence of a particular type of tree in that region of India would imply a very high probability of locating groundwater in that area. This traditional knowledge has been captured in this knowledge base and a mapping has been done. This digital library therefore contains mappings of groundwater locations in this region and is of great use to the tribal folk since it gives a consolidated view of the groundwater in their region. It also helps Governmental organisations to take effective water management measures.

The ***Traditional Knowledge Digital Library*** is a digital library of around 14 Ayurvedic books, which gives details of ancient Indian traditional medicine methods and the usage of various Indian herbs and medicinal plants based on ancient Indian wisdom. This digital library is a project of the Department of Indian System of Medicine and the National Institute of Science Communication along with the National Informatics Centre of the Government of India. This digital library could be of great use not only for its original objective of making international patent authorities aware of traditional Indian knowledge, but also to several practioners of the ayurvedic system of medicine for use in rural India. The Traditional Knowledge Digital Library, will have in the first phase classifications of around 2147 medicinal plants. The digital library will have interfaces in both Indian languages as well as foreign languages. Many developing countries with a rich traditional medicinal knowledge have approached the Government of India to help them build a similar digital library for their own countries.

The ***Mukhtabodha project*** is another attempt at building a digital library in Indian languages. Ancient texts in Sanskrit written on palm leaves and birch tree barks have been digitized and are available in the form of digital libraries. Around 262 ancient Vedic texts have been digitized and have been preserved in this digital library.

Nalanda project (Network of Automated Library and Archives) is a project of the National Institute of Technology Calicut in Kerala. This project works towards converting public domain texts in raw text format into e-books in PDF/HTML formats.

VIDYANIDHI Digital Library project is a project of the Department of Library and Information Sciences of the University of Mysore and the Department of Scientific and Industrial research of the Government of India. The objective of this Digital Library is to make available Ph.D. thesis and dissertations on the web. This project has the support of the Ford Foundation and will be of great use to students who would want to refer to the Ph.D. thesis of other students as a part of their research.

Other Initiatives:

While discussing the National and International initiatives for digital preservation, it may not be inappropriate to mention that no serious thought has gone at the national level, however at the international level we come across several such initiatives. Some of these are being mentioned here:

The Australian *PADI Project (Preserving Access to Digital Information)* at National Library of Australia has useful pointers to a number of these that can be reached at www.nla.gov.au/padi/topics/18.html that facilitates access to up-to-date information on aspects of digital preservation. The *LOCKSS project (Lots of Copies Keep Stuff Safe)* operating from Stanford University is conducting a worldwide trial with over 40 libraries and 30 publishers, addressing the issue of long-term preservation for access of electronic journal publications. LOCKSS is a set tools for marinating user access to journals, not an archive, and if this distributed project proves successful, it might provide models for long time preservation of other digital materials.

The most ephemeral content available on the web whose life is short lived, and hence such information is devoid of durable value. There are number of initiatives set-up to archive the websites of particular countries. The *National Library of Australia* (http://pandora.nla.gov.au/), the *Library of Congress*, USA (www.loc.gov/) has been awarded $100 million for developing a national programme for the preservation materials (in particular that which is only ever digital), the General Printing Office, USA (www.access.gpo.gov/) is archiving defunct government websites. In Europe, national libraries in Denmark, Sweden, Finland, UK are bogged down with the preservation issues concerning ephemeral information on the web.

There are also number of intra and inter-country collaborative endeavours underway to address digital preservation problems. Particular mention may be made of *Joint Information System Committee (JISC), the National Preservation Office (NPO)*, the British Library and other leading organizations in UK are establishing a Digital Preservation Coalition, (www.jisc.ac.uk/dner/preservation/) together with international organizations such as RLG and OCLC. Set up with an intention of dealing urgently with digital preservation issues in UK within international context.

In the more sophisticated collaborative research and development area, CMNet has had some exciting results. A few collaborative activities for illustrative purposes are Intelligent Agent and Image Retrieval, Semantic Sensitive Content-based Image Retrieval and Emperor's Digital Video and Informedia Technologies.

As a joint endeavor of National Science Foundation (NSF), Department of Defense Advanced Research Projects Agency (DARPA) and National Aeronautics and Space Administration (NASA) the formal project of DL started in 1994 under the DLI Phase I (http://dli2.nsf.gov/dlione/) for a period of 4 years (1994-98) that involved around US$ 24 million. This phase focused on investigation and development of underlying technologies for digital libraries and hence the research activities were targeted around three aspects i.e.; information storage (capturing, organization, categorizing); searching (browsing, filtering etc); and access (networking protocols, standards, etc). The major six projects undertaken in DLI in Phase I (1994-98) are:

* **University of California at Berkeley** - *Environmental Planning Library and Geographic Information Systems.*
* **University of California at Santa Barbara** - *Alexandria Digital Library project*; Spatially reference Map Information.
* **Carnegie Mellon University Project** - *Informedia Digital Video Library.*

* **University of Illinois at Urbana Champaign** - *Federating Repositories of Scientific Literature.*
* **University of Michigan Digital Library Project (UMDL)** - Intelligent Agents for Information Location.
* **Stanford University** - Interoperation Mechanisms Among Heterogeneous Services.

The Phase II (1999-2004) announced by NSF in February of 1998 was sponsored by the Library of Congress; the National Library of Medicine; the National Endowment for the Humanities, besides the ones who were in Phase I. This phase is concentrating more at applying those technologies and others in real life library situations. Test beds are developed at following universities:

* University of Arizona (High-Performance Digital Library Classification Systems: From Information Retrieval to Knowledge Management).
* University of California Berkeley Ire-inventing Scholarly Information Dissemination and Use).
* University of California Santa Barbara (Alexandria Digital Earth Prototype).
* Carnegie Mellon University (*Million books project*).
* Columbia University (A Patient Care Digital Library: Personalized Search and Summarization Over Multimedia Information)
* Harvard University (Operational Social Science Digital Data Library).
* University of South Carolina (A Software and Data Library for Experiments, Simulations, and Archiving).
* Stanford University (*Stanford Digital Technologies Project*).
* Tufts University (*The Perseus Digital Library Project*).
* Open Archive Inititiative (Digital Library Federation, the

Coalition for Networked Information, and from National - Science Foundation).

* *Gutenberg Project.*

* Networked Computer Science Technical Research Library - NCSTRL (Virginia Tech and Old Dominion University).

The Phase II tried to link the application of digital libraries, especially in facilitating teaching and learning processes. One of the major outcomes of second phase is developments such as Open Archived and distributed architecture and theorizing the digital library models.

INDIAN CONSORTIA INITIATIVES:

INDEST:

The Indian National Digital Library in Science and Technology (INDEST), set up by MHRD is a very successful open-ended consortium for benefit of mainly 38 institutions including IISe, IITs, NITs, IIMs and a few other centrally-funded Government institutions. Besides, a number of engineering colleges have joined this initiative with the financial assistance of AICTE. The Consortium operates through its headquarter set-up at the IIT Delhi. A National Steering Committee takes care of inter-institutional coordination and decisions on policy issues under the overall policy direction of the Government of India. A National Review Committee is responsible for overall policy, monitoring and coordination with UGC and AICTE for this Consortium. A good number of e-resources have been made available including ScienceDirect, IEL Online, Springer Verlag's link, Applied Science & Technology Plus, ABI Inform Complete, ACM Digital Library, ASCE Journals, ASME Journals, COMPENDEX and INSPEC on Ei Village, SciFinder Scholar, MathSciNet, Web of Science, J-Gate and JCCC.

CSIR Consortia:

The Council of Scientific and Industrial Research has 40 national laboratories carrying out R&D work in the areas of

Engineering, Biological, Chemical, Physical, Environmental and Information Sciences. Put together these laboratories subscribe to about 3100 unique titles by spending about Rs. 25 crores. More than US $ 1.3 million is spent on Elsevier titles alone. Based on the recommendation of the task force and the negotiation committee appointed by CSIR all 1700 Elsevier e-journals have been made available to all 40 laboratories since July 2002. The funding being from single source, CSIR consortia did not face much difficulty to make the payment. However there have been some problems in the matter concerned continued subscriptions to print titles as per the agreement by some laboratories. Few laboratories like NAL, NCL, IMTECH, NIO, RRLT have been providing access to Elsevier titles since quite some time. The negotiations with other publishers like Kluwer (550 titles) and Springer (450 titles) is in the advanced stage. Attempts have been made to make available the J-Gate Custom Contents for Consortia (JCCC) to all laboratories.

INFLIBNET Initiatives:

Information and Library Network (INFLIBNET), under the grants of UGC has given the access to many e-sources to a number universities and institutions. The sources include full text journals published by ACS, IOP, RSC and bibliographic databases like BIOSIS, SciFinder, J-Gate, INGENTA. Few more sources are in pipeline. It has set up UGC Infonet for giving access to many in-house and outside e-sources.

FORSA:

The *Forum for Resource Sharing in Astronomy and Astrophysics*, the consortia of Raman Research Institute, Indian Institute of Astrophysics, Tata Institute of Fundamental Research, Inter University Center for Astronomy and Astrophysics, National Center for Radio Astrophysics and Physical Research Laboratories has given access to 25 e-journals of Kluwer to their users with the payment of 12.5% over and above the print subscription. This consortium has successfully negotiated with publishers of Nature to provide access to its e-version at a price of almost 1/3 of the list price.

Consortia for IIMs:

Six Indian Institutes Management have formed a consortium and jointly approached the publishers of e-journals and databases in the area of Management, Social and Behavioral science source. They have been giving IP enabled access to e-journals - Elsevier (247 titles), Blackwell (268 titles), Kluwer (33 titles), Willey (3 titles). Apart from 25 titles free against print subscription, 2300 titles as a part of EBSCO databases and 800 titles as a part of ABI Inform database have been made available to users of IIM libraries electronically.

The usual terms like maintenance of print subscription with the identified base year, 10-15% surcharge over and above print subscription did apply to this consortium. They also provide access to 13 bibliographic databases selectively to different IIMs depending upon their subscription to the titles like ABI Infom, EBSCO, ECONLIT, GMID, Psycinfo, Sociofile etc. IIM Bangalore, alone claims the annual savings of Rs. 16.42 lakhs for accessing bibliographic databases. IIM consortia did not find any difficulties dealing with the publishers as they were able to make payment directly to the publishers individually.

ICICI Knowledge Park, Hyderabad:

ICICI Knowledge Park at Hyderabad has signed an agreement with Informatics India Ltd to provide access to J-Gate Custom Contents for Consortia service to four Hyderabad based and one Pune based R&D institutions. Initially this service is free for the members with the objective of making it self-sustaining in the later stage.

ISRO Initiatives:

The resource sharing initiative taken by ISRO libraries by avoiding duplicate subscription to bibliographic databases is expected to result in savings of Rs. 41 lakhs per year. Further, the proposed cancellation of duplicate journal titles by its centers is likely to save the surplus amount that could be used to provide access to e-journals for the benefit of the all centers. A move is there to form formal consortia for providing access to e-journals and also J-Gate Custom Contents for Consortia.

Presently various digital library projects are going on successfully in various libraries / organisations. At the same time government has also realised the need of digital library and providing funds through its various agencies. Now it's the duty of library community to take initiative for the conversion and development of the digital library while following national and international standards. For this purpose it becomes essential to convert the nature of library from text based to digitized information, which requires a chain of efforts, long term planning and technology based mordernisation of library.

PART II : DIGITISATION TECHNOLOGY

2
DIGITISATION

Introduction:

Technical Standards and Guidelines during digitization are the essential issues of the digitization process that should be taken care during the planning stages and discuss techniques for creating digital files that will conform to the guidelines. There may be valid institutional reasons for following or discarding different aspects especially in relation to the handling of original materials that may make certain processes unsuitable for that class of material. The fundamental issues associated with the digitization process are as follows:

Knowledge of Original Documents:

Having a good knowledge of the contents of the collections that are intended to be digitized will make it much easier to decide on processes and techniques for converting the originals to digital form. The physical processes required to create a digitized version of an original item depend on many factors, including:

* The format of the original - is it printed text, photographic material, video, audio etc.?
* The condition of the original - will it stands up to automated procedures (if used), will conservation be required before scanning?
* The size of the original
* The color content of the original and whether those colors are important.

For paper and photographic originals, issues to consider include the following :

Photographic media (transparencies, prints, and negatives)

* What size are the originals, are they all the same size? It makes for a smoother workflow if items of a similar size are grouped together.
* What proportion of the items have color content? Is it important to capture the color?
* What condition are they in, for example, are they dirty from heavy use? If they are dirty a better scan will be achieved if the items can be cleaned first.
* What format are they in? Slides in sleeves or strips will take longer to prepare for scanning and may cost more if a bureau is scanning them. Glass negatives are prone to breakage and require careful handling.
* Are the photographs flat or have they bowed? Bowed originals cause difficulties with focus and may need weighting down.
* What is the quality of the original? A bad original (i.e. out of focus) will not be improved by scanning.

Paper media:

* What size are the pages, are all items the same size?
* What general condition is the material in? Pristine pages will produce a better result and the scanning process may be able to be automated. Any damage in an original may be exacerbated by the scanning procedure.
* Can books that are bound be stripped to loose pages for scanning? Scanning from bound volumes is more complex and therefore expensive than from loose pages.
* Is there any artwork? - Is it black and white or color photographs or line art? Color scanning is generally more complex and resource intensive.
* Is the text size particularly small or large? Very small text may need a higher resolution to extract the information.

* Objects require a different approach. Artifacts, art works and sculptures cannot generally be successfully scanned using the techniques available for 'flat' media such as photographs. It will therefore be necessary to use photography, either traditional or digital, to get an image of the original.

Digitisation: A Technical Overview:

Digital preservation issues must be observed when producing digital content. A good baseline for creating a digital file that will be long-lasting and would be scan once for all purposes, this means that all the complex and expensive preparation work will only need to be done once. The digitization project should consider the value in creating a fully documented high-quality '*digital master file*' from which all other versions (e.g. compressed versions for accessing via the Web) can be derived. This 'digital master file' should be created at the highest suitable resolution and bit depth that is both affordable and practical. This master file then becomes the source for every other version of that item that the project will require, such as Web surrogates, versions for high quality printing and so on. The '*digital master file*' will become an archive version of the data - it remains as pure a representation of the original as possible. Ideally more than one copy should be stored on more than one media type and in more than one geographical location, thus providing a degree of protection against data corruption, media failure and physical damage to equipment. 'Surrogate' or 'access' versions of the digitized item can be created from the digital master file using image manipulation software such as Adobe Photoshop or Paintshop Pro.

Resolution and Bit-depth:

Resolution is usually expressed in *dots per inch* (DPI) and relates to the density of information that is captured by the scanning equipment. Broadly speaking, the higher the DPI the more detail is being captured. The amount of resolution required to get a useful image of an item is determined by the size of the original, the amount of detail in the original and the eventual use for the data. For example, a 35mm transparency will require a higher DPI than a 5x4 print because it is smaller and more detailed. An A4 sized modern printed document that is intended to be processed into a searchable text will need less resolution than a similar sized photographic original. There are also upward limits on resolution - file size is one (increasing resolution will increase the file size) and another is preventing the capture of extraneous information. For example, postcards are often printed on poor quality paper and if they are scanned at too high a resolution the texture of the paper will be captured and can obscure the content. There is also a point where putting more resolution into the capture process will no longer add value to the information content of the digital output. Suitable resolutions for digital master files for various media types are discussed in the HEDS Matrix and the JIDI Feasibility Study contains a useful table of baseline standards of minimum values of resolutions according to original material type. *Bit-depth* relates to the level of color that will be captured. A 'bit' is the binary digit that represents the tonal value of the pixel. As an overview, a 1-bit image is black and white (the pixel has 1 bit and is therefore black or white with no shades in between), an 8-bit image has 256 shades of either grey or color (28 = 256 shades), and a 24-bit image has millions of shades of color (224 = 16,777,216 shades). A detailed discussion of resolution, binary and bit depth can be found on TASI's Web pages and a good basic guide to color capture can also be found on the EPIcentre Web pages .

SCANNING EQUIPMENT:

Digitization equipment can be separated into 'contact' and 'no-contact'. 'Contact' equipment, i.e. flatbed scanners, requires that the original be flat against the scan bed to get a scanned image. This approach will only work if the original is flat or can be pressed flat without damage to it. No-contact equipment includes overhead scanners or book scanners and digital cameras that are able to obtain a digital image with the bare minimum of contact with the original. The equipment for scanning the originals will depend largely on the characteristics of the collection. In general terms, photographic materials are usually scanned on a flatbed or a transparency scanner while bound volumes and oversized flat materials such as maps and plans require a digital camera or an overhead scanner. The Feasibility Study for the JIDI project gives information about the type of equipment that is most suitable for broad groups of media types. If you have a mixed media collection then it may not be possible to use one scanner for everything. A flatbed that is ideal for high speed, high volume paper scanning may not be capable of the resolution required for high quality scans of transparencies. A digital camera studio set-up will be overkill for loose-leaf paper scanning and for most general photographic materials. Generally, it should make sure that requirements match the capability of the scanner. Look carefully at the resolution that the scanner is capable of, the scanner will often be listed with a maximum *optical resolution* and an interpolated or software resolution. The optical resolution is the figure to look for - *interpolated resolution* uses software to 'guess' the values of pixels that are between those that the scanner can optically register. Interpolation should be avoided in an archive-quality scanning exercise. Where resolution is listed as, for example, 600x1200 DPI the maximum optical resolution will be 600. The dynamic range of the scanner is important - it describes the tonal density of the information that the scanner will be able to capture and generally speaking the higher this is the better, particularly for dense originals such as photographic prints and transparencies. A good flatbed scanner is often the keystone to a scanning unit. Production level flatbed scanners usually have either an A4 or an A3 sized scanning area. Larger ones are available but are specialist equipment and therefore rather expensive. In order to choose a flatbed it is required to know the size of the originals, whether they are reflective (i.e. light is bounced off them to capture the image, as in photographic prints) or transmissive (light is passed through the original to capture the image, as in transparencies), the resolution and bit depth to be capture and the volume of the work to be done. The software that runs the scanner is also important. It should be straightforward to use and an ability to run batch scans will save time as the scan bed can be loaded with originals and more or less left to get on with it. The Digital Eyes Web site lists flatbeds by suitability and price. Color management software is essential to ensure that the digital representation is as accurate as possible. This can often be purchased with the scanner. RLG DigiNews December 1997 (Vol 3 number 3) has a technical review of color management software which is a good starting point. Transparencies can be scanned on a flatbed if it is capable of sufficient resolution and has a transparency adapter fitted that will shine light through the transparency into the scanning head. However, faster and potentially better results will be gained from a dedicated transparency scanner. These scan strips or mounted 35mm negative or positive transparencies to high resolutions. Scanning unmounted strips or single frame transparencies on a flatbed is difficult and time consuming because they have to be either placed in holders or taped to the scan bed to stop them moving in the heat of the light - using a transparency scanner can alleviate some of this effort and would be a good investment if 35mm is a considerable part of the collection.

Digital cameras:

Digital cameras are developing for both the home and professional market and are priced from several hundred to thousands of pounds. 'Home use' cameras are aimed at non-professional users for taking general casual photography. There are two kinds of professional digital camera; the first has developed from medical and industrial uses and is a complete unit. The second is where the film from a traditional camera is replaced with computer sensors that transmit the image to a computer rather than to film; this is known as a digital scanning back. The first type has been around for longer and has been used in imaging projects for several years. Digital scanning backs are developing for professional photographers as a replacement for traditional film cameras. One of the advantages of the scanning backs is that they use the lenses and camera body of a traditional professional camera. Professional digital camera set-ups will generally require the operator to understand the basics of photography.

IN-HOUSE SCANNING UNIT:

The conversion of the materials can be done either in-house on specially purchased or existing equipment or sent to an external agency. Setting up a digitization unit gives the institution the value of equipment and trained staff for future projects and the movement and treatment of the materials can be closely controlled. Using an external supplier to do the scanning means that the equipment and expertise of a third party can be exploited while the project team concentrates on their specialist area of the project. Both approaches have their merits but there are certain situations where the choices are more clear cut.

Major reasons for sending materials to a external agency for digitization rather than attempting to scan them in-house include that the originals are not capable of being scanned successfully in-house (for example the equipment is excessively expensive) or that the intended product is beyond the experience and abilities of the project - for example requiring advanced color management skills. As an example, the type of equipment used for the scanning of items such as bound books or microfilms tends to be so expensive that it may be difficult for a project to justify the expenditure on such equipment, particularly given the short life-span and high maintenance costs of scanning equipment. Other reasons for outsourcing may include where there is a large volume of work to be done in a short period of time or where the project has space, infrastructure or staffing constraints that preclude the setting up of in-house facilities.

Alternatively, the digitization manager may decide to use in-house resources for several reasons including that:

* The collection cannot be moved out of the institution.
* The collection is badly organized (organizing it well enough to send to an external supplier would be an excessive overhead).
* The digitization needs to be phased in small amounts over a long period.
* The digitization task is very simple.

There are some baseline infrastructure requirements for in-house digitization:

* A robust production level scanner which will be able to scan the originals to a suitable resolution.
* A powerful PC with lots of memory (at least 256Mb RAM) - or Mac equivalent.
* Plenty of system resources such as backup and write to media (e.g. CDROM) capacity.
* Software to assist the digitization.
* Experienced/competent staff to run the equipment and staff to oversee the process and quality assurance.

This is assuming that the in-house operation wants to approach anywhere near the unit prices of production available from outside agencies. A further reason why many digitization works are undertaken in-house is that the staff time, overheads and some consumables such as file storage can often be swallowed up by the institution and do not become apparent as a costed factor of the project, thus making this appear to be a cheaper option than out-outsourcing.

DIGITIZATION FORMATS:

Since computers have been employed for general business use the phrase 'Paperless Library' has been quoted as a goal for the modern Library and Information Centre. The same principal applies to the managers of archive drawings and photographic records, who have the facilities for the storage of their archives in digital format. The conversion of the original hard copy records into digital records is known as digitization. Broadly there are two approaches to achieve the required end product.

For line drawings the question needs to be asked as to whether the drawing is likely to be used and modified or is retained as an archive. If it belongs to an archival collection, the drawing is scanned and stored as a digital file on CD-ROM or DVD. If the drawing is to be used as a working drawing on a Computer Added Design (CAD) system, then the scanned data needs to be converted into vector data in an intelligent form i.e. in a way that replicates the same drawing if it had been produced originally on CAD.

Photographs are also scanned using the original negatives or transparencies if possible, if not then photographic prints. Old and damaged photographs can be cleaned and digitally repaired.

Three major issues related to storage of Digital information:

* The format of the digital data and any compression has a major effecting file size and a minor effect on quality.
* The resolution of the scanning is a balance between quality and file size.
* The storage medium can have an effect on retrieval times.

As computer storage is becoming less expensive, it supports to move towards higher standards, i.e. higher resolution. But it should be remembered that a relatively small increase in the resolution results in a proportionately high increase in file size. For example, a three color 8-bit image (RGB) at A4 is 100 Megabytes in uncompressed form at 600 dots per inch, but rises to 400 Megabytes at 1200 dpi.

Several raster-based file formats are available to store digitized information. Several new image file formats are also emerging. Many are limited to particular applications, such as digital capture devices or image manipulation programs. Others are destined for wider use, with their developers intending them to become official or de facto standards. It is a long and difficult process to create such standard formats and longer still for them to become widely used and suppol l ed.

Presently we have mainly six formats, which may be divided into two categories:

Open (Non proprietary) Formats	:	TIFF, PNG, GIF and JPEG 2000
Proprietary Formats	:	MrSID, DjVu, Genuine Fractals and Pixel Live/ VFZoom.

Here I will discuss all of these formats along with their features. Some of the earlier common file formats are also discussed in brief.

OPEN (NON PROPRIETARY) FORMATS:

Any digitization project will need to consider the long-term usefulness and accessibility of the images and this means choosing a file that is both an established industry 'standard' as well as a non-proprietary format. Some of these formats are discussed bellow:

Graphic Interchange Format (GIF):

The *Graphic Interchange Format* is an 8-bit (and under) indexed file type. It only offers a range of 256 (or less) different colors. These can either be a standard selection or an image-dependent selection by user-choice. It was designed in the early days of the Internet by Compuserve and works best for use with vector images using block colors, such as graphics. logos and banners. GIF uses LZW lossless compression which is a patented compression algorithm and for that reason should only really be used with caution. The amount of compression will depend totally on the type of image. A full color continuous tone image is unlikely to compress to less than 30% of its original size, however a solid color vector image should compress far more. The GIF file format supports layers allowing it to offer both transparency and animation.

Portable Network Graphics (PNG) file format:

The Portable Network Graphic (colloquially called 'PING') is an open raster image format. PNG is not so new. It was developed in 1995 as a replacement for the Graphics Interchange Format (GIF). It is normally used in either an 8-bit indexed version or as a 24-bit full color version, although there is also an infrequently used 48-bit version as well. It is a very versatile format, which offers either the advantages of loss less compression in full color or as a replacement of G I F in 8-bit form. It is suppotl ed by the W3C and IETF and expected to be released as ISO/IEC International Standard 15948. The latest version is PNG1.2.

PNG has provision to support a number of different compressions, but only one is currently defined for use within the format, the loss less 'Deflate' compression (also found in zip and pkzip formats). Deflate uses a combination of LZ77 and Huffman encodings, both of which are patent free. PNG compresses better than GIF, saving 5-25% for equivalent (i.e. 8-bit) images. and in higher bit modes it achieves good savings over an equivalent uncompressed TIFF image. A small caveat, although PNG is defined as lossless, some applications that write PNG images do actually throwaway a little image information in order to optimize the file size. This introduces loss and should be avoided. It can represent a lot more color information than the G I F. In addition to an 8-bit 'paletted' mode (256 colors, as in the G I F format), PNG adds two other modes, grayscale (up to 16-bits) and true color (up to 48-bits). PNG also allows color profile information to be stored within the file, enabling applications with color management systems to accurately reproduce the color on the screen or in print. Besides these PNG is Gamma correction, the PNG can record the gamma of the image (i.e. the brightness level), as it was set when the image was created. This feature enables the image to be automatically adjusted to display well on different monitors. Alpha Transparency Channel is also a prominent feature of PNG. GIF enables one of its 256 paletted colors to be declared transparent. At the same time PNG goes even further. In addition to its palette transparency, it others a full 'alpha channel' ranging from no transparency (i.e. opaque) through 254 levels of partial transparency to full transparency). This feature is primarily used in graphic design, supporting image fade-outs, drop-shadows, and the seamless overlaying of images. The next one is two-dimensional interlacing. The GIF's interlacing feature offers a way of progressively displaying (streaming) the image. It operates in one dimension, rather like a Venetian blind. PNG offers optional interlacing in two dimensions, building up the image horizontally and vertically at the same time, in 7 distinct passes (formally known as 'Adam 7'). It also interpolates the space in between while waiting for the actual data to arrive. Interlacing a PNG slightly slows its delivery, but enables the image to be understood by the viewer before it is fully downloaded.

Tagged Image File Format (TIFF):

By the mid-nineties there was some discussion about replacing CompuServe's GIF format, but the immediate prompt for PNG's development was a patent dispute. Unisys asserted their rights to the LZW compression that lay at the heart of the GIF format, forcing those developing software to pay royalties whenever they made use of GIF/LZW. In response, the new PNG format was hastily drafted. It avoided using LZW and other proprietary technologies and took the opportunity to improve on the GIF's functionality. It extended the bit-depth (from 8-bit to 48-bit), offered better color and gamma support, and better interlacing and transparency features.

In every respect the PNG exceeds the GIF. But one feature it doesn't support is animation. This is because there is a complimentary MNG (Multiple-image Network Graphics) format, finalized in 1999 and beginning to find some support.

In practice PNG was called 'the new GIF', since it seeks to replace it, but the PNG goes far beyond the GIF. Although the

GIF technically looses less in its compression, it is inherently lossy since it first shoehorns an image's color information into a palette with a maximum of 256 colors. The PNG might just as well be regarded as the new TIFF, since it offers lossless storage with an equivalent bit-depth. Despite its head-start and growing usage, there was some possibility that the PNG might not fully take hold if the more flexible JPEG 2000 achieves a good take-up and, ironically, the GIF turns into an open format.

It is still not widely used and it has taken some time for Web browsers and image application software to support it. Now PNG files have reasonable support among the leading browsers and can be created and manipulated within many image applications.

Joint Photographic Experts Group File Interchange Format (JPEG or JFIF):

The common JPEG compression and its corresponding file format were developed in the late 1980s by independent members of the Joint Photographic Experts Group (JPEG). In its core or 'baseline' form, the common JPEG is lossy. A later, loss less, version was developed (the JPEG-LS) but is rarely used. More successful was the addition of a progressive (streamed) display for the JPEG. This formed part of the original standard was not widely implemented until 1996. It divides the file into a series of scans of increasing quality, enabling the image to build up progressively as it is displayed.

JPEG is not actually a file type, but a type of compression proposed by the Joint Photographic Experts Group. It is a lossy compression and provide the best quality and lowest file size for continuous tone images. The amount of compression given to the file is chosen at the time of saving the file and allows for variation in quality against file size, as a rule of thumb, it is normally considered that a file compressed with JPEG to 10% of its original size will be visually acceptable with no obvious compression artifacts. However it is common if required, to compress right down to 2-4% if the lower quality is acceptable.

It is an open raster image format described by the ISO/IEC standard 15444, and ITU standard T.800. It is intended as a replacement for formats using the JPEG compression, particularly the JPEG/JFIF format commonly used on the Web, It is used within the JFIF file format that uses the file extension .jpg and we colloquially call the 'JPEG'. The baseline version of JPEG 2000 is known as 'JPEG 2000 Part I', and is usually given the extension.jp2 or, less often, .j2k.

From the late 1990s work began on a successor standard, the JPEG 2000 - which defines both the compression and its corresponding file format. JPEG 2000 uses state-of-the-art wavelet compression techniques that are capable of both lossy and loss less compression. Although JPEG 2000 includes some patented technology, efforts have been made to keep the baseline version license and royalty free. As a consequence, some other proprietary compressions and display features have been reserved for later versions of the standard.

JPEG 2000 Part I became an official standard at the end of 2000 and an extended version .jpx or 'JPEG 2000 Part 2', was approved in the following year. A number of other parts of the standard are being developed. These introduce new features (some of which are patented); deal with other types of images (e.g. the 'Motion JPEG' in Part 3) or with new applications (a 'wireless JPEG' in Part II).

Some of the features available within the baseline standard (Part I) are:

It supports very good compression, both loss less and lossy. The common JPEG compression was always lossy. In contrast, JPEG 2000 supports both lossy and lossless compression. JPEG 2000's compressions are based on wavelet techniques. The wavelet compression turns the image into waves and then generates a series of increasingly simplified versions. A lossless JPEG 2000 will contain all the information necessary to rebuild a complete wave, while a lossy JPEG 2000 image will make do with the simplified versions. JPEG 2000's compression is more efficient than other common compressions. It will deliver lossy images 3-5 times smaller than comparable JPEG images. Lossless JPEG 2000 images are necessarily larger, but are still generally half the size of the original uncompressed raster image. This is better than the lossless LZW compression (used in GIF and optionally in TIFF) or Deflate (used in PNG).

The common JPEG divides an image into very small (8x8 pixel) blocks and processes these independently. Where the compression is high (and quality low) the boundaries of the blocks begin to show. In contrast, the JPEG 2000's wavelet compression processes much larger areas of the image at once - sometimes the whole image. This avoids any blocking. The wavelet compression is also able to make a distinction between significant detail in the image, like edges, and less significant areas, for example, where there are slight variations in the color. At very high compression JPEG 2000 will still introduce artifacts (visible distortion in the image), but by concentrating its compression on the less significant parts it gives much better overall quality than a JPEG of the same file size.

PROPRIETARY FORMATS:

While PNG and JPEG are the new general open formats that will be seen in increasing numbers on the Web, there are other new formats that are worth being aware of. These are proprietary and tend to be used for specialized tasks. Four of these in some depth below are: MrSID. DjVu, Genuine FractalsTM and Pixel LiveTM (formerly VFZoom). The MrSID and DjVu formats specialize in encoding particular sorts of images.

MrSID deals with large pictures, plans or maps, *DjVu*, with documents containing a mix of text and image. Genuine Fractals and PixelLive specialized in a particular task, as scaling or enlarging images. If open formats can suffer through lack of use or patchy or inconsistent support, proprietary formats can be vulnerable to commercial pressures, since they are tied to the fortunes of one company. More positively, they can also benefit from significant investment in their development, a competitive environment that rewards innovation, and from synergies with other, associated commercial 'products'.

The formats below have something useful but their proprietary nature should urge some caution. MrSID, DjVu, and PixelLive are worth considering as Web display formats (though each currently requires a special viewer). However, they may not be the best choice for image archiving.

MrSID:

Multi-resolution Seamless Image Database (MrSID) file format shows the file extension '.sid'. It is designed to compress huge images seamlessly and allow selective delivery and decompression. Originally proposed as a format suitable for many different purposes, MrSID has concentrated on Geospatial applications, to which it is well suited. It is supported by the leading GIS software and used by official mapping agencies like the United States Geological Survey (USGS) and the National Imagery and Mapping Agency (NIMA), primarily as a delivery format. Long described as 'visually loss less' (i.e. lossy, but without too much obvious degradation), the latest version (3.0) introduces a truly loss less MrSID.

Like JPEG 2000 and DjVu, MrSID is based on wavelet compression. It is a good advertisement for this form of compression, achieving efficient and high quality lossy compression which varies according to the image content and color depth, but averages 20: I for 8-bit grayscale and 50:1 for 24-bit color. Of all of the wavelet-based formats, it best illustrates the zooming potential offered by the wavelet's multi-resolution approach. Instead of storing a handful of predetermined resolutions, as some other proprietary formats do, MrSID includes all the information necessary to rebuild the image at any size (i.e. resolution) up to 100%. The process of rebuilding the image can be observed when you use the MrSID viewer's sliding zoom facility: the image is instantaneously resized, but it takes a moment or two for all the fine detail to fill in.

Although it is a proprietary format, once displayed and zoomed a MrSID image can be easily 'exported' (resaved) into a TIFF format at any chosen resolution. Its developers promote it as a storage format, because of its efficient compression, but it is believed that its chief advantage is its delivery and display potential. Several big digital library projects have chosen MrSID to deliver large format cartographic materials, including the US Library of Congress.

DjVu:

DjVu is a screen/Web format and is more suited to 'mixed documents' (i.e. text and image) than to individual images. It was developed within the AT&T research labs in the mid-nineties, and then acquired and commercialized by LizardTech in 2000. Although it is a proprietary format, DjVu's specification is available for non-commercial use and there are several open source implementations of the decoder (viewer) available. Open encoders have also been developed, but these cannot really compete with LizardTech's software, which has kept the best compression engine to itself.

DjVu produces files that are 10-30 times smaller than a comparable GIF or JPEG, between 500 and 1000 times smaller than TIFF, and 50 times smaller than PDF, although results will vary considerably depending on the nature of the document and whether it is in color or black and white. The reason DjVu is so good at compressing documents is that it divides each page image into different components, treating hard lines and continuous tones in different ways. The lines on the page (e.g. text or drawn lines) are identified and pulled into a separate layer. They are then compressed using a bi-tonal (black/white) compression technique. The softer tones and colors are pulled into other layers and subjected to different compression techniques.

DjVu's bi-tonal layer is called 'DjVu Text'. It is kept at a high resolution (300dpi) and compressed and encoded using a version of the official JBIG2 standard (ISO/IEC 14492), which is more efficient than the Group 4 compression used by TIFF or PDF for bi-tonal compression. DjVu's bi-tonal encoding can be loss less. The tone and color layers are called 'DjVu Photo'. There are usually two, a foreground and a background layer. These have lower resolutions (100dpi and 25dpi respectively) and are compressed using a wavelet transform very similar to the one used in JPEG 2000 or MrSID.

The 'DjVu Text' and 'DjVu Photo' layers can be saved and used independently, but are commonly kept together within the 'DjVu Layered' format - usually just referred to as the DjVu format. This layered DjVu format is inherently lossy. DjVu handles multiple pages in one of two ways. It either bundles everything into one file. like a PDF, or it stores each page as a separate file. Metadata can be written into the file, and OCR'd (optical character recognized) text can also be included to facilitate text highlighting or searching.

This format can handle fairly large sized documents (up to 32,000 x 32,000 pixels equivalent to 100 x 100 inches at 300dpi), so is suitable for some large drawings, maps or plans. Anything bigger or purely photographic is better handled by MrSID or another format. DjVu does a particularly good job of representing handwritten letters, manuscripts and early printed materials. It provides crisp, clear text or line art while preserving the look and feel of the material on which it was written or printed.

Genuine Fractals and PixelLive/VFZoom:

It is useful to consider LizardTech's *Genuine FractalsTM* and Celartem's *Pixel LiveTM*/YFZoom together, since they perform a similar task - enlarging images. However, they do so in slightly different ways and using different technologies. Strictly speaking, they are not raster formats, but we include them here because they are used to encode types of images typically stored as rasters (i.e. continuous tone images, like photographs).

Most of the formats discussed above enable zooming, but they are only really intended to be zoomed up to full size (100%, pixel for pixel). Anything beyond this and the images will become pixelated (i.e. show their pixels). With a raster format, the only way to avoid this is to interpolate - to insert new pixels in between the existing pixels. Imaging applications like Adobe Photoshop and JASC Paint Shop offer good interpolations, but there are also dedicated interpolation products like S-Spline (http://www.s-spline.com/) and Xfile. Genuine Fractals and Pixel Live/VFZoom other alternatives to interpolation-converting the raster into a different form of information (fractal or vector) before enlarging and re-rasterising it.

Instead of leaving the image as a set of pixels, Genuine Fractals breaks the mage into small shapes (fractals), which are described mathematically and can be redrawn at a larger scale. This is done by opening up a raster image within the Genuine Fractals software or a Photoshop plug-in and specifying its new dimensions. Depending on the size and complexity of the image, the fractal encoding and enlarging can take a long time, often a number of minutes. Once enlarged, the images can be left in the Genuine Fractal "STiNg" format (with an .stn file extension) or can be re-saved into another format for printing or Web display.

In addition to resizing, a fractal approach has the potential to offer efficient image compression, by finding identical or near-identical shapes within the image and replacing them with the same equation. This functionality is available within Genuine Fractals, but the format is being promoted more for its scalability rather than its compression. It has attracted a strong following within the professional photographic community where it often used to enlarge images for printing.

Celartem's new *Pixel Live format* (launched mid 2003) is based on its earlier *VFZoom format* and still retains a .vfz or .pfz file extension. Like Genuine Fractals, it also avoids the simple raster matrix. In Pixel Live the pixels are converted into vector information (e.g. lines and shapes and fills), which, like the fractal, are capable of being mathematically described and drawn at a bigger size. The vector nature of this format is most easily seen when low quality versions of Pixel Live images are enlarged.

Unlike Genuine Fractals, the Pixel Live format serves as both a scaling and a display format (using a free Pixel Live Viewer). What is particularly interesting about Pixel Live as a display format is that the raster image is encoded at its original dimensions and delivered to the user at this size. Any vector enlargement takes place within the user's viewer, where it looks and acts like a zoom function. The earlier VFZoom format even allowed the user to resave and print the image at its increased dimensions. However, the newer Pixel Live format removes this functionality, making a greater distinction between the activity of scaling or resizing the image (which can now only be done within a PhotoShop plug-in called pxl Smart Scale) and merely zooming the image when viewing (which is what happens within the Pixel Live Viewer).

The Pixel Live format has other features that are intended to support its delivery and display. It offers a quality setting with 6 discreet levels (0-5). At level 5, the image is losslessly encoded and capable of being returned to its original raster format. But it is also possible to encode and view the image without its higher levels. This will reduce the file size, but will obviously involve some image loss. Another feature is Pixel Live's password protection option. When saved it is possible to set a username and password, which the user must enter if they are to view the image. A password-protected Pixel Live file is given a .pfz file extension.

FILE FORMAT FOR SPECIFIC PURPOSES:

There have been a number of image file formats that have been used. Of course, every year, this choice gets larger and larger as new file formats are introduced and it is not always immediately clear which tile format is the best one to use in any particular case. The choice should depend on a number of factors, which may vary according to how the users intend to use the file and what will be the pattern of usage in the information center. Each stage of the process, from capturing until delivery has its own requirements that may affect this choice. A brief look at some of these factors and guidelines for making the best choice from what is available.

File Formats for Capture:

This is the first step in the digitization process. When capturing images, it is important that they are all created at the highest possible quality and at a size appropriate for all subsequent uses. Errors at this point will certainly compromise the quality of the whole project and the only recovery option will be to go back and re-capture the original.

All digital capture devices originally capture values of Red, Green and Blue. The number of different describable colors (or tones of gray) will depend upon the 'bit-depth' of the device. Any modern device will be able to capture in at least 24-bit color (or 8-bit B& W), although many modern devices now offer to capture at higher bit depths, right up to 48-bit. The suggested format for this purpose is *TI FF* or the proprietary format of capture device.

File Formats for Master Archive:

The requirements of a file format for archiving are the same as for creation, the suggested formats: *TI FF* and *PNG*.

File Formats for Optimisation and Manipulation:

All image optimization and manipulation is undertaken within image processing software. Whilst carrying out this work, it can be useful to save the image in the proprietary format of the image processing software. Suggested formats for this purpose are image processing proprietary formats such as PSD for Photoshop, PSP for Paint Shop Pro and PNG for Fireworks.

However *TIFF* is still a good choice if the increased functionality of the proprietary formats is not required.

File Formats for Delivery:

Choosing the correct image file format for delivery probably poses the hardest decision with the biggest variety of choice. These are just some of the issues that will need to be considered:

* What is the intended use of the image after delivery?
* How much image resolution is needed to convey the intellectual content to the user?
* On what output device is the image going to be used - monitor, printer, projector?
* What are the capabilities of the output device?
* What bit depth can it handle?
* What is the required resolution?
* What bandwidth is available for delivery?
* Is the image for photo-realistic or presentation use?
* How is the image going to be delivered? CD-ROM, tape, W AP, Internet (modem or LAN/W AN connection)?
* Is there a requirement to add any watermarking or deal with any other digital rights management issue?
* Do the users require the image to be provided with any color profile or other color management information?

With so many considerations, combined with the proliferation of file formats, each designed for a specific use.

File Formats for Web Delivery:

For most digitization projects, the most common delivery format is simply a monitor with the images viewed through a Web browser interface. This makes the choice of file format easy as the current selection of Web browsers only support a small range of image file formats (*JPEG, GIF & PNG*), although this range can be extended with the use of the appropriate plug-in.

Delivering images through a Web browser has some inherent advantages and unfortunately some challenges. The main advantage is that (in common with all monitor delivery) images naturally look 'good' on a monitor where their perceived 'brightness' (the light is being transmitted to you, rather than reflected) hides many small deficiencies in quality that would compromise quality if the image was printed. On the other hand, present browsers have only limited image-viewing capabilities and are unable to 'zoom' in and out of the images. These browsers provide compression, however the amount and method of compression varies.

Web browsers currently support the following file formats:

JPEG (JFIF): *JPEG* is not actually a file type. but a type of compression proposed by the Joint Photographic Experts Group. It is used within the JFIF file format that uses the file extension .jpg. It is a lossy compression and will provide the best quality and lowest file size for continuous tone images. The amount of compression is varied on various range of colors (these can either be a standard selection or a image-dependent selection by user-choice). It was designed in the early days of the Internet by Compuserve and works best for use with vector images using block colors, such as graphics, logos and banners. GIF uses LZW loss less compression which is a patented compression algorithm and for that reason should only really be used with caution. The amount of compression will depend totally on the type of image. A full color continuous tone image is unlikely to compress to less than 30% of its original size, however a solid color vector image should compress far more. The GIF file format supports layers allowing it to offer both transparency and animation.

PNG: *The Portable Network Graphic* (colloquially called 'PING') file is an open source 'standard' that was introduced to overcome the possible patent problems associated with the GIF format. It is normally used in either an 8-bit indexed version or as a 24-bit full color version, although there is also an infrequently used 48-bit version as well. This makes it a very versatile format offering either the advantages oı lossless compression in full color (as an archive format) or as a GIF replacement in 8bit form. However it cannot compete with the JPEG in terms of producing high quality and small, full color images for viewing on the Web. The compression available from PNG in 24-bit mode is typical for a loss less compression providing a file of about 60-75% of the original size and in 8-bit mode it is much the same as G I F. PNG supports transparency (even variable opacity, although browsers do not!) but is not able to provide animation. Suggested formats and relevant uses are *JPEG, PNG, and GIF* file formats for PowerPoint or other Multimedia Programs.

The main influence on choice will be the available bandwidth for the delivery of this material. If there are still some bandwidth or performance restrictions (Internet, need to save on floppy or deliver on slow machine) then it will make sense to use some of the file formats suggested for Web delivery, however if the presentation is to be delivered locally from a fast machine, then there is no reason to not use images of a correspondingly higher quality. Suggested formats for monitor delivery are *JPEG. PNG and GIF*.

PROCESS OF DIGITIZATION:

Now it is clear that digitization is an exciting preservation option while providing unparalleled access available to all. The technology is advancing rapidly and this raises the question of accepted standards for digital preservation technology. The standards for image capture, resolution, data transfer protocols, indexing, access, and file types must be of sincere consideration. Some of the important considerations are as follows:

Defining your requirements:

The first consideration before even thinking about equipment is to define the end use of the images. On this will depend what resolution of images and what file sizes are required, and hence the equipment and time scales involved. It is also essential to consider how you will store and access the scanned images and to ensure that your budget includes the cost of the right software to meet your requirements.

Choose the right equipment:

It is important to remember that scanning technology advances quickly and enhancements are regularly incorporated into new products meaning hardware has a high depreciation rate and may quickly become obsolete and uneconomical to maintain. The main types of capture devices available are:

High end A3 flatbed scanners:

These are suitable for all types of photographs, transparencies, negatives and pages up to A3 size that may be laid absolutely flat. They are best used to produce files of 20 Mbyte plus. They are not suitable for bound volumes, glass plates, mounted slides, formats larger than A3 or, because they use very bright light, anything that is in danger of fading.

Drum Scanners:

These are used by reprographic houses. Whilst they produce very high quality results they are expensive and the originals have to be fastened around a drum, which means they need to be very flexible and unmounted.

Medium format scanning backs:

Scanning backs are essentially the devices that convert a medium format conventional camera into a hi-resolution camera. With the right accessories, they are ideal for capturing items that cannot be placed on a scanner.

Digital cameras:

Digital cameras come in a variety of standards. To be suitable for digitization work these must be of a professional standard and capable of 18 Megabytes plus, with interchangeable lenses and accessories.

mm scanners:

These would seem to be ideal for collections made up of slides only. However, many of them are aimed at the domestic market and will not be robust enough for any reasonable sized collection. They often struggle to produce up to 18 Megabyte files of a good dpi.

Workstations:

All capture devices will need a dedicated workstation of good specification and with monitors capable of proper calibration, appropriate scanning software, a CD writer and the ability to store a reasonable number of images, either on the hard drive or server.

SET UP YOUR SCANNING LABORATORY:

Before digitization can start there are a number of things needed to consider. Over and above the environment needed to run computers the following are essential:

* A stable power supply - fluctuations can ruin scans and make consistency impossible.
* The scanning equipment must be installed in a proper clean area - dust and dirt is exaggerated when viewed on-screen.
* The workstation must be co-located with the scanner - The person who digitize, must be able to view the scan on–screen while working.
* Check links to networks or servers are available - you will be moving large files.
* If cameras are used, the ambient light should be fully controllable - overhead lighting or the variability of daylight will add a permanent color cast and make consistency impossible.
* The studio should have solid floor to prevent vibration - no digitizing is instantaneous.
* There must be sufficient room and suitable surfaces to clean

items, handle and store them before, during and after scanning.

* The area must be secure.

DECISIONS ON PROCEDURES ON DIGITISATION:

Sorting and Cataloguing:

Every item to be digitized must be clearly identifiable. If the digital file name is not marked or labeled on the original item, then it should carry some other unique identifier, such as an accession number, which can be associated with the file name during the scanning process.

Job Specification:

Before starting the work, the rules and conventions must be decided for the job. For example:

* What file type and final size or resolution is required?
* Should monochrome prints be captured as RGB or greyscale.
* Should images to be rotated for upright orientation?
* Should operators crop to edge of item or inside edge of print/negative? It should be specified whether captions are to be included if they are located outside the regular cropping convention, or exclude all or some types of captions.
* Should color casts to be corrected? Film transparencies and negatives very often have a color cast created by the film material, lighting conditions or processing - or a combination of all three. There are methods for detecting the presence of and correcting such irregularities.
* Is re-touching to be done? If so, to what extent, at what screen size and what is the maximum time to be spent on each item?
* Is the original unprocessed scan to be retained?

* If visible or digital watermarks are to be applied - to which resolution versions and when in the process?

Prepare your materials:

Before scanning you need to prepare your equipment and originals.

Batching:

Where possible group original items in batches of same size/format materials, say 100 - 150 in a batch. This will make the work easier to manage and improve productivity. It also means quality issues can be more easily isolated and corrected.

ICC Profile Checking:

Ensure the monitors are all calibrated and profiled to the same standard, that the capture devices are individually profiled and that the final files are all tagged with the required device independent of ICC color profile.

Pre-cleaning:

If materials have been in storage for any length of time a degree of controlled cleaning may be desirable. Cleaning processes should be carried out well away from the digitization area using lint free cotton and surgical gloves.

Oil mounting:

Oil mounting is a specialist technique that can significantly reduce effect of scratches, ground in dirt and other damage to negatives or transparencies.

Adjust and check your scans:

This is an important step and often overlooked in the planning. Once the image is captured it must have basic checks carried out, either immediately after capture or in batches at a later time.

Color range and balance:

Check that the capture device's sample range has been

utilized at either end of the tonal. If color cast correction is to be carried out, this is the time to do it.

Cropping and rotating:

Carry out cropping as decided in your job specification and, if necessary, rotate the image for correct orientation.

Re-touching:

Carry out re-touching to the standard decided in the job specification - this needs training and/or experience. Retouching on photographic image will always show if not done to a professional standard.

Compression:

Where required create a compressed version of the image.

Multi-pack creation:

Where required create screen resolution multi-pack versions.

Water-marking:

Where required apply visible or digital watermarking to specified versions of the image.

Quality inspection:

It is advisable for a quality inspection of say 20% of output to be carried out by a qualified person who hasn't been involved in either scanning or post-processing.

IDEAL STEPS FOR DIGITISATION :

Ideally a digitization process should involve following steps:

1. Image preparation;
2. Preparation of the volumes, issues and pages of the document for scanning;
3. Scanning pages of the document;
4. Editing images of the document;

5. Using *Optical Character Recognition Software (OCR)* on images to edit text versions. (OCR is the process whereby a computer program "reads" the text from an image of a document and converts it into ASCII text);
6. Creating a searchable database of the text; linking text to images;
7. Mounting on Web.

Image preparation:

The first step is to take all measures that are necessary to preserve the hard copy of the documents. A physical review of the document revealed much variance in the condition of the pages and that, while some could withstand scanning without any preservation, other pages would not. Consultation took place with the preservation library assistant in the rare book section at the university library and procedures were set up to follow:

1. Trim each page so that no rough edges are left;
2. Mend rips and tears with acid-free binding tape;
3. Put each issue in an acid-free envelope and store each volume in an acid-free storage box.

Important factors to consider for format:

At this stage it is necessary to decide the most appropriate file format for the online version of the document. The integrity of each page had to be maintained and in order to do this, save the pages after scanning as images. There are two primary options:

1. Save the image as a PDF (Portable Document Format) file using Adobe Acrobat; or
2. Save the image as a *GIF (Graphical Interchange Format)* or *JPEG (Joint Photographic Experts Group)* file.

It is advised to save the images as JPEG files, which would be most appropriate. JPEG will allow the entire project to be uploaded as an HTML file and furthermore, JPEG retains more information as it compresses an image:

* Each page had to be kept intact so that the user could view the page online just as it appeared in the paper copy;
* User-friendliness was important. Therefore, the online version had to be searchable, had to have a minimum of side-to-side scrolling, had to load fairly quickly and the pages had to be clear and easy to read;
* *Optical Character Recognition (OCR)* would work on scanned images of the document. This was a consideration as several different fonts were very small and that cannot always be recognized by OCR programs;
* With standardization the maximum number of users should be able to view it.

Scan pages of the document:

Having determined the type of file to be used for the online version, several preliminary scans were conducted to determine the appropriate image type, brightness, contrast, height and width, as well as the length of time it would take for each page to be scanned. To ensure uniformity in scanning the following parameters have been investigated for set up:

Height: 12.65 in.

Width: 8.18 in.

Brightness: 125 (approx.)

Contrast: 130 (approx.)

Image Type: Black and White Photo

File Type: JPEG

Image Quality: 600 dpi

The process of deciding what to digitize anticipates all the major stages of project implementation. Digital resources not only depend on the nature and importance of the original source materials but also on the nature and quality of the digitization process itself. Besides this how well relevant information is captured from the original text and is organized, indexed, delivered to users, and maintained over time.

For taking a decision on to the selection of documents, these are presented in a sequence that moves from relatively abstract assessments of intellectual value to nuts-and-bolts issues concerning whether available resources and technology can provide a product that meets expectations. In practice, the pieces interact in ways that are often complex. Decisions about what to digitize must first and foremost address the intellectual value of the original sources. We are likely to be able to convert only a small percentage of existing scholarly materials to electronic form, and doing even this will require substantial investments. We therefore need to determine what it is truly worthwhile to convert. Some scholarly resources are heavily used; others are consulted infrequently. With only limited funds available for reformatting, types and levels of use can help to shape priorities.

A person reading a book, looking at a photograph, or consulting a manuscript encounters few barriers to use. One might have to handle an object carefully, or use a magnifying glass to read fine print, but in general the work is immediately approachable. The same resource, when digitized, should be equally accessible and approachable. Ideally, the electronic version will also permit new kinds of use and more sophisticated types of analysis.

Decisions to digitize must take into account the physical size, nature, and condition of source materials as they affect the characteristics of the desired product. They must likewise address whether available means of conversion can satisfy expectations for the result. Projects must also, from the very first, consider how users will be guided through the electronic version.

After an extensive analysis of the above mentioned issues it is sorted out that a librarian or an information officer should consider following points while planning for the digitization of documents in his library and information centre:

Assessment of scholarly value of Library material:

Materials with marginal scholarly value are best left in

their original form or made accessible in a less costly manner. Scholarly value, of course, is a subjective assessment and even the most marginal materials can support some kinds of research. Most users, nonetheless, would opt for electronic access to original monographs rather than to derivative works, or to the papers of a prominent scholar over the administrative records of a university department. Bibliographers regularly make purchase decisions that reflect their evaluation of the intellectual quality of single items or collections of materials. Similar judgments apply in choosing what to digitize.

Digitization and the intellectual value of the digital material:

Scholarship can be facilitated when texts are made fully searchable by rekeying (retyping) them or by employing OCR software. Comparisons between successive drafts of a text and the final published work, for example, or with later editions and translations, are vastly simplified when the words and phrases are searchable. A concordance or thesaurus is likewise most easily mined when it is in searchable form. Electronic texts can be moved readily from one environment to another (from the World Wide Web onto the hard drive of a personal computer, and then into a word processing program, for example), shared with other users, and manipulated and reconfigured for multiple purposes. Digitized prints, drawings, and other visual resources can be viewed in groups at low resolution or inspected individually for very fine detail. Digital charts and tables, appropriately coded, can be loaded directly into statistical software packages for additional analysis.

Electronic accessibility of body of information of original books, manuscripts, photographs, or paintings:

A collection of thousands of portrait images, however promising a resource, might be nearly unapproachable because of its size and the condition and dimensions of individual items. Well-indexed and in digitized form, however, the collection could be searched with relative ease for images of a particular person or for some indexed characteristic (the country from which the portrait originates, for example). Likewise, the digitization of large-format architectural drawings could enable comparisons of small- and large-scale drawings, different views of the same architectural feature, or sequential phases of construction.

Increased value of the combination or aggregation of original sources increase their value:

Digitizing related scholarly monographs, like building a coherent collection of paper copies, can strengthen the context within which each title is approached. Ephemera-leaflets from a political campaign, for example-are often most useful when studied in the aggregate, as are posters, broadsides, and popular literature. Harvard has digitized daguerreotypes from thirteen repositories to facilitate the combinations and comparisons that are otherwise precluded by the fragility, value, and dispersion of the original images.

Popularity of digitized source material which is being consulted among scholars:

Intensive use does not automatically make a collection a good candidate for digitizing. If the primary audience is local, for example, and if competition for a particular resource is not a problem, access may already be sufficient. Ephemera produced by a community political organization may be of great interest to local scholars and of limited value to a worldwide audience. On the other hand, if use is heavy and widespread, digitizing may at once guarantee convenient and reliable access, and make it possible for some institutions to discard their original copies. The JSTOR project, through which a large array of core scholarly journals is being made accessible in digital form, is a prime example of an initiative focusing on high-use materials.

Digitization may provide wider access:

Low use may signal that a collection has marginal intellectual value, but there are many other reasons for valuable materials to have generated little interest. A collection may be held in a remote location, for example, or be owned by an institution with highly restrictive access policies. Bibliographic records may be poor, as is often the case with pamphlets. The value of digitizing such materials may go beyond the simple fact that the resulting files can be widely distributed. Broader access, as it creates a new community of users, can also facilitate more active scholarship.

Physical condition of the original materials limit their use:

Some resources are too fragile to be consulted. Aging newspapers or palm-leaf manuscripts that break at the slightest flex simply cannot be browsed. In such cases, a digital copy might be provided to improve access, and a microfilm or other photographic surrogate made to ensure long-term survival. (Film can be made from a digital file or vice versa.)

Sources may also be at risk because of high user demand or extraordinary monetary value:

A nation's founding documents, glass-plate negatives of vanished architectural sites, or rare maps may benefit from the creation of digital copies that satisfy the purposes of most users. These files do not necessarily need to meet archival standards. They are created to protect the originals from handling.

Related materials are so widely dispersed that they cannot be studied in context:

Cooperative efforts to digitize disparate pieces of a greater whole can create or restore a more usable collection. Papyrus fragments, a prominent individual's far-flung correspondence, scattered photographs of a particular subject or by a specific photographer and broken serial runs are among the many materials whose coherence, accessibility, and scholarly utility can be enhanced through digitization.

Manageable size and format of Digital files:

Digital resources need to match users' technical capabilities and equipment. Most require Internet access and standard web browsers, or a CD-ROM drive. Images delivered to the Internet in formats other than *JPEG* or *GIF* require additional software for viewing or printing. Even when electronic resources are optimized for on-screen delivery, some network connections, particularly those via modem, are still far too slow to support browsing of digital collections at satisfactory speeds. And scholars in some locations may lack training opportunities or the ongoing technical support needed to take advantage of the electronic environment. These limitations, however, are not necessarily reasons to rule out digitizing. The worldwide trend is toward greater capabilities. Moreover, the more important the resources available electronically, the greater the incentive to acquire the network, viewing, and printing technology necessary to use those resources. Digitization may, in and of itself, stimulate improved access.

Digitization and the needs of local students and scholars:

Immediate demand can inject a measure of practical reality into decisions to create electronic resources. A historian may choose to teach from digitized images of manuscripts that would otherwise be unavailable to a large class. Because ready access to shared electronic files can transform the classroom, proposals to digitize in support of immediate teaching needs may garner faculty support.

Various approaches of Digitization and its facilitation to a researcher:

Different digitizing techniques result in electronic files with different characteristics. These in turn can correspond well or poorly with scholarly needs. If the goal is to provide an image-based finding aid that helps users identify original materials of interest, for example, mounting slow-loading high-resolution images would be counterproductive. If, on the other hand, the intention is to reduce or eliminate handling of original materials, an image that fails to convey all critical information embodied in the original will fail to serve its intended purpose.

The simplest approach to digitizing involves use of a scanner or digital camera to create electronic pictures (bitmap images) of original materials:

Decisions concerning the number of dots recorded by the scanner (resolution), how many shades of gray or colors will be recorded (bit depth), and other factors related to scanning equipment and settings will determine how well the digital product replicates the original. High-quality bitmap images can usually capture all the significant detail in texts or graphics. Scanning rare and unique texts or visual resources can make them accessible to users who would otherwise never see them. In such a case, merely reproducing the original in electronic form represents an extraordinary enhancement.

For textual materials, post-scan processing can support expanded capabilities:

Scanned text can be processed with Optical Character Recognition software to produce searchable indexes. OCR software is now only occasionally employed in digitizing projects because it cannot yet interpret accurately all fonts and alphabets, and because it adds significantly to per-page costs. Text can also be rekeyed to create ASCII files-very straightforward digital text files that permit searching by keywords or phrases. In some cases this enhancement is the primary justification for digitization. Directories, dictionaries, and indexes are all significantly easier to use when specific words can be searched within a well-designed digital file.

ASCII texts accommodate key-word searching (e.g., searching for all instances of the word "temperance") and some kinds of analysis, but they do not readily replicate the structure and format of an original document. Without special coding, researchers cannot directly consult the seventh paragraph of the third chapter of a particular text. Nor can they search for all occurrences of "welcome" used as a verb rather than a noun. These capabilities become possible in marked-up texts, which are coded to highlight elements of structure, format, and syntax. The Standard Generalized Markup Language (SGML) is the emerging model. One SGML application, the Encoded Archival Description (EAD), is being used to create electronic versions of archival finding aids.

These and other approaches to digitizing carry very different costs, benefits, and resource requirements. While electronic versions can be more versatile than original materials, in some cases they hinder research. A scholar studying bookbinding or papermaking, for example, is poorly served by a reproduction of any kind. So too is the scholar whose immediate access to a large and important collection of literary works is sacrificed in order to serve a worldwide constituency-perhaps because bound volumes have been disbound for scanning.

Digitization increase the utility of the source materials:

Digitization can enhance original materials in many ways. Image quality can be improved by eliminating extraneous stains and marks. Thumbnail images of visual resources (photographs, drawings, and paintings) can be browsed to discover patterns, trends, and relationships among individual items, and specific images can then be scrutinized at higher resolution. Likewise, patrons can review scanned images to identify needed materials before requesting that they be retrieved from storage.

Electronic transcriptions of texts, in ASCII format or marked-up files can be linked to bitmap images of original documents. Readers can then decide for themselves whether "authoritative" transcriptions are in fact accurate. Comparisons of different versions of a text are likewise simplified. Related texts and images can be assembled together within a single, unified corpus. Examples such as the *Geet Govind project* of UNDP, administered by *Indira Gandhi National Centre for Arts*, New Delhi is an interactive, multimedia document on Archaic and Classical India, suggest the potential of electronic texts.

Almost all electronic products will provide basic links that allow users to navigate them (to locate a particular map within a printed text, for example). The degree to which a digitization project exploits electronic links will depend upon its intended use. For digital resources created as pedagogical tools, predetermined connections are part of the package. Products intended for research tend to be less aggressive in ordaining relationships among sources, since their creators assume that researchers will build their own structures of meaning.

Critical features of the source material must be captured in the digital product:

The cost and nature of digitizing hardware and software continue to evolve, and preferred solutions are likely to shift as well. It may sometimes make sense to defer certain digitizing projects so that technology can catch up to needs. The success of a project to digitize oversized maps at Columbia University, for example, depended partly on the ability of users to see detail and read place names. As a result, the maps were scanned at relatively high resolution, thereby creating challenges for digital image delivery and presentation. File sizes were very large and initially outran the capacity of the library's computers and network. Greater bandwidth and more powerful machines have enhanced functionality.

Digitization process retained source material:

Automatic sheet feeders are fast and efficient, but they may destroy brittle paper. Digital cameras can minimize the manipulation of source materials, but subjecting certain media-watercolors, for example prolonged lighting is problematic.

Issues of hardware which is used for conversion:

Color slides, for instance, cannot be fully represented by scanners that create only black-and-white images. Even a color scanner with limited capacity to reproduce tonalities will be inadequate when high-quality images are important. Digitizing equipment can be expensive, and the costs may be difficult to justify when use is sporadic. Some projects may thus be done most economically if they are contracted out. Agreements with external vendors, in addition to specifying technical conditions, performance expectations, and handling guidelines, must fully define ownership and distribution rights for all digital products.

Digitization of information resources which continue to grow:

Ongoing commitments and extended arrangements for copyrights may be required when collections are still expanding, as is the case with current journals and annual reports, or the papers of a living individual. Consultations with scholars and other experts can be particularly useful, since the long-term value of current materials is often difficult to discern.

Users navigation within and among digital collections:

Printed sources orient readers by means of tables of contents, chapters and sections, pagination, indexing, and formatting cues. Manuscript materials often rely on finding aids linked to the organization of file folders. Photographs may be mounted in albums. At a minimum, electronic products need to provide the same kind of functionality. The process may require several steps. For a multi-volume work that has been scanned page by page, for instance, each page is a separate computer file that must be individually labeled and stored. The files for critical pages of the work-for example, the title page, table of contents, and the first page of every new chapter-must then be linked to electronic navigational tools so that they can be easily located.

Existence of Digital files in the Information Centers:

Bibliographic records, finding aids and indexes can all be adapted to include references to electronic resources. Nonetheless, our ability to determine what has been digitized remains well behind what we know about materials that have been microfilmed or photocopied.

One of the principal challenges is to determine what

information is essential in describing an electronic product. The "*Dublin Core*" and other special initiatives for structuring and standardizing descriptive data propose to combine information about the technical characteristics of digital files, their location, and a summary of their contents. The resulting records are known as "*metadata.*" Their function is to provide users with a standardized means for intellectual access to digitized materials. Despite these and other initiatives, projects to catalog digital files are only in the developmental stage. No system has yet been widely adopted for tracking the digitizing activities of libraries, although new approaches continue to emerge.

Better delivery of Digital products to users:

Alternative modes of digital storage and delivery must be considered from the outset of a project. CD-ROMs, for instance, are distributed and used differently from information made accessible over the Internet. The differences are reflected in hardware requirements, software, and ease of use. CD-ROMs are sometimes bundled with software for searching and analysis that is superior to that generally provided for Internet files. On the other hand, access to CD-ROMs is limited to individual workstations or small networks, while Internet files can be made available to a very broad audience. And Internet resources, by nature, can be updated or augmented without requiring users to replace objects that have become obsolete.

Internet products, however, generate questions of their own. How immediate must access be?

Files can be mounted on a server so that they are instantaneously available on-line. They can be stored on disks in a jukebox and loaded on demand ("near-line" access), or kept off-site ("off-line") and retrieved and delivered on demand. Near-line and off-line access can save on server space and requirements, though there are countervailing staff costs associated with retrieving and mounting the files. Expected demand, file sizes, fee structures, and available staffing and equipment must all be considered.

Authorization of use of the digital resources, and required circumstances:

Copyright holders may limit distribution rights, institutions may be unable or unwilling to provide the infrastructure needed to support universal access, and cost-recovery enterprises cannot by definition make their products available without restriction. Digitizing projects must thus consider access policies and control, pricing mechanisms, and billing procedures. Access issues impinge upon selection decisions in a number of ways. A university may mount high-resolution images of unique holdings for scholarly use (a medieval manuscript, an important collection of drawings), but would not allow unauthorized publication of those images. Moreover, electronic resources cost money that must be secured through subsidies or fees. When neither internal budgets nor external subventions provide adequate financial support, digitization will require a paying audience.

Access, when it is not universal, must be managed:

Current alternatives include passwords, direct user fees, and limitations according to organizational affiliation. Different capabilities for viewing, downloading, and printing may be offered at different prices or to different sets of users. There are many options, each reflecting a different pathway toward a self-sustaining endeavor.

Ensure the integrity of the digitized data:

The malleability of electronic products makes them particularly useful for many kinds of scholarship. Digitized files must be embedded with detailed information concerning the methods used to create them. The same information should be included in external bibliographic or descriptive records. Users who are consulting or copying the sources must also be able to confirm that the files they see or receive match the originals. Means to authenticate and protect digital products, long available in financial and industrial applications, are only beginning to take hold in the scholarly world.

Adequacy of the existing technology infrastructure to fulfill local demands:

Robust computer systems and an appropriate number of work stations are perhaps more easily provided than such ancillary features as network printing capabilities in the library and in offices, classrooms, and residences.

The Goal of the project is to long-term preservation of deteriorated materials:

Preserving documentary resources in electronic format presumes that, to the greatest extent possible, all the information contained in the original material has been captured completely and accurately. This requires careful attention to significant detail, whether the smallest text characters on a page or all the shades and tones of blue and green in a seascape. Targets for resolution, grayscale, and rendition of color either exists or is being developed to ensure the needed detail and fidelity.

Digital preservation also requires a supporting organization and infrastructure dedicated to storing the electronic files and to migrating them to new formats and/or media as technology change. Unless these capacities are all in place, digital files cannot be regarded as permanent. Creating an enduring digital preservation master file is a multidimensional task with long-term implications. Hybrid projects, in which digital files are complemented by copies on microfilm, alkaline paper, or some other stable medium, provide the insurance that exclusively electronic projects do not.

Availability of already digitized source material:

As we have seen, it can be difficult to determine whether a specific item has been digitized and by what means. If an electronic copy does exist, is it accurate, satisfactorily functional, and accessible? Does it take advantage of the capabilities of current technologies? If the existing product does not serve the intended purposes of the proposed project, a new version may be warranted.

Benefited User Group of the proposed digital product:

It is important to consider whether the product will support better teaching or research and enable students to learn more, or in different ways-if, for example, texts or images are more fully revealed. Digitization may allow librarians to manage collections and provide services more effectively, or to provide traditional services such as copying or interlibrary loan at lower cost or at less risk to collections.

Commensuration of the intellectual value of the proposed product with the expense:

The limited resources available for digitization might have greater impact if they were directed at another project, or directed toward an entirely different approach to providing access-through exhaustive indexing perhaps, or microfilming, or some other type of reformatting that would prove in the end more useful to scholars.

Creation of acceptable digital product at lower cost:

When materials are scanned to support short-term course work, for example, careful (and expensive) post-scan processing to eliminate extraneous marks and speckles or to deskew misaligned images may be a waste of time. Likewise, an adequate substitute for full-text scanning of little-used journals might be provided by linking scanned tables of contents and indexes to bibliographic records and relying on traditional forms of document delivery.

The accumulated body of digital products may enable savings elsewhere in the institution-for example, by reducing staff costs for reshelving bound journals, or by lowering the costs of storage, circulation, and preservation-and these savings could offset some or all of the expense of digitizing. But such savings as may be realized are difficult to predict. It is essential to realize that the costs of digitization are just beginning at the time of initial capture. The programmatic capacity to distribute and maintain electronic resources, and to migrate them to new forms as original digital platforms fail and formats and software are superseded, is fundamental to long-term efforts. In addition, there are staff costs associated with training and user support. Finally, rising user expectations may require that existing digital files be reprocessed in new ways. When OCR software is perfected, for example, unsearchable bitmap images of texts could be thought unsatisfactory. Projects that do not plan for change may become obsolete, and therefore irrelevant.

Research libraries are eagerly embracing the digital world:

They are acquiring access to great quantities of electronic materials produced outside their walls. At the same time it becomes essential to maintain digital versions of all worthwhile existing text material of their own holdings. A careful review, analysis, and planning can yield electronic resources that are functional and faithful to the original sources, and that support new kinds of scholarship. A detailed plan of work, regular assessment of progress, closely documented adjustments and corrections, and the retention of other project-related data can strengthen the knowledge base for future efforts.

QUALITY ASSURANCE:

It is imperative that all digitization undergoes a series of quality control analyses at various stages, regardless of whether the material has been produced in-house or via an outside agency. This is an accepted method of verifying that all reproduction is up to standard. Bearing in mind limits on time and finances, some form of sampling may be necessary to reduce the costs of this process, as with the NARA who state that at a minimum 10 images or 10% of images (whichever number is higher) need to undergo quality control (these should be selected randomly from the entire collection). Ideally *Quality Assurance (or QA)* must be performed on all master images and their derivatives with each step being fully documented. The types of things one should look for are:

* size of image
* resolution of image
* file format
* image mode is correct (i.e. colour images are in colour, not greyscale)
* bit depth
* details in highlights and shadows
* tonal values
* brightness
* contrast
* sharpness
* interference
* orientation
* noise
* alignment of colour channels
* cropped and border areas, missing text, page numbers, etc.
* alignment of image (i.e. excessive skewing that is not the result of the such things as the tight binding of a book)
* missing lines or pixels
* dithering
* poor quality interpolation with access and thumbnails
* text legibility

The overall return should be checked for file name integrity, completeness of job, and overall meeting of digitization project scope. NARA recommend that if more than 1% of images looked at fail the above quality control checks then the job needs to be redone. The Library of Congress concurs with many of these findings. For the *American Memory Project* running under the *NDLP (National Digital Library Program)* it established a fifteen-point workflow practice for the Quality Review stage covering such areas:

* Verify delivery of 100 percent of files
* Inspect 10 percent of file contents
* Ensure technical requirements have been met
* Provide feedback to contractor
* Review any re-work

Aids and more specific guidelines to help in the testing of such ideas as contrasts and noise are available with accepted test cards and procedures. A good place to start to look for these is the Photographic and Imaging Manufacturer's Association/IT10 Still Picture Imaging web page has a growing list of standards.

DIGITIZATION STANDARDS:

As with costs, any attempt to establish a set of standards for digitization (i.e. resolutions, bit-depth, khz, fps, etc.) is fraught with difficulties. Not only is there no recognised standard to which everyone adheres even for the most basic of scanning (the variance in the source documents means that nothing could be derived to suit all purposes), there is also the short life of the technology. For example, any recommendations made now would most probably be redundant in a year's time with the changing capabilities of the capture devices, software, and falling prices. Instead, as with the rest of this section, all one can do at the moment is outline the general issues and indicate present practices.

Specifications:

The specifications suggested for any digitization project will be variable for all the reasons outlined throughout this book. At the outset, however, projects should derive a set of standards which will allow full informational capture of the originals, following accepted practice in benchmarking. Having done this, there may be a need for accommodation of available resources. The standards should not just specify requirements for the archival master, but should also state the parameters for the derived products:

High resolution (*Archiving resolution*) used for highest quality digitization (e.g. Oxford's Celtic and Medieval Manuscript project), for archiving file format with 'full informational capture', for outputting to high-quality print and film surrogates (in the case of graphics/text documents). The distinction between preservation copies and preservation quality images should be noted.

With graphics one of the most important factors is resolution. Different resolutions are required for different purposes, with high resolution often equating to an increase in unit costs. Furthermore, the digitization industry at present is awash with various projects digitizing at different resolution levels, and there are no archival or access standards available to which everyone adheres. Take for example a picture of a map. The digitizer scans the picture in at 600 dpi (e.g. a 5" x 4" print, with the image of the map filling the whole photograph exactly). However, if the original map was in fact 25 inches across (i.e. five times the width of the picture) the 'effective dpi' would be 600/5, i.e. 120dpi. Franziska Frey notes that 'a growing consensus within the preservation community is that a number of image files must be created for every photograph to meet a range of uses'.

COPYRIGHT ISSUES:

There are many interdependent and interacting factors to be weighed in selecting materials to digitize. The specific choices that result from the selection process will reflect subjective judgments, any of which may change over time. Nuance assessments, ambiguity, and shades of gray are all to be expected.

Questions concerning *copyright*, however, are far more clear-cut. Simply stated, if a proposed digitization work involves materials in the public domain, the work can proceed. If the source materials are protected by copyright but rights are held by the institution or appropriate permissions can be secured, the work can move ahead. If permissions are not forthcoming for copyrighted sources, however, the materials cannot be reproduced. Copyright assessments thus play a defining role with regard to digitization projects.

Copyright issues in the digital environment are still very much in flux and have provoked ongoing international discussion. While the broad thrust of digital technology is toward enhanced access, diminished costs, and more versatile capabilities, it is far less clear that copyright law will likewise encourage wider use. The legal strictures applicable to a particular project will vary depending on the country in which the project is based, the country in which the source materials were produced, and prevailing international agreements. Different kinds of materials, moreover, usually pose different types of rights-management issues. The performance rights associated with musical scores, for example, or exhibition rights for films, differ from rights for nonperformance materials such as electronic journals or documentary photographs. To complicate matters, all these rights are susceptible to change over time.

Digital projects must be undertaken with a full understanding of ownership rights, which is difficult as they often are to ascertain, and with full recognition that permissions are essential to convert materials that are not in the public domain. Rights that must be negotiated with the copyright holder often entail fees. The institution hosting a project may also have policies and procedures that inform intellectual property negotiations. The legal office of most institutions can provide guidance. The Internet site of IFLA Days: Copyright and Intellectual Property Resources is a good resource for maintaining current awareness. It includes articles, reports and white papers, discussions, and information about organizations related to copyright issues, intellectual property in general, and electronic distribution of intellectual property.

DIGITISATION EFFORTS IN INDIA:

* Several libraries, large and small, in the country are

involved in digitisation projects. While many of these are by nature experimental exercises, there are several national level projects involving the investment of large resources. Among the more significant projects are digital conversion projects at research institutes and university libraries and include some collaborative efforts. A few of these are highlighted below.

* The *National Library* (Kolkata) under a pilot project entitled "*Down Memory Lane*" from February 1999 and June 2001 digitised 6601 of its rare and brittle English books through a local private agency. Books published prior to 1900 and Indian books published before 1920 were converted; in all, more than 2.5 million pages were scanned and archived in 548 CD-ROMs (in duplicate). (http://www.nlindia.org) The Central Secretariat Library has also been involved in converting some of its rare books.
* The National Institute of Technology, Calicut has set up a Etext Conversion Project aiming at converting the Public Domain Etexts in raw text format into eBooks in easily Screen-Readable PDF/LIT Other /HTML Formats. By the end of 2003, 881 texts had been thus converted and made available in its Digital Library. The PDF books are optimized for screen-reading using Adobe Acrobat Reader 4.0 or higher and Adobe eBook Reader 2.0 or higher and the font size is selected for easy reading on screen. The titles covered under this Nalanda eText Conversion Project can be searched by words in title or author names. (http://www.nalanda.nitc.ac.in)
* In addition to academic and national level libraries, research organisations are also involved in digitisation projects. Munshi (2003) has described the Indian National Science Academy's (INSA) efforts towards digitisation of its own journals. Other research organisations are also following suit.

* Building up a digital archive is a major component of the Archives of Indian Labour set up in July, 1998 as a collaborative project of V.V. Giri National Labour Institute and the Association of Indian Labour Historians. The Archives of Indian Labour is dedicated to the cause of preserving and making accessible the fast depleting documents on the working class. The Archives was instituted in order to address the urgent need for preservation of rapidly decaying documents and material on labour and to provide for greater public access to them. This is said to be the first fully digital archives in the country and aspires to be the prime repository of labour related records. A total of 9 special collections comprising 1,00,000 printed pages, 400 hours of taped interviews have till date been stored in digital form. (http://www.indialabourarchives.orgl).

* In addition to these representative institutional efforts, two collaborative projects need to be mentioned. Under the Carnegie Mellon University's international project of Digitising a Million Books, the Digital Library of India is taking shape. Coordinated by the Indian Institute of Science, Bangalore, the project involves more than 15 partner institutions that include universities, research institutes, colleges, maths and public libraries. More than 27,000 documents have been digitised including books in English (approx. 12,000) and Telugu (approx.l0,000), Sanskrit, Urdu Tamil and other Indian languages. While English and a few Telugu and Tamil books have been converted to text, the other Indian language resources have been stored as digital images (http://www.dli.gov.in/).

* Another collaborative endeavor limited to universities is the Vidyanidhi project which seeks to digitise theses and build up an open archive of this elusive but rich source of information. More specifically it seeks to digitise, archive and provide wider access to doctoral theses in india by

making them available online. While bibliographic data about several thousand theses are available, only a few hundred of these are available as full-text electronic copies; this is partly due to technical reasons and partly because of the intellectual rights issue (http://www.vidyanidhi.org.in).

* In addition to these efforts by academic and research organisation, attempts to digitise information required by the the citizen are on Land records, cartographic materials, legal judgements, policy documents, parliamentary discussions, various forms needed by the public are being digitised. A few corporate houses, too are digitising their institutional archives and their working documents required across the enterprise.

A digitization project can cover a wide range of complex activities and it is often easy to lose track of the underlying project aims and objectives. Digitization is a tool and not a purpose and should always be used to facilitate the end result of the project rather than becoming the sole focus of it. It is hoped that the above mentioned information will help to make the process of digitization less fearsome and more tangible and therefore something to be harnessed to help to create useful and exciting digitization practice.

3
DIGITISATION TOOLS

Introduction:

In the process of creation of digital library we, information officers use to procure information in computer readable format, we organize it and maintain it for its best usage. For presenting an ideal example of digital library, it is essential to think about on our present text based collection and this is the real challenge for any practicing information officer. When we think about it, we need to convert all of this in the computer readable format while using latest tools and techniques of digitisation.

Presently we will discuss about Scanners and Digital Camera as digitisation equipments. In theory, a 24-bit scanner offers an 8-bit range (256 levels) for each primary colour - the difference between 256 levels is commonly accepted to be indiscernible to the human eye. Unfortunately, a few of the least significant bits are lost in noise, while any post-scanning tonal corrections reduce the range still further. That's why it's best to make any brightness and colour corrections in one go from the scanner driver before making the final scan itself. More expensive scanners with 30- or 36-bit depths have a much wider range to start with, offering better detail in the shadow and highlight areas, allowing you to make tonal corrections and still end up with a decent 24-bits at the end. A 30-bit scanner collects 10-bits of data each for the red, green and blue colour components while 36-bit scanners collect 12-bits for each. The scanner driver allows the operator to control which 24 of those 30 or 36 bits are kept and which ones are discarded - this adjustment being made by changing the Gamma Curve, accessed through the TWAIN driver's Tonal Adjustment control.

ISSUES ON INFORMATION CAPTURING:

Bit Depth:

It is essential to understand the term *bit depth* for knowing the complete process of scanning. For each pixel in an image, the scanner can remember a certain number of bits, which is known as bit depth. The higher the bit depth, the better the scanner is at distinguishing between really close shades of the same colour. This results in higher image quality. The minimum bit depth for decent image quality is 24. So for each pixel, the scanner remembers 8 bits of information for each of three colour levels (red, blue and green). Overall, this means the scanner can theoretically represent around 16.8 million colours.

Inherent in the scanning process is a certain loss or distortion of information which is caused by a number of factors. This is commonly referred to as "noise." In practice, noise cuts 24 bit depth down to around 18 which decreases the number of colours represented. As a result, scanned photos will lose some image quality in the highlights and shadows. But the average user with a regular printer should find 24 bits adequate for most documents and web graphics.

The next couple of steps up in bit depth are 30, 32, 36, 42 and 48. If somebody plans on getting a scanner for slides, negatives or transparencies he will need at least 30 bits, while 36 bits would be preferable. But what happens if somebody get a scanner with 30 bits, his monitor or printer can only handle 24 bits of colour data. The extra information at higher bit depth will still produce smoother colour gradations and better overall image reproduction.

Resolution:

There are two types of *resolution*, optical and interpolated; the first one is the most important. The ***optical resolution*** of a scanner is measured in dots or pixels per inch (dpi or ppi). More pixels mean better resolution and sharper image quality. The number of pixels a scanner can generate is based on how many *charged-couple devices (CCDs)* are arranged horizontally and vertically in the scan head. Remember one CCD produces one pixel. Resolution is quoted both horizontally and vertically (eg. 600x300). When comparing resolutions always use the smaller number. If you need to pick up fine details, small fonts or complex lines or edges more optical resolution you will require.

The ***interpolated resolution*** for a scanner is always higher than its optical resolution. To get interpolated resolution the scanner takes the information from two true pixels and by using mathematical algorithms it fills in a third pixel between them. Since more pixels are being mathematically generated, the interpolated resolution is higher. Optical resolution is a more reliable indicator of image quality. Higher interpolated resolution will be sufficient if you just need to enlarge images.

An optical resolution of 300 dpi should be enough for the average user. It will produce an image that will look good on the web or printed out on an inkjet or laser printer. Graphic artists who want to scan line art or images with lots of detail will want to go up to 600 dpi. The people who are looking for a scanner to scan slides, negatives or transparencies need 1200 dpi resolution. Such a high resolution is needed to compensate for the small size of the original.

Even if the printer has lower resolution than by that particular scanner, scanning at higher resolutions will produce better image quality in the finished document. You will have to scan at higher resolution than what you want to print at because the image quality degrades when you process the image with editing software like PhotoShop. A scanner with a higher resolution will also produce better images even at resolutions below the maximum. For example, a 150 dpi scan from a 600 dpi scanner looks better than the same scan from a 300 dpi scanner.

Dynamic Range or Optical Density:

Those who need a good graphics scanner or want really

high image quality, need to consider dynamic range, also called *optical density (OD)*. It is a measure of how well the scanner can capture the tonal range of an image, the gradations from bright highlights all the way to dark shadows. *Dynamic range* is measured on a logarithmic scale (like the Richter scale) from 0-4 with zero as pure white and four as pure black. Dynamic range is the difference between the darkest and brightest optical densities a scanner can capture. The bigger the difference the larger the dynamic range.

Most flatbed scanners have an OD around 2.8-3.0 which is fine for the tonal range of photographs. To scan slides, negatives and transparencies which have broader tonal ranges, a higher OD will be required. For slides and transparencies OD must be around 3.2, a bit higher at 3.4 will be required for negatives. When comparing scanners with the same bit depth, choosing one with a higher dynamic range will give you better image reproduction.

Speed:

Scanners for personal use won't be too concerned with the speed. The speed depends on the scanning resolution, the higher the resolution lesser the speed. An efficient time for a 600 dpi colour scan is about 100 seconds but only 30 seconds for a monochrome 300 dpi scan.

Softwares : The software bundle probably contains

* driver program,
* colour calibration software,
* image-editing software and
* optical recognition software (OCR).

For Windows the driver program is usually TWAIN compatible. A *TWAIN driver* allows imaging devices like scanners to be compatible with TWAIN-supported software. Since TWAIN is an industry standard most bundled software will operate off TWAIN. Colour calibration software tries to maintain the original colors of the image throughout its processing. This means that what you see on the monitor and what you print out should be reasonably close to the colors of the original. Out of these variety of software, Optical Recognition Software is most important for any information officer.

Optical Recognition Software (OCR):

When a page of text is scanned into a PC, it is stored as an electronic file made up of tiny dots, or pixels; it is not seen by the computer as text, but rather, as a 'picture of text'. Word processors are not capable of editing bitmap images. In order to turn the group of pixels into editable words, the image must go through a complex process known as *Optical Character Recognition (OCR)*. Optical recognition programs examine the scanned image and convert it into a format that can be read by a word processor, spreadsheet or database.

OCR research began in the late 1950s, one of the earliest OCR techniques was something called matrix, or *pattern matching*. Most text is either in Times, Courier, or Helvetica typefaces in point sizes between 10 and 14. OCR programs, which use the pattern matching method, have bitmaps stored for every character of each of the different font and type sizes. By comparing a database of stored bitmaps distributed to the bitmaps of the scanned letters the program attempts to recognize the letters. This early system was only really successful using non-proportional fonts like Courier where letters are spaced regularly and are easier to identify. Complex multi-font documents were well beyond its scope and an obvious limitation to this method is that it is only useful for the fonts and sizes stored.

Feature extraction was the next step in OCR's development. This attempted to recognise characters by identifying their universal features, the goal being to make OCR typeface-independent. If all characters could be identified using rules defining the way that loops and lines join each other, then individual letters could be identified regardless of their typeface.

For example, the letter "a" is made from a circle, a line on the right side and an arc over the middle. The arc over the middle is optional. So, if a scanned letter had these "features" it would be correctly identified as the letter "a" by the OCR program.

In terms of research progress, feature extraction was a step forward from matrix matching, but actual results were badly affected by poor-quality print. Extra marks on the page, or stains in the paper, had a dramatic effect on accuracy. The elimination of such "noise" became a whole research area in itself, attempting to determine which bits of print were not part of individual letters. Once noise can be identified, the reliable character fragments can then be reconstructed into the most likely letter shapes.

No OCR software ever recognizes 100% of the scanned letters. Some OCR programs use the matrix/pattern matching and/or feature extraction methods to recognize as many characters as possible and complement this by using spell checking on the hitherto unrecognized letters. For example, if the OCR program was unable to recognize the letter 'e' in the word 'th~ir', by spell checking 'th~ir' the program could determine the missing letter is an 'e'.

Recent OCR technology is far more sophisticated than the early techniques. Instead of just trying to identify individual characters, modern techniques are able to identify whole words. This technology, developed by *Caere*, is called *Predictive Optical Word Recognition (POWR)*. Using higher levels of contextual analysis, POWR is able to virtually eliminate the problems caused by noise. It enables the computer to sift through the thousands or millions of different ways that dots in a word can be assembled into characters. Each possible interpretation is then assigned a probability, and the highest one is selected. POWR uses sophisticated mathematical algorithms which allow the computer to hone in on the best interpretation without examining each possible version individually.

When probabilities are assigned to individual words, all

kinds of contextual information and evidence is taken into account. The technology makes use of neutral networks and *predictive modelling techniques* taken from research in Artificial Intelligence (AI). These involve extensive use of *'experts'* - algorithms set up to be specialists in various areas of character recognition. One expert might know a great deal about font styles, another about dictionary information, another about the degradation caused by faxes. By combining the use of expert systems with modelling techniques taken from Cognitive Science, a mathematical, probabilistic infrastructure can be created that dynamically 'investigates' all the different possibilities of characters that make up a word in question by querying a variety of experts, and generating an initial set of general hypotheses. The evidence for and against each hypothesis is weighed and a probability assigned to each hypothesis. The investigation continues until a clear and compelling answer emerges. At each stage in the investigation, a new set of experts is selected based on the relevance of their areas of expertise to the particular situation.

The net result is that POWR is able to identify words in a way, which more closely resembles human visual recognition. In practice, the technique significantly improves the accuracy of word recognition across all document types. All the possible interpretations of a word are assessed by combining all sources of evidence, from low-level pixel-based information to high-level contextual clues. The most probable interpretation is then selected.

Although OCR systems have been around for a long time, their benefits are only just being appreciated. The first offerings were extremely costly, in terms of software and hardware, and they were inaccurate and difficult to use. Consequently many of the early adopters became frustrated with the technology. Over the past few years, however, OCR has been completely transformed. Modern OCR software is highly accurate, easy to use and affordable and for the first time OCR looks set to be adopted in all kinds of work environments on a mass scale.

Unless there is a specific need to preserve colour information from the original document, its best to scan documents for OCR in greyscale. This uses a third of the space of an RGB colour scan. Line-art mode makes for even smaller file sizes - but this often loses detail, reducing the accuracy of subsequent OCR processing.

Interface:

Connecting a scanner to the computer can be done in a number of ways. Plugging a scanner into the parallel port and configuring it is fairly easy. Most of them come with pass-through connectors to attach the printer to the scanner, one should not try to use both at once. Parallel ports tend to be the slowest way to connect, but the latest models can be almost as fast as the other two options, USB and SCSI.

The Universal Serial Bus (USB) is quickly becoming popular, offering straight-forward installation, flexible configuration and faster data transfer. **Small Computer System Interface** (SCSI) commonly known as "*scuzzy*"is used to connect most high-end scanners, however, connect via a port.. This type of connection is fast but can require more work to configure and install. Macintosh systems support SCSI connection. If somebody wants to get a SCSI scanner then he may have to open up the computer to install a SCSI controller card. Most SCSI scanners come with controller cards and SCSI cables. Even if he already has a SCSI card for another device, it may not be compatible with the scanner or the provided cables.

Scanning Process:

All scanners work on the same principle of reflectance or transmission. The image is placed before the carriage, consisting of a light source and sensor; in the case of a digital camera, the light source could be the sun or artificial lights. When desktop scanners were first introduced, many manufacturers used fluorescent bulbs as light sources. While good enough for many purposes, fluorescent bulbs have two distinct weaknesses, they rarely emit consistent white light for long, and while lightening they emit heat which can distort the other optical components. For these reasons, most manufacturers have moved to 'cold-cathode' bulbs. These differ from standard fluorescent bulbs in that they have no filament. They therefore operate at much lower temperatures and, as a consequence, are more reliable. Standard fluorescent bulbs are now found primarily on low-cost units and older models.

By late 2000, Xenon bulbs had emerged as an alternative light source. Xenon produces a very stable, full-spectrum light source that's both long lasting and quick to initiate. However, xenon light sources do consume power at a higher rate than cold cathode tubes. To direct light from the bulb to the sensors that read light values, CCD scanners use prisms, lenses, and other optical components. Like eyeglasses and magnifying glasses, these items can vary quite a bit in quality. A high-quality scanner will use high-quality glass optics that are colour-corrected and coated for minimum diffusion. Lower-end models will typically skimp in this area, using plastic components to reduce costs.

The amount of light reflected by or transmitted through the image and picked up by the sensor, is then converted to a voltage proportional to the light intensity- the brighter the part of the image, the more light is reflected or transmitted, resulting in a higher voltage. This *analogue-to-digital conversion (ADC)* is a sensitive process, and one that is susceptible to electrical interference and noise in the system. In order to protect against image degradation, the best scanners on the market today use an electrically isolated analogue-to-digital converter that processes data away from the main circuitry of the scanner. However, this introduces additional costs to the manufacturing process, so many low-end models include integrated analogue-to-digital converters that are built into the scanner's primary circuit board.

The sensor component itself is implemented using one of three different types of technology:

* PMT, a technology inherited from the drum scanners of yesteryear
* CCD, the type of sensor used in desktop scanners
* CIS, a newer technology which integrates scanning functions into fewer components, allowing scanners to be more compact in size.

PMT:

PMT (photomultiplier tube) is the sensor technology used by the high-end drum scanners used by colour prepress companies. Expensive and difficult to operate, these were the devices used to load images into a computer before the advent of desktop scanning.

Technicians would carefully mount originals onto a cylindrical drum which would then be spun at high speed. The machine would then be moved - via a mechanically accurate threaded shaft - initially to align its optical sensor with the original and then slowly across its entire span as the item was scanned. Variation to output size can be assisted with variable sideways carriage movement, different lenses for various reproduction ranges and different drum circumferences.

PMT scanners have two light sources, one for reflective original and one for transparent originals. The light detected by the sensor is split into three beams which are passed through red, green and blue filters and thence into the photomultiplier tubes - where the light energy is converted into an electrical signal. PMTs have a much higher sensitivity to light and lower noise levels than CCD scanners. Consequently, drum scanners are capable of excellent tonal resolution, being less susceptible to errors due to refraction or focus than their flatbed counterparts. However, drum scanners are slow compared to CCD scanners and are expensive. These days they're are generally used only for specialised high-end applications.

CCD:

CCD (charge-coupled device) technology is responsible

for having made scanning a desktop application and has been in use for a number of years in devices such as fax machines and digital cameras. A charge-coupled device is a solid state electronic device that converts light into an electric charge. A desktop scanner sensor typically has thousands of CCD elements arranged in a long thin line. The scanner shines light through red, green and blue filters and the reflected light is directed into the CCD array via a system of mirrors and lenses. The CCD acts as a photometer, converting the measured reflectance into an analogue voltage, which can then be sampled and changed to discrete digital values by an analogue-to-digital converter(ADC).

CIS:

CIS (contact image sensor) is a relatively new sensor technology which began to appear at the budget end of the flatbed scanner market in the late 1990s. CIS scanners employ dense banks of red, green and blue LEDs to produce white light and replace the mirrors and lenses of a CCD scanner with a single row of sensors placed extremely close to the source image. The result is a scanner that is thinner and lighter, more energy efficient and cheaper to manufacture than a traditional CCD-based device - but that is not, as yet, capable producing as good results.

The technology employed by its sensor mechanism is not, however, the only factor that governs a scanner level of performance. The following are equally important aspects of a given unit's specification:

* resolution
* bit depth
* dynamic range

Scan resolution:

Resolution relates to the fineness of detail that a scanner can achieve, and is usually measures in *dots per inch(dpi)*. The more dots per inch a scanner can resolve, the more detail the resulting image will have. The typical resolution of an inexpensive desktop scanner in the late 1990s was 300 x 300.

A typical flatbed scanner has a CCD element for each pixel, so for a desktop scanner claiming a horizontal optical resolution of 600 dpi(dots per inch) - alternatively referred to as 600 *ppi(pixels per inch)* - and a maximum document width of 8.5inch there will be an array of 5,100 CCD elements in what is known as the scan head.

The scan head is mounted on a transport which is moved across the target object. Although the process may appear to be a continuous movement, the head moves a fraction of an inch at a time, taking a reading between each movement. In the case of a flatbed scanner, the head is driven by a stepper motor, a device which turns a predefined amount and no more, each time an electrical pulse is fed.

The number of physical elements in a CCD array determines the x-direction sampling rate, and the number of stops per inch determines the y-direction sampling rate. Although these are conveniently referred to as a scanner's 'resolution', the term is not strictly accurate. The resolution is the scanner's ability to determine detail in an object and is defined by the quality of electronics, optics, filters and motor control, as well as the sampling rate.

The actual scan head, though capable of reading a raster line 8.5in wide, will be much smaller than that, typically around 4in wide. The reflected light is presented to the scan head through a lens, and the quality of the optics can have a greater effect on the resolution of the scan than the sampling rate. High resolution optics in a 400dpi scanner is likely to produce better results than a 600dpi device with poor optics.

By late 1998 the physical limit as to how many CCD elements could be placed side by side in one inch stood at 600. It is, however, possible for the apparent resolution to be increased using a technique known as interpolation, which under software or hardware control guesses intermediate values and inserts them between the real ones. Some scanners do this much more effectively than others.

The determination of the appropriate resolution at which to scan an image is important both in terms of achieving the desired quality and in terms of the efficiency of the scanning process itself. Since modern advertising has conditioned us to think that more is always better, it is not difficult to understand why many users have a tendency to scan at too high a resolution. The key point is that scan resolution should always be determined by the capability of the output device. If the chosen scan resolution does not properly match the given output device, there will be adverse consequences. If it is lower than the output resolution, the display or printing process will interpolate the extra pixels that are needed and the final result will lose detail and sharpness. If, on the other hand, the chosen scan resolution is higher than the output resolution, the display or printing process will discard the extra pixels. The result will look fine, but the same quality result could have been achieved with lower resolution and a smaller image file.

The following discusses rules for determining an appropriate scan resolution for each of:

* a glossy magazine
* an inkjet printer, and
* a computer monitor

Printed images use a technique called *halftoning* to reproduce different levels of colour. In magazines an ordered halftone is used, where regular dots of differing sizes produce the varying levels of colour. The typesetters used in offset lithography - the technology used for printing glossy magazines - are capable of printing at 133 lines per inch. This technology is not quite the same as laser or inkjet printer technology and the general rule here is for layout artists to scan at 1.5 times the printing resolution - an equivalent of 200dpi.

Most inkjet printers use *dithering*, where the dots are scattered across the area of each pixel. This produces better looking results at lower resolutions. The use of halftoning means that the number of pixels per inch the printer can reproduce is lower than its stated "dpi" resolution. When scanning for output on a printer, the scan resolution should match the intended output resolution as closely as possible, taking into account the relative sizes of the original and the reproduction. If these are to be the same, no adjustments are necessary. If, however, the scanned image is to be printed at a different size - either larger or smaller than the original - the scan resolution needs to be adjusted accordingly.

This is best illustrated by an example. Suppose the intention is to print the scan of a 1x1.5in stamp at a size of 2x3in on an inkjet printer that has a print resolution of 600dpi. If the stamp were to be scanned at a 600dpi resolution, the scanned image would have 600 pixels vertically (1in times 600dpi) and 900 pixels horizontally (1.5in times 600dpi). Enlarging the image to the intended print size of 2x3in reduces the effective resolution to 300dpi - the 900 horizontal pixels will be spread out over 3in (900 divided by 3 equals 300), and the same is true in the vertical dimension. This is only half of the printer's resolution and the output quality will be less than optimal. For the best quality final printed output - which actually uses the 600dpi resolution the inkjet is capable of - the image should be scanned at 1200dpi.

A similar adjustment needs to be made if the output size is smaller than the original. Suppose the intention is to scan a 4x5in cover that is to be displayed on a Web page at half size, 2x2.5in. Computer monitors typically have a resolution of 72 or 90dpi. Scanning the cover at 72dpi would produce an image with 288x360 pixels. Reducing this to half the size would still give an image with a vertical resolution of 144dpi, twice that necessary. In this example, therefore, the original image could be scanned at 36dpi with no loss of quality in the resultant displayed image.

The rules used in these examples can be summarised by the following formula:

SR = (DR x DW) / OW, where

SR = ideal scanning resolution, in dpi

DR = resolution of final display device, in dpi

DW = width at which the image will be printed or displayed, in inches

OW = width of the original being scanned, in inches.

Interpolation:

Scanners typically offer resolutions of 2,400dpi, 4,800dpi and 9,600dpi. It is important to realise that scanners simply are not capable of picking up this level of detail. The actual optical resolution of the CCDs in most modern scanners is 600 x 1,200dpi at best and all higher figures are based on interpolation. Note that the specification of a *non-uniform resolution*, for example, 600 x 1200dpi - necessarily implies hardware interpolation, since the acquisition of data at 600dpi in one axis and 1200dpi in the other clearly cannot result in a 'square' of data. At 600 x 600dpi such a scanner will interpolate the 1200dpi dimension down to 600dpi (usually done by merely running the stepper motor that moves the light bar at twice its minimum rate), or at 1200 x 1200dpi they interpolate up the x dimension. Basically, an integrated circuit chip in the scanner generates new data by taking the dots the scanner actually sees, and calculating where the dots in between would most likely fall, using an algorithm to realise the colour of the new dots by averaging the colour of adjacent dots.

Software interpolation can increase the resolution even more than hardware interpolation. It is performed by the PC's processor under the control of the scanner's *TWAIN driver* software. Interpolated images will always seem too smooth and slightly out of focus. This doesn't matter so much with line-art where interpolation has the effect of smoothing out jagged edges. But for continuous-tone images like photographs, it is often better to stick with a scanner's actual optical resolution.

Colour scanners:

Colour scanners have three light sources, one for each of red, green and blue primary. Some scanning heads contain a single fluorescent tube with three filtered CCDs, while others have three coloured tubes and a single CCD. The former produce the entire colour image in a single pass, the target being illuminated by the three rapidly changing lights, while the latter have to go back-and-forth three times.

Single-pass scanners have problems with the stability of light levels when they're being turned on and off rapidly. Older three-pass scanners used to suffer from registration problems along with being slow. More modern three-pass units are much improved and able to match some single-passers for speed. However, by the late 1990s most colour scanners were single-pass devices. These scanners use one of two methods for reading light values: *beam splitter* or *coated CCDs*. When a beam splitter is used, light passes through a prism and separates into the three primary scanning colours, which are each read by a different CCD. This is generally considered the best way to process reflected light, but to bring down costs many manufacturers use three CCDs, each of which is coated with a film so that it reads only one of the primary scanning colours from an unsplit beam. While technically not as accurate, this second method usually produces results that are difficult to distinguish from those of a scanner with a beam splitter.

Bit-depth vs. coloured scanning:

When a scanner converts something into digital form, it looks at the image pixel by pixel and records what it sees. That part of the process is simple enough, but different scanners record different amounts of information about each pixel. How much information a given scanner records is measured by its bit-depth.

The simplest kind of scanner only records black and white, and is sometimes known as a 1-bit scanner because each bit can only express two values, on and off. In order to see the many tones in between black and white, a scanner needs to be at least 4-bit (for up to 16 tones) or 8-bit (for up to 256 tones). The higher the scanner's bit-depth, the more accurately it can describe what it sees when it looks at a given pixel. This, in turn, makes for a higher quality scan. Most modern colour scanners are at least 24-bit, meaning that they collect 8 bits of information about each of the primary scanning colours: red, blue, and green. A 24-bit unit can theoretically capture over 16 million different colours, though in practice the number is usually quite smaller. This is near-photographic quality, and is therefore commonly referred to as *"true colour" scanning.*

Recently, an increasing number of manufacturers are offering 30-bit and 36-bit scanners capable, so they claim, of producing better quality colour images. Whilst the fact is that very few graphics software packages are capable of handling images with more than 24 bits, the additional bits are still worth having. When a software program opens a 30-bit or 36-bit image, it can use the extra data to correct for noise in the scanning process and other problems that hurt the quality of the scan. With more inherent information present in 30- and 36-bit scanned images, users can more precisely alter image detail and RGB luminance values via the scanner's driver software.

The alternative route to improved quality - simply by building better 24-bit scanners - that provide cleaner data, less affected by random noise in the lower-order bits - is actually much less economic. This approach would require highly precise optics for focusing reflected light to the *CCDs (charge-coupled devices)* that capture the data; minimal-distortion glass free from internal contaminants; CCDs that capture light and convert it to electrical signals with high accuracy; and a smoothly-moving scanning head with little vibration. Such a device would cost considerably more than one that used lower-cost and lower-quality components with slightly more expensive *ADCs*, capable of capturing 10-bits and 12-bits of data each - for the red, green and blue colour components respectively - rather than just 8.

Scan modes:

PCs represent pictures in a variety of ways - the most common methods being are *line art*, *halftone*, *greyscale*, and *true colour*:

* *Line art* is the smallest of all the image formats. Since only black and white information is stored, the computer represents black with a 1 and white with a 0. It only takes 1-bit of data to store each dot of a black and white scanned image. Line art is most useful when scanning text or line drawing. Pictures do not scan well in line art mode.
* While computers can store and show greyscale images, most printers are unable to print different shades of grey. They use a trick called *halftoning*. Halftones use patterns of dots to fool the eye into believing it is seeing greyscale information
* *Greyscale* images are the simplest of images for the computer to store. Humans can perceive about 255 different shades of grey - represented in a PC by a single byte of data with the value 0 to 255. A greyscale image can be thought of as equivalent to a black and white photograph
* *True colour* images are the largest and most complex images to store, PCs using 8-bits (1 byte) to represent each of the colour components (red, green, and blue) and therefore 24-bits in total to represent the entire colour spectrum.

File formats:

The format in which a scanned image is saved can have a significant effect on file size - and file size is an important consideration when scanning, since the high resolutions supported by many modern scanners can result in the creation of image files as large as 30MB for an A4 page. Windows bitmap (BMP) files are the largest, since they store the image in full colour without compression or in 256 colours with simple *run-length encoding (RLE)* compression. Images to be used as Windows wallpaper have to be saved in BMP format, but for most other cases it can be avoided.

Tagged image file format (TIFF) files are the most flexible, since they can store images in RGB mode for screen display, or CMYK for printing. TIFF also supports LZW compression, which can reduce the file size significantly without any loss of quality. This is based on two techniques introduced by *Jacob Ziv* and *Abraham Lempel* in 1977 and subsequently refined by Unisys researcher *Terry Welch*. *LZ77* creates pointers back to repeating data, and *LZ78* creates a dictionary of repeating phrases with pointers to those phrases.

CompuServe's *graphics interchange format (GIF)* stores images using indexed colour. A total of 256 colours are available in each image, although what these colours are can change from image to image. A table of RGB values for each index colour is stored at the start of the image file. GIFs tend to be smaller than most other file formats because of this decreased colour depth, making them a good choice for use in WWW-published material.

The PC Paintbrush (PCX) format has fallen into disuse, but offers a compressed format at 24-bit colour depth. The JPEG file format uses lossy compression and can achieve small file sizes at 24-bit colour depth. The level of compression can be selected - and hence the amount of data loss - but even at the maximum quality setting *JPEG* loses some detail and is therefore only really suitable for viewing images on-line. The number of levels of compression available depends on the image editing software being used.

Unless there is a need to preserve colour information from the original document, images stored for subsequent OCR processing are best scanned in greyscale. This uses a third of the space of an RGB colour scan. An alternative is to scan in line-art mode black and white with no greyscales but this often loses detail, reducing the accuracy of the subsequent OCR process.

The table below illustrates the relative file sizes that can be achieved by the different file formats in storing a 'native' 1MB image, and also indicates the colour depth supported:

File format	Image size	No. of colours
BMP - RGB	1MB	16.7 million
BMP -RLE	83KB	256
GIF	31KB	256
JPEG - min. compression	185KB	16.7 million
JPEG - min. progressive compression	150KB	16.7 million
JPEG - max. compression	20KB	16.7 million
JPEG - max. progressive compression	16KB	16.7 million
PCX	189KB	16.7 million
TIFF	1MB	16.7 million
TIFF - LZW compression	83KB	16.7 million

TWAIN driver:

TWAIN is a very important standard in image acquisition, developed by *Hewlett-Packard, Kodak, Aldus, Logitech and Caere* which specifies how image acquisition devices such as scanners, digital cameras and other devices transfer data to software applications. TWAIN allows software applications to work with image acquisition devices without knowing anything about the device itself. If a device is TWAIN compliant and a software application is TWAIN compliant, the two should work together regardless of whether or not the software was bundled with the image acquisition device when it was purchased.

It is possible to attach more than one TWAIN compliant image acquisition device to a PC at the same time. Each of the devices will have it's own separate TWAIN module. This makes it necessary for TWAIN compliant software applications to provide a means for the end user to select which TWAIN device to use during a session. In practice the "acquire" option in the File menu of an application such as PhotoShop would be selected. The user would be prompted to select a suitable TWAIN source which would launch the device's own driver, all without leaving the main application. After scanning, the driver automatically closes, leaving the scanned image open in the main application. No unnecessary quitting, launching, or saving of potentially large and possibly useless files.

Increasingly, manufacturers are shipping scanners with two TWAIN drivers. The first will be a basic, simplistic driver, aimed at the novice scanner. With this, scanning is basically a one-button affair. Click the preview button, and a small preview of the image appears on-screen, in a preview pane. From here, the scanning area may be adjusted along with the resolution and pixel depth. When completely happy with the preview results the Scan button is clicked to initiate the actual scan.

For more advanced there should be an Advanced Scanning Options button somewhere on the first driver. This will open the second driver, the one offering a higher degree of overall image adjustment such as brightness, contrast, colour and Gamma Correction. This allows adjustments to be made to specific ranges of tonal values, either as a whole, or to each primary colour in turn.

Colour calibration:

Any image scanned by desktop scanner can look different on screen than it does when printed, and both can vary quite a bit from the original. The solution to this problem is a colour calibration (or colour matching) system. Such software is really valuable only for scans of high-quality images (transparencies, professional-quality prints, etc.) that need to meet rigorous quality standards. For most people using a desktop scanner, accurate colour is not as important as fast, pleasing colour. This is just as well, as the complexities of colour and human perception have made calibration a daunting challenge and as a consequence, there are several different solutions already available, with more on the way. One of the most comprehensive systems is the *Kodak's Colour Management System (CMS)*, which uses its own colour definitions together with profiles for each different scanner, monitor, and printer in the system to translate and standardize colours. Elements of the Kodak system are bundled with Adobe PhotoShop and other software, and CMS is rapidly becoming the favorite of graphic artists and others who depend on closely matched colours. Other systems have been developed by individual scanner manufacturers and software publishers. These proprietary profile-based systems can also do the job, provided that they include profiles for all of the different devices that will be used for scanning, viewing, editing, and outputting the final image.

A final approach is known as output-based correction, and involves scanning and outputting a standard calibration target, and then making adjustments to colour profiles in order to standardize colours. This is a less sophisticated process, and is probably inappropriate for users who want to continually re-calibrate their systems for optimum results. For basic colour scanning, however, output-based correction is often sufficient.

Photo-retouching:

While scanners provide an effective means of capturing colour images, that's often just the beginning. Once a photograph has been digitized, it's appearance can be dramatically altered by use of a bitmap editor or paint package.

In advertising and publishing, very few images are used 'raw-models' features are 'cleaned up', wrinkles ironed out, eyes sharpened and coloured, and untidy hair trimmed. There is also a trend towards producing attention-grabbing images by distorting and montaging elements of photographs.

Generally the photo-retoucher is trying to do one of two things - change some elements of a picture in a natural way that cannot be detected (like changing the colour of someone's eyes) or produce something unreal and impossible-looking. Either way, the hand of the retoucher must be invisible.

Most of this kind of work is produced using Adobe PhotoShop, but even the simplest paint packages allow these kinds of alterations. However, while a lot can be achieved with the cheaper packages such as PaintShop Pro and PC Paintbrush, packages like PhotoShop, Xres and Corel PhotoPaint make complicated effects much easier to achieve.

Maintenance Aspect:

For cleaning the scanner's glass bed of any scanner use mild soap or an ordinary glass cleaner. Put it on a soft cloth, do not pour it on the glass. Whatever you do, do not get the 'inch' ruler scales wet enough to damage them. The bottom of the rulers is often used for the scanner's internal calibration area before beginning a scan. Don't do anything foolish or excessive in that area. Don't get the glue wet either. Don't pour the cleaning fluid directly on the glass bed due to this risk. Instead put it on the cloth and then wipe with the cloth. You don't notice this film on windows or mirrors, but the scanner's bright light causes the scans to show it. It can cause some odd 'oily' or speckled effects in your scans from such residue between the photo and the glass. Be careful to inspect the glass closely under the scanner's bright light to be certain all of the cleaner film is removed. Inspect the glass (down low from the side) in the bright light for streaks, to make sure you have removed all of it.

Whatever you do, do not scratch the glass. Paper towels are rough, and can make fine scratches on optical surfaces (for example, you would never consider using paper towels on a camera lens), and a soft cloth should be used instead. It would be wrong to recommend it, but I admit that I do use the better softer paper towels on the scanner bed. But I apply them 'easy' without much pressure. Whatever you use, crumple it up real good so that any grit hopefully can find a crevice to get into, away from the glass. Grit is a real issue, keep that in mind, and don't scrub hard.

To check your work, open or remove the scanner's lid, and scan a large area of 'nothing'. Don't put anything on the glass, simply scan nothing with the lid off or fully open. 100 dpi is more than enough. You will get an all-black image, there is nothing to reflect the light back to the scanner. View it both at Actual image size, and also view it reduced to fit on the screen. See any faint haze or cloudy areas? Then you didn't do a good job cleaning the glass. White spots seen there may be dust on the glass, or may be noise. Dust is spots in repeatable locations, noise spots will vary from scan to scan.

Vernon Kinslow suggested as "An old clean diaper or an old clean T-shirt leaves very few lint specks. Also if you clean one side right to left and the other side up and down, if you leave a streak you can go straight to it and correct the problem." This is surely better than a paper towel, but any grit can still scratch.

Normally the scanner's top cover is removed very easily, for the purpose of cleaning the bottom side of the glass. Be certain to unplug the power cord first. There is high voltage on the lamp and line voltage too. Stick to the purpose of cleaning the glass and leave the rest alone.

SCANNERS:

At its most basic level, a scanner is just another input device, much like a keyboard or mouse, except that it takes its input in graphical form. A scanner is a device that captures and converts images to a computer readable format. Its eyes are an array of photosensitive cells that detect light reflected off or transmitted through the object being scanned. This array of receptors, referred to as a *charged-couple device (CCD)*, measures light intensity and converts it into an electrical charge. On the simplest level, a scanner is a device which converts light into 0s and 1s. In other word, scanners convert analogue data into digital data.

An *analogue to digital converter (ADC)* is then required to digitize the information. Each cell in the CCD array creates one pixel and for each pixel a certain number of bits is stored. The more bits of information assigned to each pixel, the better the image quality is produced.

There are also scanners that use *CIS (Contact Image Sensor)* technology. With a CCD scanner, the light reflected from the original document passes through a system of mirrors and lenses which redirect the light to the CCD array. In a CIS scanner, the array of image sensors lies just under the document to be scanned so the sensors catch the reflected light directly. CIS scanners are cheaper to manufacture, smaller and more durable, however their image quality is not as good as CCD. They are more suited to cramped desktops and make useful portable scanners.

There are a number of types of scanner available in the market. While choosing the particular type it is essential to check the priorities and type of document to be scanned. Main types of them are as follows:

Flatbed Scanners:

Flatbed scanners are constructed with a flat glass plate over the photosensitive array and a cover to go over the glass. One can place paper or objects like open books on top of the glass. Light emitted from under the glass reflects off the object being scanned and is picked up by the moving CCD array in the scan head. Flatbeds are a popular and flexible type of scanner available in both monochrome and colour. Their only draw back is that they engage a lot of desktop space.

Sheetfed Scanners:

Unlike a flatbed scanner, the photosensitive array in a *sheetfed scanner* is stationary, and the page being scanned is moved over the array. This is a good type of scanner for someone who intends to scan a lot of documents to produce editable text. If you combine a sheetfed scanner with an *automatic document feeder (ADF)*, you don't need to feed in each sheet by hand. Sheetfeds are available in both monochrome and colour. Although you can feed pictures or small pages into the scanner, the scanned images can get warped so flatbeds are still more flexible. Sheetfed scanners are compact so they are good for limited spaces.

Handheld Scanners:

Handheld scanners have scan heads 4-5 inches wide, which makes them very portable. They plug into the parallel port so they are easy to share among people and can be a good addition to a laptop. The down side of the handheld scanner is that you will have to make several passes over a regular sized document to scan the whole thing. Usually, software is provided that will put the small scans back together, like stitching a patch-work quilt, but this is often time consuming. Moreover, unless you have the slow steady hands of a surgeon, your scans can turn out unevenly.

Pen Scanners:

In case of *pen scanners* you can drag a pen scanner over a line of print like a highlighter. The built-in optical recognition software turns the scan into text that can be downloaded to a computer via serial or *USB port*. Pen scanners can hold hundreds of text pages.

Portable Scanners:

These are like mini versions of sheet-fed or flatbed scanners that are compact enough to fit in a briefcase. Portable sheet-fed scanners are about the size of a three-hole punch while flatbed models are smaller than a hardcover book. These types of scanners plug into a PC Card or *USB port* and can scan in colour or black and white. Portable and handheld scanners have weaker light sources so their image quality is not close to a full-fledged scanner.

Slide, Film, and Transparency Scanners:

Usually people do not need to scan slides or transparencies, but people in the graphics or publishing industry often do. Slides, film, negatives and transparencies have to be scanned so that light transmitted through them is picked up by the photosensitive array. Most scanners have the light source and the scan head on the same side so they can not accommodate these types of images. Since slides and film are so small you need very high-resolution scanners to do the job. There are a few options to scan slides. Some flatbed scanners support a *transparency adapter* (TPA or TPU). This is a backlight that you attach instead of the scanner cover. These adaptable flatbeds sometimes have a special section on the glass bed that is magnified especially for slides. Other kinds of flatbeds come with a pull out drawer where you can place slides, but they are fairly costly. The last option is to get a dedicated slide scanner. These scanners have small scanning areas 4"x5", high resolution and high bit depth, which makes them much more expensive.

DIGITAL CAMERA:

It is easy to understand the booming business that digital camera manufacturers are doing these days. The host of easy-to-use personal and business publishing applications, the dramatic expansion of the Web and its insatiable appetite for visual images, and the proliferation of inexpensive printers capable of photo-realistic output make a digital camera an enticing add-on. Those factors, combined with improving image quality and falling prices, put the digital camera on the cusp of becoming a standard peripheral for a home or library PC.

In principal, a digital camera is similar to a traditional film-based camera. There is a viewfinder to aim it, a lens to focus the image onto a light-sensitive device, some means by which several images can be stored and removed for later use, and the whole lot is fitted into a box. In a conventional camera, light-sensitive film captures images and is used to store them after chemical development.

Digital photography uses a combination of advanced image

sensor technology and memory storage, which allows images to be captured in a digital format that is available instantly without any need for earlier 'development' process. Although the principle may be the same as a film camera, the inner workings of a digital camera are quite different, the imaging being performed either by a *charge coupled device (CCD)* or *CMOS (complementary metal-oxide semiconductor) sensors*. Each sensor element converts light into a voltage proportional to the brightness which is passed into an *analogue-to-digital converter (ADC)* which translates the fluctuations of the CCD into discrete binary code. The digital output of the ADC is sent to a *digital signal processor (DSP)* which adjusts contrast and detail, and compresses the image before sending it to the storage medium. The brighter the light, the higher the voltage and the brighter the resulting computer pixel. The more elements, the higher the resolution, and the greater the detail that can be captured.

This entire process is very environment-friendly. The *CCD* or *CMOS* sensors are fixed in place and it can go on taking photos for the lifetime of the camera. There is no need to wind film between two spools either, which helps minimise the number of moving parts.

Most of the digital cameras are based on the CCD technology and replaces both the shutter and film found in conventional cameras. It's origins lie in 1960s, when the hunt was on for inexpensive, mass-producible memory solutions. It's eventual application as an image-capture device hadn't even occurred to the scientists working with the technology initially.

At Bell Labs in 1969, *Willard Boyle* and *George Smith* came up with the CCD as a way to store data. The first imaging CCD, with a format of 100x100 pixels, was created in 1974 by *Fairchild Electronics*. By the following year the device was being used in TV cameras for commercial broadcasts and soon became commonplace in telescopes and medical imaging systems. It was some time later before the CCD became part of the high-street technology that is now the digital camera.

It works like an electronic version of a human eye. Each CCD consists of millions of cells known as *photosites* or *photodiodes*. These are essentially light-collecting wells that convert optical information into an electric charge. When light particles known as photons enter the silicon body of the photosite, they provide enough energy for negatively-charged electrons to be released. The more light that enters the photosite, the more free electrons are available. Each photosite has an electrical contact attached to it, and when a voltage is applied to this, the silicon below each photosite becomes receptive to the freed electrons and acts as a container for them. Thus, each photosite has a particular charge associated with it, the greater the charge, the brighter the intensity of the associated pixel.

The next stage in the process passes this current to what's known as a read-out register. As the charges enter and then exit the read-out register they are deleted and, since the charge in each row is 'coupled' to the next, this has the effect of dragging the next behind it. The signals are then passed as free of signal noise as possible to an amplifier and thence on to the ADC.

The photosites on a CCD actually respond only to light, not to colour. Colour is added to the image by means of red, green and blue filters placed over each pixel. As the CCD mimics the human eye, the ration of green filters to that of red and blue is two to one. This is because the human eye is most sensitive to yellow-green light. As a pixel can only represent one colour, the true colour is made by averaging the light intensity of the pixels around it, a process known as colour interpolation.

Recognising a glass ceiling in the conventional charge coupled device (CCD) design, Fujifilm have developed a new, radically different CCD with larger, octagonal-shaped photosites situated on 45 degree angles in place of the standard square shape. This new arrangement is aimed at avoiding the signal noise that has previously placed limits on the densities of photosites on a CCD, providing improved colour reproduction, a wider dynamic range and increased sensitivity, all attributes that result in sharper, more colourful digital images.

During 1998 *CMOS* sensors emerge as an alternative image capture technology to CCDs. The CMOS manufacturing processes are the same as those used to produce millions of processors and memory chips worldwide. As these are established high-yield techniques with an existing infrastructure already in place, CMOS chips are significantly less expensive to fabricate than specialist CCDs. Another advantage is that they have significantly lower power requirements than CCDs. Furthermore, whilst CCDs have the single function of registering where light falls on each of the hundreds of thousands of sampling points, CMOS can be loaded with a host of other tasks, such as analogue-to-digital conversion, load signal processing, handling white balance and camera controls, and more. It is also possible to increase CMOS density and bit depth without bumping up the cost.

For these and other reasons, many industry analysts believe that eventually, almost all entry level digital cameras will be CMOS based and that only midrange and high end units will use CCDs. Problems remain to be solved such as noisy images and an inability to capture motion correctly and at the start of the new millennium CMOS technology clearly had a way to go before reaching parity with CCD technology.

However, it's prospects were given a major boost in late 2000 when Silicon Valley based Foveon Inc. announced it's revolutionary X3 technology and the manufacture of a CMOS image sensor with about 3 times the resolution of any previously announced photographic CMOS image sensor and more than 50 times the resolution of the most commonly manufactured CMOS image sensors low-end consumer digital cameras of the time.

Hitherto, CMOS image sensors had been manufactured using 0.35 or 0.50 micron process technology, and it had been generally accepted that 0.25 represented the next round of product offerings. Foveon's 16.8 million pixel (4096x4096) sensor is the first image sensor of any size to be manufactured with 0.18 micron process technology, a proprietary analogue CMOS fabrication process developed in collaboration with National Semiconductor Corporation and represents a two generation leap ahead of the CMOS imager industry. The use of 0.18 micron processing enables more pixels to be packed into a given physical area, resulting in a higher resolution sensor. Transistors made with the 0.18 micron process are smaller and therefore do not take up as much of the sensor space, which can be used instead for light detection. This space efficiency enables sensor designs that have smarter pixels, which can provide new capabilities during the exposure without sacrificing light sensitivity. Comprising nearly 70 million transistors, the 4096x4096 sensor measures 22mm x 22mm and has an estimated ISO speed of 100 with a dynamic range of 10 stops.

Picture quality:

The picture quality of a digital camera depends on several factors, including the optical quality of the lens and image-capture chip, compression algorithms, and other components. However, the most important determinant of image quality is the resolution of the CCD. The more elements, the higher the resolution, and thus the greater the detail that can be captured.

In 1997 the typical native *resolution* of consumer digital cameras was 640x480 pixels. A year later as manufacturing techniques improved and technology progressed the emergence of "megapixel" cameras meant that the same money could buy a 1024x768 or even a 1280x960 model. By early 1999, resolutions were as high as 1536x1024 and before the middle of that year the two megapixel barrier had been breached, with the arrival of 2.3 million CCDs supporting resolutions of 1800x1200. A year later the unrelenting march of the megapixels saw the three megapixel barrier breached, with the advent of 3.34 megapixel CCDs capable of delivering a maximum image size of 2048x1536 pixels. The first consumer model 4 megapixel camera appeared in mid-2001, boasting a maximum image size of 2240x1680 pixels.

At this level, raw resolution is arguably little more than a numbers game and secondary to a digital camera's other quality factors. One of these and almost as important to the quality of the final image as the amount of information the CCD is capable of capturing in the first place - is how cleanly the information is passed to the *ADC*.

The quality of a CCD's colour management process is another important factor and one of the prime reasons for differences in the output of cameras with the same pixel count CCD. The process should not be confused with the interpolation method used by some manufacturers to achieve bitmap files with a resolution greater than their true optical resolution. This method is more accurately referred to as resampling, adds pixels using information already present, and although it increases the effective resolution, it does so at the cost of a reduction in sharpness and contrast. It works by quantifying pixels and qualifying them according to the common traits they possess. In place of the standard interpolation, in which pixels are copied and pasted to create larger images, some cameras employ a software enlargement technique, which it is claimed produces results better than can be achieved by conventional interpolation. This copies and pastes pixels - according to where the enlargement software thinks they are needed to make lines, shapes, patterns and contours - to create larger images.

Another limiting factor is the image compression routines used by many digital cameras to enable more images to be stored in a given amount of memory. Some digital camera store images in a *proprietary format*, requiring the manufacturer's supplied software for access, but most digital cameras compress and save their images in the industry-standard *JPEG* or *FlashPIX* formats, readable on almost every graphics package. Both use slightly lossy compression leading to some loss of image quality. However, many cameras have several different compression settings, allowing the user a trade-off between resolution quality and image capacity, including the option to store images in with no compression at all for the best quality.

LCD Panel:

A colour *LCD panel* is a feature that is present on virtually all modern digital cameras. It acts as a mini GUI, allowing the user to adjust the full range of settings offered by the camera and is an invaluable aid to previewing and arranging photos without needing to connect to a PC. Typically this can be used to display a number thumbnails of the stored images simultaneously, or provide the option to view a particular image full-screen, zoom in close and, if required, delete it from memory.

Few digital cameras come with a true *single-lens reflex (SLR)* viewfinder, where what the user sees through the viewfinder is exactly what the camera's CCD 'sees'; most have the typical compact camera separate viewfinder which sees the picture being taken from a slightly different angle and suffer the consequent problems of parallax. Most digital cameras allow the LCD to be used for composition instead of the optical viewfinder, thereby eliminating this problem. On some models this is hidden on the rear of a hinged flap that has to be folded out, rotated and then folded back into place. On the face of it this is a little cumbersome, but it has a couple of advantages over a fixed screen. First, the screen is protected when not in use. Second, it can be flexibly positioned so as to allow the photographer to take a self-portrait or to hold the camera above their head whilst still retaining control over the framing of the shot. It also helps with one of the common problems in using an LCD viewfinder, viewing difficulty in direct sunlight. The other downside is that prolonged use causes batteries to drain quickly.

In a step designed to try to address this problem, some LCDs are provided with a power-saving skylight intended to allow it to be used without the backlight. In practice, however, this is rarely practical. If there is sufficient light to allow the skylight to work, the chances are that it will also render the LCD unusable.

Digital cameras are often described as having lenses with equivalent focal lengths to popular 35mm-camera lenses. In fact, most fixed-length lenses on digital cameras are auto-focus and have focal lengths around 8mm; these provide equivalent coverage to a standard film camera - somewhere between wide-angle and normal focal length, because the imaging CCDs are so much smaller than a frame of 35mm film. Aperture and shutter speed control are also fully automated with some cameras also allowing manual adjustment. Although optical resolution is not an aspect that features greatly in the way digital cameras are marketed, it can have a very important role in image quality. Digital camera lenses typically have an effective range of up to 20feet, an ISO equivalency of between 100 and 160 and support shutter speeds in the 1/4 of a second to 1/500th of a second range.

Zoom Feature:

Digital cameras offer two distinct varieties of zoom feature: optical zoom and digital zoom. *Optical zoom* works in much the same way as a zoom lens on a traditional camera. Produced by the lens system, it is the magnification difference between minimum and maximum focal lengths. Importantly, in digital cameras this magnification occurs before an image is recorded in pixels. *Digital zoom*, on the other hand, is arguably little more than a marketing publicity.

By the early 2000s many digital cameras came equipped with motorised *optical zoom lenses* which provided an effective range from wide-angle to telephoto. These generally come in a range between 3x and 10x, but it can be higher. The 'times' notation can be confusing, with '3x', for example, having a different precise meaning for different cameras. This is because the actual focal length of a digital camera relates to the size of its sensor. Digital camera specifications therefore generally also cite a '35mm equivalent' lens rating. A 3x zoom lens is the standard offering and generally implies an 'equivalent' focal length of some range between 35mm and 140mm. Some cameras have a gradual zoom action across the total focal range, others provide two or three predefined settings.

Digital zoom is nothing more than the cropping of the middle of an image by a digital camera's software. When an image that has been digitally zoomed 2x is reproduced, either on a display monitor or by being printed, it will effectively be viewed at half its original resolution. A more sophisticated from of digital zoom uses the digital camera's software to interpolate the cropped image back to its original resolution. In this event, fewer of the original pixels are used to represent the enlarged image, which will appear less sharp as a result. Some digital cameras provide a digital zoom feature as an alternative to a true optical zoom, others provide it as an additional feature.

For close-up work, a macro function is often provided, allowing photos to be taken at a distance as close as 3cm but more typically supporting a focal range of around 10-50cm. Some digital cameras even have *swivelling lens* units, capable of rotating through 270 degrees and allowing a view of the LCD viewfinder panel regardless of the angle of the lens itself.

Exposure Mode:

Every digital camera has a fully automatic mode metering that allows a user to simply point and shoot. However, in common with traditional film cameras, they also offer a number of different ways of controlling the exposure of an image. A good exposure will result in an image that has balanced contrast and brightness, with no areas that are too bright and washed out or too dark which also creates loss of detail. *Center weighted metering* is the system used by many digital cameras to measure the correct exposure. With this system, the camera measures the amount of light mostly around the centre area of the lens and less towards the edges. For many situations this works well, but in some lighting situations, centre weighted metering can produce poorly exposed photos. If the scene to be photographed has light areas and dark areas, for example in the shade of trees on bright sunny days with lots of sunlight and shadowed areas, centre weighed metering will often either over expose the bright sections, or underexpose the dark sections. Some digital cameras offer *matrix type metering systems*, which break the scene into several areas and measures each individual area's exposure. This results in an image with a balanced exposure throughout. Spot metering is another option included on some digital camera models. This measures the exposure at a small, precise portion in the centre of the lens, allowing the user to ensure perfect exposure on a particular section of the scene.

Programmed auto-exposure modes keep the basic exposure settings automatic while providing manual access to other camera settings. Some offer aperture and shutter priority modes, which allow the user to set the f-stop or shutter speed, and then automatically calculate the other settings needed to expose an image correctly.

Some cameras provide a manual exposure mode, allowing the photographer a significant degree of artistic licence. Typically, four parameters can be set in this mode: white balance, exposure compensation, flash power and flash sync. Different types of light (outdoor, fluorescent, and so on) will have an impact on the colours in images. *White balance* provides a means to correct for the effect of the lighting conditions, such as sunny, cloudy, incandescent or fluorescent. *Exposure compensation* alters the overall exposure of the shot relative to the metered 'ideal' exposure. This feature is similar to that a SLR cameras, allowing a shot to be intentionally under or over exposed to achieve a particular effect. A *flash power* setting allows the strength of the flash to be incrementally altered and a *flash sync* setting allows use of the flash to be forced, regardless of the camera's other settings.

Some cameras offer what is referred to as '*automatic exposure bracketing*'. With this, several frames are shot when the shutter is released, each at a different exposure setting. The exposure that gave the best result can then be selected.

Most digital cameras offer a number of image *exposure timing options*. One of the most popular is a *burst mode* that allows a number of exposures to be taken with a single press of the shutter. The speed and number of sequential shots that can be captured in a burst is dependent on the amount of internal memory the camera possesses, the image size selected and the degree of compression applied to the photos. Cameras with fast burst rates - specified as a fps rate - generally have a large amount of '*buffer memory*', which is used as a temporarily store prior an image being processed and written to the camera's primary image storage medium. By the early 2000s, the capability to shoot up to 15 shots in a burst at rates between 2 and 6 fps was fairly typical.

Also common is time-lapse, which delays multi-picture capture over preselected interval. Other examples are the ability for four consecutive shots to each use only a quarter of the available CCD array, resulting in a single frame with four separate images stored on it and to take multiple exposures at a preset delay interval, tiling the resulting images in a single frame.

Features allowing a variety image effects are becoming increasingly common. For example, a user may have the option to select between monochrome, negative and sepia modes. Apart from their use for artistic effect, the *monochrome mode* is useful for capturing images of documents for subsequent optical character recognition (OCR). Some digital cameras also provide a '*sports mode*', which adds sharpness to the captured images of moving objects and a '*night shooting mode*', which allows for long exposures.

Panoramic modes differ in their degree of complexity. At the simpler end of the spectrum is the option for a letterbox aspect image that simply trims off the top and the bottom edges of a standard image, taking up less storage space in the process. More esoteric is the ability to produce pseudo-panoramic shots by capturing a series of images and then combining them into a single panoramic landscape using special-purpose software.

Self Timer:

A *self-timer* is a common feature, typically providing a 10-second delay between the time the shutter is activated and when the picture is taken and all modern day digital cameras have a built-in automatic flash, with a manual override option. The best have a working range of up to 12feet and provide a number of different modes, such as auto lowlight and backlight flash, fill flash for bright lighting shadow reduction, force-off for indoor and mood photography and red-eye reduction. Red-eye is caused by light reflected back from the retina, which is covered in blood vessels. One system works by shining an amber light at the subject for a second before the main burst of light, causing the pupil to shrink so that the amount of red light reflected back is reduced.

Watermark:

Another feature commonly available with film cameras that is now available on their digital counterparts is the ability to watermark a picture with a date and time, or indeed some other chosen text. The recent innovation of built-in microphones provides for sound annotation, in standard *WAV format*. After recording, this sound can be sent to an external device for playback, or played back on headphones using an ear socket. Some cameras even offer an audio made that effectively allows it to be used as a voice recorder.

A couple of other features which demonstrate the digital camera's close coupling with other aspects of PC technology are a function that allows thumbnail images to be e-mailed directly by camera-resident software and the ability to capture short video clips that can be stored in MPEG-1 format. Some cameras record silent video only and limit the length of the clips; others sound with the video and allow the clip to be as long as the camera is capable of saving to its storage media.

Borrowing from technology developed for their video camcorder brethren, some digital camera's feature image stabilisation systems. This is particularly useful when used in conjunction with high powered zoom lenses, when it can be very difficult to keep the camera still enough to create a clear image, especially in low light situations and when using a slow shutter speed. Image stabilisation is employed to help overcome the effects small movements of the camera.

Higher-end models also provide support for two memory cards and features more commonly associated with SLR-format cameras, such as detachable lenses and the ability to drive a flash unit from either the integrated hot shoe or an external mount. Indeed, by early 2000 a number of major manufacturers, including Nikon and Kodak, were preparing to follow rival Minolta's lead in pushing digital cameras into the mainstream professional market by offering single lens reflex technology at 'affordable prices'. While the difference between professional and consumer models remains significant, it decreased dramatically during the late 1990s, as has the gap between digital cameras in general and their analogue counterparts.

PIM technology:

In 1998, the Photographic Industry Association comprising most of the world's digital camera manufacturers came up with a set of standards called the *Design Rule for Camera File System (DCF)*. This defined colour parameters for digital camera images which took into account the limited colour range supported by the WWW and computer display monitors. This digital camera image 'target colour space' was, in fact, identical to the sRGB colour space originally developed by Microsoft Corporation and Hewlett Packard in the mid-1990s. The implications of this were that after being shot, an image's hues were compressed by a digital camera to make them fit within the DCF-defined colour spectrum.

The DCF colour standard worked well enough until early in the new millennium. However, by then the sRGB colour space was not as large, nor as rich in colour as the spectrum available on even the inexpensive photo-printers of the day. Users were thus being deprived of the opportunity to produce output with the nuances of colour their equipment was capable of.

In early 2001 Epson unveiled a solution to this problem, in the shape of its *Print Image Matching (PIM) technology*. PIM works within the structure of DCF, while allowing devices with extended colour capabilities to print the greater spectrum of colour captured by a digital camera. It does this by getting a digital camera to store the complete colour information for a captured image before it is converted to the DCF standard. When images are output to a printer the PIM printer driver software reads the associated PIM data, thereby allowing them to be reproduced with the extended range of colour. PIM doesn't interfere with a digital camera's operation in any way. Specifically, it has no impact on image processing and therefore shot-to-shot time. Indeed, users can turn PIM off if it is not required. In the event that images shot with PIM enabled are subsequently transferred to software applications or printers that don't support PIM, the PIM data is simply ignored.

PIM can be viewed as both an open and adaptable standard. Open in as much as the technology is available to any printer manufacturer who chooses to license it and adaptable since it can evolve as CCD sensors and printers improve, ensuring that the colour fidelity of printed images will continue to be preserved in the future. It also offers the prospect of digital camera manufacturers being able to add user selectable image enhancements for use at picture taking time, allowing photographers to preset the intensities of such controls as contrast, colour balance, highlight point, shadow point, brightness, saturation, and sharpness to suit their personal preferences.

Memory storage:

Many first generation digital cameras contained one or two megabytes of internal memory suitable for storing around 30 standard quality images at a size of 640x480 pixels.

Unfortunately, once the memory had been filled no more pictures could be taken until they'd been transferred to a PC and deleted from the camera.

Modern digital cameras use removable storage. This offer two main advantages: first, once a memory card is full it can simply be removed and replaced by another; second, given the necessary PC hardware, memory cards can be inserted directly into a PC and the photos read as if from a hard disk. By early 1999 two rival formats were battling for domination of the digital camera arena:

* **CompactFlash:** First introduced in 1994 by SanDisk corporation, and based on *flash memory technology*, *CompactFlash (CF)* provides non-volatile storage that doesn't require a battery to retain data. It is essentially a PC Card flash card that's been reduced to about one quarter of its original size and uses a 50-pin connection that fits into a standard 68-pin Type II PC Card adapter. This makes it easily compatible with devices designed to use PC Card flash RAM. CompactFlash cards measure 43mm by 36mm. They are available in both Type I and Type II cards, although predominately the former. A Type I card is 3.3mm thick and will operate in both a Type I and a Type II slot. A Type II card 5mm and will operate in a Type II slot only. By late 2001 maximum capacities had reached 512MB.

* **SmartMedia:** Originally known by the awkward acronym *SSFDC (Solid-State Floppy Disk Card)* when it first appeared in 1996, the *Toshiba*-developed *SmartMedia* cards are significantly smaller and lighter than CompactFlash cards, weighing 0.48g with a form factor of 45 by 37mm and a thickness of only 0.78mm. It uses its own proprietary 22-pin connection - but like its rival format is PCMCIA-ATA-compatible and can therefore be adapted for use in notebook PC Card slots. Capacities are less than for CompactFlash - 128MB was still the maximum capacity

by late 2001, capable of storing 560 high-resolution (1200x1024) still photographs - and cost per megabyte is similar to that of CompactFlash.

Devices are available for both types of media to allow access via either a standard floppy disk drive or a PC's parallel port. The highest performance option is a SCSI device which allows PC Card slots to be added to a desktop PC. CompactFlash has a far sturdier construction than its rival, encapsulating the memory circuitry in a hard-wearing case. SmartMedia has its gold-coloured contact exposed, and prolonged use can cause scoring on its surface. Its memory circuitry is set into resin and sandwiched between the card and the contact. CompactFlash can operate between temperatures of 25°C to 75°C and claims a 100-year usage life; SmartMedia can be used between 0°C to 50°C and claims that it can be written to at least 250,000 times.

With the 24-bit colour, 1800x1200 resolution images being produced by consumer models by mid-1999 occupying a massive 6.2MB - storage capacity is becoming an increasingly important aspect of digital camera technology. It is not clear which format will emerge as winner in the standards battle. SmartMedia has got off to a good start, but CompactFlash is used in PDAs as well, and this extra versatility might prove an important advantage in the long run.

By the end of 1999 a third memory technology had emerged, in the shape of Sony's *Memory Stick*. Smaller than a stick of chewing gum and initially available with a capacity of 32MB, Memory Stick is designed for use in small AV electronics products such as digital cameras and camcorders. It's proprietary 10-pin connector ensures foolproof insertion, easy removal, and reliable connection and its unique Erasure Prevention Switch helps protect stored data from accidental erasure. Capacities had risen to 128MB by late 2001, with the technology roadmap for the product going all the way up to 1GB. By the end of 2001 the digital camera memory market share for CompactFlash, SmartMedia and Memory Stick was estimated to be around 44%, 33% and 6% respectively.

Disk storage:

Some higher-end professional cameras use PCMCIA hard disk drives as their storage medium. Although they consume no power once images are recorded, and have much higher capacity than flash memory (a 170MB drive is capable of storing up to 3,200 images 'standard' 640 by 480 images), the hard disk option has some disadvantages. An average PC Card hard disk consumes around 2.5W of power when spinning idle, more when reading/ writing, and even more when spinning up. This means it is impractical to spin up the drive, take a couple of shots and shut it down again; all shots have to be taken and stored in one go, and even then the camera's battery will last a pitifully short length of time. Fragility and reliability are also a major concern. The moving parts and extremely tight mechanical tolerances to which hard drives are built make them inherently less reliable than solid-state media.

With the resolution of still digital cameras increasing apace and the emergence of digital video cameras, the need for flexible, high-capacity image storage solutions has never been greater. In 1999 omega launched an innovative removable storage device intended for use in digital cameras as well as notebook and handheld devices. The battery-powered Clik! drive supports the PC Card interface and provides a capacity of 40MB on its 10g, 50x50mm media. It comes complete with an adapter, allowing the transfer of images from CompactFlash and SmartMedia cards to its significantly cheaper 40MB magnetic disk media. The following year Agfa's ePhoto CL30 Clik! became the first digital camera to use Clik! disks as its primary mode of storage.

Mid-1999 also saw IBM enter the fray with the launch of the world's smallest hard disk drive, its revolutionary Microdrive. The *Microdrive* uses a single one-inch diameter platter that weighs just 16g and spins at 4,500rpm. Using the Type II CompactFlash interface, the new device, initially available in capacities of 170MB and 340MB - took CF-style storage into a new dimension. By the end of 1998 the largest available

CompactFlash memory card held just 64MB and in mid-2000 digital cameras rarely came with more than an 8MB card. In 2000 IBM announced 512MB and 1GB versions of the Microdrive. As well as their increased capacity, these second-generation drives also boasted improved sustained data rates, and thus extended battery life and a non-operating shock rating that had been improved by 50%, from 1,000 G to 1,500 G.

One of the major advantages of a digital camera is that it is non-mechanical. Since everything is digital, there are no moving parts - and subsequently a lot less that can go wrong. However, this didn't deter Sony from taking a step which can be viewed as being imaginative and retrograde at the same time - including an integrated 3.5inch floppy disk drive in some of its Mavica range of digital cameras. While the integrated drive obviously added both weight and bulk to a device that's usually designed to be as compact as possible, it is true that some users actually prefer designs that lend themselves to a double-handed grip. Its potential unreliability was addressed to some extent by the provision of a 'Whole Disk' copy facility that allowed users to easily make copies of disks. This copied images from the original disk to the camera's internal memory and thence to a second disk.

In the second half of 2000 Sony updated its innovative approach with the introduction of a Mavica model which stored images on 8cm/185MB CD-R media. A so-called 'mini CD' provides sufficient capacity to store around 300 640x480 resolution images using JPEG compression. In early 2001 the concept advanced a step further with support for mini rewritable media as well as write-once CD-R media. Performance implications that would have been unacceptable for digital camera applications made certain (write-time) trade-offs unavoidable. Notwithstanding the constraints imposed, the primary benefit of CD-RW media – it's reusability is fully realised. As well as being able to delete images one at a time, starting with the most recent and working backward, users have the option to erase an entire disc via a 'format' function.

Connectivity:

Despite the trend towards removable storage, digital cameras still allow connection to a PC for the purpose of image downloading. Until the late 1990s the principal method of transfer was via a conventional *RS-232 port serial cable* at a maximum speed of 115Kbit/s. However, since then *USB connectivity* has become the norm, with most manufacturers bundling cameras with the necessary cables and driver software. In the past some professional models offered a fast *SCSI connection*.

USB is also exploited by a method of image transfer that emerged in the early 2000s and that saves the bother of having to connect a camera to a PC at all. These 'media readers' are available for all the common media types CompactFlash, SmartMedia, MemoryStick, MultiMedia Card etc. and simply plug in to a USB port, either directly or via an extension cable. They're also available in combo units, capable of reading multiple media formats. They draw power from the USB port and so don't waste a camera's precious batter power. They vary in speed, the fastest being capable of data transfer rates approaching 1 mbps. For those without USB, adapters are also available that allow a CompactFlash or SmartMedia card to be inserted into a special floppy disk like device that works from a standard 3.5inch 1.44MB floppy disk drive.

Supplying a digital camera with TWAIN drivers that allow the user to simply download images to a standard image editing application has also becoming standard practice. Some digital cameras provide a *video-out socket* and S-Video cable to allow images to be displayed directly to a projector, TV or VCR. Extending the 'slide show' capability further, some allow images to be uploaded to the camera, enabling it to be used as a mobile presentation tool.

An increasing number of digital cameras have the ability

to cut out the computer and output images directly to a printer. But without established interface standards, each camera requires a dedicated printer from its own manufacturer. As well as the more established printer technologies, there are two distinct technologies used in this field: *thermo autochrome* and *dye sublimation*.

Digital vs Film:

Despite the massive strides it has made in recent years, the conventional wisdom remains that though digital cameras offer advantages in term of flexibility, when it comes to picture quality they still fall a significant way behind that of a traditional camera and film. However, since this assertion involves the comparison of two radically different technologies, it is worth considering more closely.

The first step is to consider resolution. Whilst it is easy to state the resolution of a digital camera's CCD, expressing the resolution of traditional film in absolute terms is more difficult. Assuming a capture resolution of 1280x960 pixels, a typical 1999 model digital camera is capable of producing a frame size of just over 1.2 million pixels. A modern top-of-the-range camera lens is capable of resolving at least 200 pixels per mm. Since a standard 100ASA 35mm negative is 24x36mm, this gives an effective resolution of 24x200x36x200 = 34,560,000. This resolution is rarely achieved in practice and, indeed, rarely required. However, on the basis of resolution, it is clear that digital cameras still have some way to go before they reach the level of performance as their conventional film camera counterparts.

However, this is only part of the answer. The next factor to consider is colour and here digital cameras have an advantage. Typically, the CCDs in digital cameras capture colour information in 24 bits per pixel. This equates to 16.7 million colours and is generally considered as being the maximum number the human eye can perceive. On its own this doesn't constitute a major advantage over film. However, unlike the silver halide crystals in a film, a CCD captures each of the three component colours (red, green and blue) with no bias. Photographic film tends to have a specific colour bias, dependent on the type of film and, to a certain extent, the manufacturer and this can have an adverse effect on an image, according to its colour balance.

However, its silver halide crystals that give photographic film is its key advantage. While the cells on a CCD are laid out in rows and columns, the crystals on a film are, to all intent and purposes, randomly arranged with no discernible pattern. As the human eye is very sensitive to patterns, it tends to perceive the regimented arrangement of the pixels captured by a CCD very easily, particularly when adjacent pixels have markedly different tonal values. Magnify photographic film, and though the dots will be discernible, there will be no apparent regularity. Its for this reason that modern inkjet printers use a technique known as '*stochastic dithering*', which adds a random element to the pattern of the ink dots in order to smooth the transition from one tone to the next. Photographic film does this naturally, so the eye perceives the results as less blocky when compared to digital stills.

There are two possible ways around this problem for digital cameras. Manufacturers can either develop and build models that can capture a higher resolution than the eye can perceive, or they can build in dithering algorithms that alter an image after it has been captured by the CCD. Both of these options have downsides however, such as increased file sizes and longer processing times.

X3 technology:

In 2002 after five years of research and development, the prospect of truly affordable film-quality digital cameras was given a massive boost when Foveon Corporation unveiled a digital camera imaging sensor which the company claimed was capable of obviating 35mm film. In conventional digital cameras systems colour filters are applied to a single layer of photo-detectors in a tilted mosaic pattern. The filters let only one wavelength of light i.e. red, green or blue pass through to any given pixel, allowing it record only one colour. As a result, typical mosaic sensors capture 50% of the green and only 25% of each of the blue and red light. The approach has inherent drawbacks, no matter how many pixels a mosaic-based image sensor might contain. Since they only capture one third of the colour, mosaic-based image sensors must rely on complex processing to interpolate the two-thirds they miss. Not only does this slow down the speed of image rendering, interpolation also leads to colour artifacts and a loss of image detail. Some cameras even intentionally blur pictures to reduce colour artifacts.

Foveon's new CMOS image sensor uses the company's revolutionary *X3 technology* to capture up to three times more information per pixel than modern day digital cameras at similar mega pixel resolutions. The X3 image sensors accomplish this by using three layers of photo detectors embedded in silicon. The layers are positioned to take advantage of the fact that silicon absorbs different colours of light at different depths, so one layer records red, another layer records green and the remaining layer records blue. This means that for every pixel on a Foveon X3 image sensor, there's actually a stack of three photo detectors. The result is a sensor capable of capturing red, green, and blue in each pixel location in essence, the first full-colour digital camera image sensor.

Foveon's X3 technology not only leads to better pictures, but better cameras too. In fact, it opens the door to an entirely new breed of camera, one that can switch seamlessly between still photography and digital video, without sacrificing the quality of either. Because *Foveon* X3 image sensors capture full colour at every pixel location, those pixels can be grouped together to create larger, full-colour '*super pixels*'. This capability, called *Variable Pixel Sizing (VPS)*, marks another first in digital photography.

With VPS, the signals from groups of pixels can be combined so the camera reads them as one. For example, a

2300x1500 image sensor contains more than 3.4 million pixels. But if VPS is used to group those pixels into 4x4 blocks, the image sensor would appear to have 575x375 pixels, each of them 16 times larger than the originals. The size and configuration of a pixel group is variable - 2x2, 4x4, 3x5, etc. and is controlled through sophisticated circuitry integrated into Foveon X3 image sensors.

The grouping of smaller pixels into larger pixels increases the signal-to-noise ratio. This allows the camera to take full-colour pictures in low-light conditions with reduced noise. Using VPS to reduce the resolution also allows the sensor to run at higher frame rates, accelerating the rate at which pictures can be taken. These gains in speed and sensitivity offer other benefits such as an improved focusing system.

VPS also makes it possible to switch from high-quality still photography to outstanding digital video, enabling the development of the first cameras with true dual-mode functionality. Hitherto, cameras attempting to accommodate both still and video functions have had to sacrifice performance in one mode to do the other well. The unique design of Foveon X3 image sensors enables them to handle both functions without compromise.

BATTERIES:

The fact is that a digital camera is a high drain device that uses up batteries at an alarming rate. Turning off the LCD display helps considerably as does running on AC power whenever possible, such as when transferring images to a PC or viewing images on a TV. While digital camera batteries come in all shapes and sizes, the AA format is by far the most common. However, traditional alkaline AA batteries should be relied on only in emergencies. They are simply not strong enough for a power-hungry instrument like a digital camera for more than a few dozen images.

An ordinary AA *alkaline battery* is typically supposed to have a capacity of 2.4Ah (amp hours). This means it should be able to deliver 1.2A for two hours before going flat. However, whilst this expression of cell capacity is fine for low-current applications - like personal cassette players, its not at all appropriate for a high-current device like digital cameras, which are capable of imposing loads of such magnitude that they can cause a battery's voltage to drop precipitously, with the consequence that its life is greatly reduced.

Rechargable cells are much better at handling the high output currents required by digital cameras and despite the fact that some types have a notoriously poor 'shelf life' – the length of time they'll hold a charge – they're generally the most cost-effective option in the long run. They come in a variety of types or 'families':

* *Nickel cadmium (NiCd)*: Probably the most robust and commonly available rechargeable battery. Good for on average 700 charge and discharge cycles, they lose about 1% of their power a day when not in use and suffer badly from 'memory effect' - the accumulation of gas bubbles on the cell plates of a battery that has only been partially discharged before recharging, which causes a reduction in the plate area within the battery and thus its capacity.
* *Nickel metal hydride (NiMH)*: Good for between 500-1000 charge and discharge cycles, NiMH batteries offer about 40% more capacity than NiCDs but at a significantly higher cost. They have a slightly worse shelf-life than NiCds but, in the main, have the important advantage of not being prone to 'memory effect'.
* *Lithium ion (Li-ion)*: Li-ion batteries offer about twice the capacity of a similarly sized NiMH battery and are good for about 500 charge and discharge cycles. However, they require their own special charger and are more expensive than other battery types. Their big advantage is a long shelf

life: up to ten years. For that reason, they make great emergency spares.

* ***Zinc-air batteries:***

Zinc-air batteries have been around for decades and have found practical use in hearing aids and pagers where their lightweight and high energy density have enabled them to dominate the market for a number of years. In recent years electrical and mechanical enhancements have allowed the technology to be adapted for use in portable electronic systems.

Zinc-air battery cells are chemically similar to the everyday alkaline battery. However, in place of the magnesium dioxide paste used by the former is a thin carbon electrode used to catalyse oxygen from air for reaction with zinc. This significantly increases the energy density, giving zinc-air one of the highest energy densities for conventional battery systems.

By the early 2000s disposable zinc-air batteries had emerged as an increasingly popular back up or emergency power source in digital photography, compatible with more than 50 digital camera models. They offered a long shelf life and sufficient power for several hours of continuous use. Packaging typically included a recloseable foil pouch that allowed the user to extend battery life after initial use, a built-in belt clip for easy carrying and a cord that allowed connection through a camera's DC jack.

LABORATORY BASED STANDARD REQUIREMENTS:

Basic requirements for an ideal image/text capturing laboratory are as follows:

General:

* One type of camera only. Both still and moving images will be produced by the same camera.
* Moving image photography, both film and television, integrated into a single electronic system offering extremely high definition, without the scanning lines used in present television systems.

* Still photography catered for by the same camera.

A moving image camera is a stills camera capable of taking pictures in very rapid succession. A stills camera with a very fast motordrive may be regarded as a moving image camera.

Types of Cameras:

* Digital electronic.
* Both Colour and Black & White outputs.
* No film used in the camera.

Photo-sensitive emulsions and 'wet' processing will be things of the past. Toxicity considerations will rule out our present system of photography, long before resistance to change dies out.

Lens:

* Electronic zoom of fixed focal length.
* No moving parts, including lens elements.
* Focusing accomplished by varying the refractive index of the lens.
* Zooming accomplished by varying the sensor's scanned area, not by the physical movement of lens elements.
* Widest lens angle of 180° horizontal angle of view produced by scanning the whole of the sensor.
* Narrowest lens angle of 1° horizontal angle of view produced by scanning a small area of the sensor.
* Angle of view the only parameter of a lens which needs to be referred to. The angle of view is the only important measurement for the photographer. It is independent of format. Reference to lenses by their focal length, as an indicator of 'narrow', 'standard' or 'wide' angle, will become meaningless.
* Electronic Iris diaphragm, with no moving parts.

  Its operation will be similar to liquid crystal, darkening

the edges of an internal element.Its only importance will be to control depth of field.

Lens hoods:

No longer required. Protection from flare will be by liquid crystal darkening of the outer part of the front lens element, restricting the light entering the lens to only that, which is actually used in the formation of the image. This masking will automatically follow the zoom demand and format selection, adapting its shape and size to suit. Image contrast will thus be increased, flares eliminated.

Matte boxes:

No longer required. Filters, including colour correction filters and effects filters such as Star and Diffusion, will all be electronic. Even Dior silk stockings, much used in film and television photography, will be electronic.

Format:

* Any aspect ratio may be set, to match an existing format or to suit user-preference
* Shape and size infinitely variable.

Image sensor:

* '*Photon dimension' resolution*, from a new type of sensor replacing both film and the CCDs (charge coupled devices) used in present electronic cameras.
* The 'grain' or 'pixel' size of the new sensor will be related to one photon.
* The limiting resolution factor will be that of the lens.

One of the main problems with present day video, based on scanning lines, is that the line structure imposes intrinsically poor resolution, resulting in the inability to enlarge sections of the picture without severe loss of quality. Even the CCDs used in digital still cameras have resolutions that are only just adequate for their intended purpose.

Sensitivity

* Inherent relative sensitivity extremely high, in the order of ISO 10 to the power of 6. (ISO 1,000,000)
* Inherent sensitivity reducible by electronic attenuation to permit more workable lens apertures and for the control of depth of field.
* Sensitivity may be changed on a scene-by-scene or frame-by-frame basis. No longer do photographers have to expose the whole roll of film at the same speed rating.

Motor drive:

* Built-in 200 frames per second silent electronic '*motor drive*'.
* Much higher speeds available for special scientific applications.
* Single frame exposure capability, for both still images and time-lapse moving image applications.

Being a combined motion picture and stills camera, the camera will offer still photographers a built-in silent electronic 'motor drive'.

Spectral response:

* Spectral sensitivity both within and beyond the visible spectrum.
* Infra Red, Ultra Violet and X-Ray sensitivity selected by the user.
* Settings may be invoked or modified on a scene-by-scene or shot-by-shot basis.

Colour balance:

* Any colour temperature may be selected.
* Any ambient light (including mixed light) may be balanced to. Colour balance not restricted to 'Daylight' (approximately 5500K) or 'Studio' (approximately 3200K).

* Non black-body radiators (such as fluorescent and discharge lighting) can be balanced.
* Settings may be stored and modified on a scene-by-scene or shot-by-shot basis.

Stereoscopy:

* Stereoscopic.
* Anti-phase sensors at the lens nodal point give a stereoscopic separation equal to the diameter of the front element of the lens.
* Spatial separation electronically increases this to give separation equal to the human eye.
* Greater separation available for scientific purposes and special effects.

Movements:

* Full view camera movements a standard facility.
* These will be carried out either in the camera or in post production - in 'D4' (*Desktop Digital Daylight Darkroom*)
* Other effects (for example, line curvature) provided electronically.

Automatic picture leveling:

* Special circuitry to cancel out unsteadiness caused by camera shake or vibration.
* May be switched off when an unsteady effect is especially called for by the script.

Like a built-in *SteadiCam* or *gyroscope*, this will be especially useful for news cameramen working under critical conditions.

Viewfinder:

* Flat screen, viewable in ambient light using both eyes. No more squinting into a darkened hole with one eye. Ambient light falling onto the *viewfinder* will be reflected back to

the photographer, whilst being electronically attenuated where the areas of the picture are lower than peak level. Thus, viewfinder brightness will be directly proportional to ambient light falling upon it. This effectively eliminates the problems encountered with conventional cathode ray tube based viewfinders, which suffer because the more stray light that falls onto the screen, the more difficult it is to view the picture.

* Ability to be used on or off the camera, without cable connection.
* Stereoscopic or two-dimensional display, selected as required by the photographer.
* Internal illumination option, for use in low ambient light situations.
* Alternative Head-Up Display or Virtual Reality-type helmet, to enable the camera to be used quite separately.

Storage device/recorder:

* Integral electron-dimension storage device.
* Advanced real-time compression techniques record only the changes in successive frames.

Size and weight:

* Small size
* Light weight

Ergonomics

* Equally easy to use for both left- and right-handed photographers.
* Easy to hold in the hand with stability.
* Most operational controls easily accessible and operable by thumb and forefinger.

Processing:

* *Desktop Digital Daylight Darkroom - D4* - enables full

post-production control and editing of the recorded images, with non-linear editing of moving images allowing instant access to any part of a lengthy recording.

* Direct output, without the need for complex processing via computers, to give instant viewing on television-type displays.
* Direct (filmless) link to plate making.
* Special applications, such as multi-camera control for large television outside broadcasts, continue to use additional application specific processing add-ons.
* Special 'looks', such as those of old (1990s) film stocks, will be able to be imparted to images.

RAM based requirements:

When you open an image, Photoshop loads the data into the computer's *RAM* and reserves an additional equal amount of RAM in which to store an 'undo' version (in case you change your mind or make a mistake), plus the same amount again for computation of effects. This adds up to three times as much RAM as the size of the image. If you have allocated 10Mb of RAM to Photoshop, everything is fine if you are working on images up to 3.3Mb. For larger images, when it doesn't find enough RAM, Photoshop cleverly uses hard drive as temporary storage or 'virtual memory'. Photoshop calls this a 'scratch disc'. Writing and reading to and from a scratch disc takes time - much more than to and from RAM.

How much RAM you need depends on the size of data you will be handling. Prints 8x10 inches at 300 ppi need a 20.6Mb file, so you need 61.8Mb of RAM plus enough for the operating system and any other applications you may want to open at the same time, say 80Mb in total. If you want to work on 4x5 inch Base*64 Pro Photo-CD images at 72Mb each, the amount of RAM required jumps up to 216Mb - so round the total up to 256Mb. They can handle large image files with much less RAM than Photoshop.

If you are a Mac user, while you have the Photoshop icon highlighted, press Command+M to make an alias of it. Drag this alias to the desktop, where it will be conveniently placed to drag and drop images onto - much quicker than going File>Open and then navigating to the image. Dragging and dropping an image file to the alias also launches the Photoshop application itself. I find such shortcuts essential.

PART III : WEB ENABLING OF LIBRARY

4

WORLD WIDE WEB (WWW)

HISTORICAL DEVELOPMENTS:

During the past two decades, the world has witnessed a technological evolution that has provided a medium of communications entirely new to mankind. Through the use of networks, information in all forms has been disseminated throughout the world. This is known today as the World Wide Web (WWW) grew out of a project that began with a different intent (ARPANET). The ARPANET was designed and developed in 1969 by *Bolt, Beranek and Newman* under a contract for the Advanced Research Project Agency (ARPA) of the US Department of Defence. The purpose of the Network was to study how researchers could share data and how communications could be maintained in the event of a nuclear attack. The ARPANET Project was eventually turned over to the National Science Foundation (NSF) and ultimately became known as "Internet", by which the NSF allowed access to businesses, universities and individuals. In the beginning, many resources such as electronic mail, news, telnet, FTP, and Gopher were offered through the Internet to its users.

One of the early applications of the Internet was its most popular application, the World Wide Web (WWW) or sometimes known as "the Web". The WWW is one of the software tools that through the use of hypertext allows computers to link information in new ways, different from a sequential reading approach, to make it easy to retrieve and add information from different computer sources through the use of communication links. In the short time since its inception, the Internet has indeed revolutionized business, in that it redefines the methods used in traditional business practices and offers another important channel for mass communication.

During the early days of the Internet, the technology was primarily utilized as a medium for communication (e.g. e-mail) purposes. Soon afterwards many organizations from both the public and the private sectors began to discover that, in addition to use of the Internet and its popular WWW, they could utilize this technology in support of marketing and information dissemination purposes. This resulted in companies realizing that the greatest payback in investing in the technologies of WWW would be in sharing information about the firms' products and services to the firms' stakeholders. As a result, successful organizations of all sizes and types have been adopting different applications/technologies of WWW in discovering emerging ways of doing business that even a decade ago could not be imagined. In recent years, the WWW has become the glittering palace of information and electronic trading that some visionary pundits promised. The Web has provided many improvements in the marketing business sector, particularly in areas such as "identification of sales prospects", "immediate access to information (i.e. product/service specifications and pricing) and allowing customers to obtain goods regardless of their geographical locations around the world.

According to Bird the main reasons why businesses are utilizing the Web are primarily marketing related. They use the Web to:

* establish a presence;
* network;
* make business information available
* serve customers;
* heighten public interest;
* release time-sensitive data;

* sell products and services;
* reach a highly desirable demographic market;
* answer frequently asked questions;
* stay in contact with salespeople;
* open international markets;
* create a 24-hour service;
* make changing information available quickly;
* allow feedback from customers;
* test-market new services and products;
* reach the media; and
* reach a specialized market.

The data illustrate the changing foundation of marketing based on the emergence of the Web. Although the financial marketing advantages are not yet proven, the Web remains a fairly inexpensive form of communicating with potential customers.

In addition to the use of the Web for communication and marketing purposes, during the past two decades, there have been many other emerging Web-enabled technologies, including:

* mail technologies;
* electronic interchange;
* electronic data interchange (EDI);
* electronic commerce (EC);
* network management;
* organizational intranets/extranets;
* online analytical processing (OLAP); and
* teleconferencing, etc.

CRITICAL ISSUES OF WEB-ENABLED TECHNOLOGIES:

The Web-enabled technologies are not free of associated risks and controversies. Like many other emerging technologies, this technology has its share of associated problems and limitations. In order to clearly understand the total potentials of these technologies, one must also assess the limitations, stipulations and provisions of these technologies in modern organizations. Some of the many issues, problems and limitations of the Web-enabled technologies are given below.

Bandwidth restrictions and latency:

A large percentage of the Web users run low-speed modems 56K, which in reality cause considerable delays in obtaining web-based materials when the corresponding downloads incorporate images, animation and audio. A recent study by a popular server revealed that about one in five users was connecting with graphics turned off to eliminate the annoying latency of loading web. *Latency* issues are also being experienced with some of the more popular Web documents. In this case, the slowness relates to the number of requests an individual Web server can handle at once. Since the Web has evolved into a multimedia intensive tool, gridlock has become an even bigger problem than for the other part of the Internet.

Cyberloafing:

Surfing the Internet, wasting time and accessing inappropriate materials are the primary concerns, which have been labeled as cyberloafing. Studies show that, once users become more familiar with the Web, the cyberloafing practice becomes a common phenomenon. Cyberloafing can also take place in a different form, where users receive unsolicited messages about all kinds of decent and indecent offers. In this case the user is not searching sites to explore; however, in the act of reading the unsolicited e-mail message they can be tempted to explore inappropriate materials.

In the latter case when the cyberloafing takes place at work by an employee of an organization, besides the productivity lost, there is also the liability concern associated with cyberloafing, if the act involves the downloading of indecent materials. These actions can create a company liability that potentially involves allegations of "harassment", "free speech", "privacy", "jurisdiction" and even "copyright infringement".

Equity:

Some argue that the Web will bring forth a better democracy within the USA by returning the power to the people. This may not come to pass if the issues of equity and demographic trends are poorly addressed. According to Pitkow the users joining the Web, their estimated median income ($64,700 annually) is well above the national median of $36,950 as estimated by the 1993 US Census and they are predominantly male (70 per cent). Whether the explanations for the lack of utilization by some groups lie in the issue of availability, affordability or usability remains a topic for additional research. However, all statistics clearly indicate that this technology is not equally utilized by all classes of society in the USA as well as other countries.

Exposure points:

As more companies utilizing Web-enabled technologies incorporate the ability for remote access to their computer systems by their employees, there is a higher risk of information exposure. In other words, these emerging exposure points are inroads which can lead to sloppy data entry into the systems, as well as savvy hackers breaking into the system, where inadequate control measures might not be applied at every exposure point.

Flooding of the Web with content for content's sake:

With the ease of access to the Internet and the availability of access to Web development tools, there is an abundance of slick and costly Web Pages on the Internet. Many of these WebPages include information that is not helpful to their viewers. They are merely on the Internet so the individuals or company that owns the site can claim that they have a web site. In recent years, many companies have been beginning to view content for content's sake as a wasteful exercise and instead are beginning to understand that the role of the Web site is to facilitate business processes.

Inadequate search facilities on the WWW:

One of the important issues of the Internet is that of inadequate search facilities with the lack of a high level query language for locating, filtering and presenting WWW information. Some search engines search the document headers, some look for the document themselves, while others look for indices or directories. As a result, one can conclude that much of the information on the Web is presented in a dynamic and somewhat chaotic fashion. In a recent survey of Web users, 34.5 per cent of the participants were not able to locate a site which was known to exist and 23.7 per cent were not able to figure out how to return to a site that they had previously visited.

Maintainability and integrity of data:

The task of keeping up with commercial WebPages by maintaining the latest information is considered to be a costly issue facing many organizations. As a company's Web site becomes more elaborate and complex, the task of maintaining and validating information included in their Web sites becomes much more costly and complex too. Ultimately, it will reach a point where maintaining and ensuring the accuracy of information becomes difficult. Inaccurate and out-of-date information included in the Web site can contribute, in part, to decisions being made by the user of the information that are based on data that are either inaccurate or outdated which can harm the organization's business processes.

Security:

The issue of *Web security* is considered as being among the most important challenges of many organizations. Many security experts believe that the existing layers of security are considered to be inadequate and in some cases fragile. It is important to note that security is a broad term. In some instances the term security is related to privacy, while in other contexts the term refers to the integrity of data. Security issues can be better understood by examining the concrete examples of security threats and risks.

E-mail risks:

It is identified that several unique risks related to e-mail, including volume levels that overload systems, *junk mail*, *mail bombs*, "*flaming*" or flooding a user with messages, interception and unauthorized reading of electronic mail, and improper representations by employees.

False store fronts:

A false store front risk is presented when a hacker sets up a Web page that looks legitimate for business but uses the site to gather credit card numbers, account numbers or other confidential information from unsuspecting consumers, after which, the "business" disappears and the information obtained is utilized for unauthorized transactions.

Industrial espionage:

There is a growing concern that the Web requires additional methods to secure the confidential data accessible on the Web against interception and decryption by unauthorized users. "Sensitive about anything that touches their legacy applications and custom-built accounting and inventory tools that run the business side of the corporation, most companies have tiptoed carefully into so-called. *Webification*". Most of the attacks launched at industry systems take advantage of simple holes largely attributed to misconfigured systems, poorly written software, mismanaged systems, or user neglect.

Information vandalism

Vandalism in this context is the unauthorized modification of data that are available on the Web. Often this takes the form of "graffiti" placed in the text of a home page, which are unauthorized, often embarrassing and potentially harmful. The contents of certain transactions are modified, such as the payee of an electronic check or the amount of a bank account transfer.

ISP linkage alterations:

Internet Service Providers (ISP) provide access to the

Internet via the maintenance of a domain name server, which provides a direct translation of a WWW address into an Internet address. If a link established within a Web Page is altered, then the user may be erroneously linked to an inappropriate, potentially embarrassing location within the web.

Viruses:

With the increasing number of networked computers, the ability of a developer to place a virus within any number of programs and have that virus become widespread to all who download, open or execute the program or file is great .

Webware:

Many systems allow software developers to attach programs which are executed upon access to a WebPage. This software is termed Webware. "Simply visiting a WebPage may cause you to unknowingly download and run a program written by someone you don't know or don't trust".

With the advent of Electronic Commerce (EC) and the overwhelming interest in utilization of this technology for modern commerce, there are many challenges presented by the security issues and risks. Although there are perceived issues with security, especially related to EC, there is still substantial interest in utilizing the Web technology for EC.

System incompatibilities:

The issue of system incompatibilities has been dominant during the past several years. In many cases, cross-platform compatibility is not always available in all of the emerging technologies being developed which, can result in difficulty when trying to make them function in unison.

Unauthorized use of computer resources:

Today's emerging interconnectivity technologies have presented opportunities for computer misuse which were not previously possible. The Boeing corporation recently has begun reviewing the issue of URL filtering of objectionable material.

According to the Computer Fraud and Abuse Act, computer usage in excess of one's level of authorization can result in personal liabilities for any harm caused. Many companies are debating the best solution to this issue. In response, Boeing has decided that "restricting site access is a cumbersome management process, but unrestricted access to public web sites could open the company up to legal issues".

User ignorance and perceptions:

The lack of adequate understanding of the Internet and its usage and risks has been a contributing factor in maintaining secure systems. Modern information systems comprise many different components of distributed hardware, software and data maintained on different locations by different systems. According to Prawitt *et al.*, while it is becoming increasingly critical for users to exercise sound control practices, most are not adequately trained to do so.

Web performance tracking:

With the explosive growth of Web applications, services, traffic volumes and contents, a management void has been created. If the performance and availability of the Web services are not managed and information cannot be accessed quickly, it is likely that the user will jump to a competitor's site, which results in the loss of business McConnell states as "To achieve peak performance, the IT department must harmonize many critical elements, including the transport network and its Featured Sites service levels, if any, Web server hardware and software and information content."

Low overhead e-payment facilities:

Low overhead e-payment facilities, micropayments, are needed as a service on the WWW, so that advertising is no longer necessary to cover the costs of running services and so that the content providers can sell information in the same fashion as the purchase of newspapers or a single. The process typically works, whereby an account is opened with a micropayment system and the software required is downloaded to work with the user's browser. Digital Equipment Corporation has developed a system that "will eliminate minimum purchase requirements of ten to 25 cents now imposed by other electronic payment methods, allowing users to buy and sell information profitability down to fractions of a cent".

Failure to adhere to standards:

Failure of primary companies and their products to adhere to the standards that exist (e.g. HTML and JavaScript) is an issue that was ranked highly by the expert panel on the study. The primary importance of this issue lies in the fact that many companies, which have monopolistic power, such as Microsoft, do not abide by those standards that exist in the industry. Their lack of following the industry standards can be viewed as an attempt in creating a new "standard" with their products.

Unsolicited e-mail (spamming):

Spamming occurs when an endless stream of mail is received, which can overflow the user's mailbox and can even choke the user's system. In recent years, with the easy to obtain free e-mail addresses from many different sources such as "Hotmail", "Juno", and "Netscape", the act of forwarding unsolicited e-mail messages has reached a crisis level for many users everyday. Users all around the world receive unsolicited e-mail messages for promoting products or services.

Use of metadata:

The World Wide Web currently has a huge amount of data with practically no classification information and this makes it extremely difficult to handle data/information effectively. Many systems can support knowledge management by establishing a metadata - information about information - standard, so that users of data can obtain the raw materials that enable them to capture, store and share knowledge that is gathered from different sources. This task can be accomplished by adding to Web objects a metadata classification which will assist search engines and Web-based digital libraries to properly classify and structure the information on the WWW.

Ensure a continued global body:

Many users of the WWW are concerned that the body of knowledge created on the Internet consists of some kind of global understanding to which users from all over the world can relate. This task has been assigned to the World Wide Web Consortium (W3C) to accomplish. W3C is a global body that was founded to lead the WWW to its full potential by developing common protocols that promote its evolution and ensure its interoperability. The primary services offered by W3C to users and developers consist of:

* acting as a depository of information about the World Wide Web;
* providing reference code implementations to embody and promote standards; and
* providing various prototype and sample applications to demonstrate use of new technology.

Privacy and confidentiality agreements:

The privacy and confidentiality agreements issue entails an aspect of the security issue in that it is a violation of users' privacy. This issue addresses the dilemma of individual right to privacy and the sharing of confidential information about people in society. With the technology advances of the past two decades, many users believe that more information about their lives is now shared with others through the use of the Internet. Despite many existing laws with regard to the "right to privacy" of users of the Internet, everyday there are many cases of the violation of users' privacy and confidentiality, where information that should not be shared by others is passed throughout the Webs of this modern technology.

Global laws for Net crimes:

Despite the fact that there is a global perception that crimes and criminals should be punished, there is considerable confusion regarding what is a criminal act in one society in comparison with another. Global laws for *Net crimes* are considered to be a mplex issue that is anticipated to remain unresolved for a long based on the current dilemma of establishing national laws regarding Internet.

Required labeling of sites:

With millions of Web sites in existence and millions added constantly, there is a concern about how to differentiate Web sites from one another regarding their contents. This particular issue can be considered an offset of two other critical issues discussed in this chapter, "inadequate search facilities" and "global laws". Supporters of this issue claim that by labeling sites search engines can provide more effective and efficient search processes, and also labeling will assist the enforcement of any global laws related to Net crimes. This issue becomes valid after having global laws in place to deal with Net crimes.

System utilization:

The issue of system utilization deals with the overall question of what functionality or information sharing is best served on the World Wide Web. During the past decade, many users have seen the transformation of this technology into a business tool, where businesses all over the world can conduct their commerce through this medium. Many users question what should be the overall functionality of the Internet in the future, as this becomes more acceptable as a common medium for communication purposes.

Expressibility of HTML:

The expressibility of HTML issue is primarily concerned with the ability of the user to create documents that contain complex layouts. This is very important for the functionality of the Web because of its usefulness in presenting information with all its characteristics and potentials. As more users rely on the use of this technology to share information with other users, the role of HTML or other tools will become more recognized. These tools should allow users at all levels to create documents that contain the full picture and are not limited by the shortcomings of the tool that they used.

Lack of standardized vector graphics:

This issue deals with the lack of incorporation of vector graphics in Web design. The adoption of vector graphics in Web design would enable programmers to present better user interfaces to Web applications - "Vector graphics scale easier, download faster and print better than their bit-mapped graphics counterparts GIF and JPEG". Standardization in this facet of the Web is at an early stage, whereby a couple of proposals have been placed before the W3C for consideration.

Hype:

Web sites are effective if used imaginatively and intelligently. Many firms boast that their Web sites are showcases for the firm's goods and services. Few, however, are very effective at serving the cause of the firm's betterment. Despite this reality, there is a considerable degree of hype among organizations and their Web designers that their Web sites should consist of more whistles and bells in order to compete with their rivals, as well as to attract more customers.

Access appliances that avoid computer software management:

This particular issue was added by one of the expert panel members to the list of critical issues of this study during round one. (Other panel members questioned the real meaning of this issue but, regrettably, the expert who suggested the issue did not provide any clarification or further responses after the first round. At the time of writing, there is no clear explanation concerning this issue.

WORLD WIDE WEB CONSORTIUM (W3C):

The W3C was created to lead the Web to its full potential by developing common protocols that promote its evolution and ensure its interoperability. It is an international industry consortium jointly run by the MIT Laboratory for Computer Science (MIT LCS) in the USA, the National Institute for Research in Computer Science and Control (INRIA) in France and Keio University in Japan. Services provided by the Consortium include:

* A repository of information about the World Wide Web for developers and users,
* Reference code implementations to embody and promote standards,and
* Various prototype and sample applications to demonstrate use of new technology.

At present over 500 organizations are Members of the Consortium.

5
WEB DESIGNING TECHNOLOGIES

HYPERTEXT MARKUP LANGUAGE (HTML):

HTML is the lingua franca for publishing hypertext on the World Wide Web. It is a non-proprietary format based upon SGML, and can be created and processed by a wide range of tools, from simple plain text editors - you type it in from scratch to sophisticated WYSIWYG authoring tools. HTML uses tags such as <h1> and </h1> to structure text into headings, paragraphs, lists, hypertext links etc.

EXTENSIBLE HYPERTEXT MARKUP LANGUAGE (XHTML):

The Extensible HyperText Markup Language (XHTML) is a family of current and future document types and modules that reproduce, subset, and extend HTML, reformulated in XML. XHTML Family document types are all XML-based, and ultimately are designed to work in conjunction with XML-based user agents. XHTML is the successor of HTML, and a series of specifications has been developed for XHTML.

HTML Working Group:

To develop the next generation of HTML as a suite of XML tag sets with a clean migration path from HTML 4. Some of the expected benefits include: reduced authoring costs, an improved match to database & workflow applications, a modular solution to the increasingly disparate capabilities of browsers, and the ability to cleanly integrate HTML with other XML applications.

XML LINKING:

XML Linking Language (XLink) allows elements to be inserted into XML documents in order to create and describe links between resources. It uses XML syntax to create structures that can describe the simple unidirectional hyperlinks of today's HTML, as well as more sophisticated links.

Tools:

* X2X from empolis UK Ltd. is an XML XLink Engine. X2X allows linking between documents and information resources without needing to change the resources that are being linked. X2X removes the requirement to insert link information inside document content.
* Fujitsu XLink Processor: Fujitsu XLink Processor, which is developed by Fujitsu Laboratories Ltd., is an implementation of XLink and XPointer.
* xlinkit.com is a lightweight application service which provides rule-based XLink generation and checks the consistency of distributed documents and web content. One can request xlinkit.com to link desired information along with required rules. xlinkit.com will generate the links that can be used for navigation. It will also diagnose inconsistent information.
* Mozilla: The Open source browser has support for XLinks simple links.
* Amaya: The W3C editor/browser now supports XLinks simple links too.
* XTooX is a free XLink processor that turns extended out-of-line links into inline links. It takes as its input a link base- a document containing only XLinks - and puts the links into the referenced documents.

XML BASE:

This specification proposes syntax for providing the equivalent of HTML BASE functionality generically in XML documents by defining an XML attribute named xml base.

XML POINTER LANGUAGE (XPointer):

XML Pointer Language (XPointer) is the language to be used as a fragment identifier for any URI-reference that locates a resource of Internet media type. XPointer has been split into a framework for specifying location schemes, and three schemes. The xpointer() scheme, which is based on the XML Path Language (XPath), is still under development. It supports addressing into the internal structures of XML documents. It allows for traversals of a document tree and choice of its internal parts based on various properties, such as element types, attribute values, character content, and relative position.

Tools:

* Fujitsu XLink Processor: Fujitsu XLink Processor, which is developed by Fujitsu Laboratories Ltd., is an implementation of XLink and (almost all of) XPointer.
* libxml: the Gnome XML library has a beta implementation of XPointer. The full syntax is supported but the test suite does not cover all aspects yet.
* 4XPointer: this is an XPointer Processor Written in Python by Fourthought, Inc.
* At the University of Bologna two different implementations of XPointer are in progress, one in JavaScript for ASP pages and another in Java.
* XPointerLib from the Connexions project, a mozdev.org project providing XPointer support for Mozilla / Netscape 7 / Phoenix browsers. It is an XPCOM service written in JavaScript that creates and resolves a subset of the XPointer language.

MATHEMATICAL MARKUP LANGUAGE (MATHML):

The Mathematical Markup Language (MathML) is a way of describing math syntax so mathematical ideas can be exchanged using the web. A W3C recommendation means the consortium considers the specification to be stable makes a contribution to web interoperability and has been thoroughly reviewed by the W3C membership. The MathML spec provides for two sets of markup tags, first set presents the mathematical notations and second set relays the semantic meaning of expressions. MathML is not intended as user language; it is meant for use with software tools that translate mathematical equations into a human-readable format. The consortium says such tools are already under development, both as freeware and as commercial products. *XML, or eXtensible Markup Language*, is a version of the ISO- standardized Standard Generalized Markup Language (SGML), and is viewed as the successor to HTML. It provides for more wide-ranging applications than merely displaying text and pictures. For instance, the sets of tags are extensible, as the name suggests, so developers can make up their own tags as required, which can be used to identify a particular piece of text as belonging to a particular group. It also retains some of SGML's basic features, such as complex structures, validation and human readability. Users who want to publish a mathematical equation on the Web must render and display the equation as an image. MathML shares XML's capability to retrieve data objects in real time from external databases and monitors being used as retrievable computer entities.

MathML 1.0 provides a solid foundation for representing mathematical expressions. However, a number of critical requirements dating back to the original HTML-Math Working Group Charter remain to be accomplished, and other goals developed as a result of MathML implementations or of feedback from the community remain to be met. MathML 1.0 offered a unique opportunity to ensure effective math on the Web through its widespread acceptance, and it seems very desirable to maintain the present MathML 1.0 Recommendation, and to further develop the specification.

The current Math Working Group proposes that the W3C establish a new Math Working Group to continue the work of the W3C Math activity. The proposed revision MathML aims to reduce the overhead involved in publishing scientific and technical Web content, while increasing its scope to accommodate new areas of science. We expect that as a result of a new MathML the suite of tools for authoring, managing, transforming and rendering MathML will continue to evolve and leverage the relationship between MathML and other W3C specifications.

World Wide Web Consortium (W3C) released of the Mathematical Markup Language (MathML) 2.0 in February, 2001 as a W3C Recommendation. MathML 2.0, an XML application, provides encoding mathematical notation and content for use on the Web. A W3C Recommendation indicates that a specification is stable, contributes to Web interoperability, and has been reviewed by the W3C Membership, who are in favor of supporting its adoption by academic, industry, and research communities. *MathML 2.0* Extends the Foundation for Math on the Web. MathML 2.0 consist of a number of XML tags that can be used to markup an equation in terms of its presentation and also its semantics. As a result, MathML 2.0 attempts to capture something of the meaning behind equations rather than concentrating entirely on how they are going to be formatted out on the screen. This is because mathematical equations are meaningful to many applications independent of how they are rendered aurally or visually.

SYNCHRONIZED MULTIMEDIA INTEGRATION LANGUAGE (SMIL):

The World-Wide Web has grown up in an ad hoc way, starting with text, then adding images, sounds and video. So the simultaneous use of these multimedia elements has never been addressed properly. In particular, the only way to create a constantly changing flux of text, sounds and images is to create a video stream. This approach is both inflexible and inefficient, as video tends to require high bandwidth.

The Synchronized Multimedia Integration Language

(SMIL, pronounced "smile") enables simple authoring of interactive audiovisual presentations. SMIL is typically used for "rich media"/multimedia presentations which integrate streaming audio and video with images, text or any other media type. SMIL is an easy-to-learn HTML-like language, and many SMIL presentations are written using a simple text-editor. SMIL permits multimedia streams to be played sequentially or in parallel, and for different elements to be placed in absolute positions on the screen. Its hotlinks can be embedded in video multimedia elements, as well as in text and images. This would allow SMIL presentations to offer full interactivity.

SMIL enables authors to bring television-like content to the Web, avoiding the limitations of traditional television and significantly lowering the bandwidth requirements for transmitting this type of content over the Internet. With SMIL, producing audio-visual content does not require learning a programming language and can be done using a simple text editor. SMIL was developed by the W3C *Synchronized Multimedia (SYMM) Working Group*, a mix of experts from the four divergent industries (CD-ROM, interactive television, Web, and audio/ video streaming) interested in bringing synchronized multimedia to the Web. *Philipp Hoschka*, chairman of the W3C SYMM Working Group and editor of the SMIL specification says "Such an agreement is the necessary signal for content providers to start creating synchronized multimedia content for the Web, and, thus, a prerequisite for market growth in this area."

Features:

SMIL offers the following key features:

* Easy-to-learn synchronization primitives: 90 percent of the power of SMIL can be tapped by mastering only two tags, "parallel" and "sequential."
* Temporal hyperlinking: This feature offers all the capabilities of hyperlinks in HTML and adds capabilities required in time-based presentations.

* Reusability of media objects: All components of the multimedia presentation are referenced via URLs rather than physically embedded into a SMIL file. For example, videos stored in a digital video library can be reused in many presentations.
* Load balancing: Different media objects in a presentation can be stored on different servers—another benefit of using URLs rather than physically including media objects within the SMIL document.
* Language selection: Authors can indicate that an audio track is available in several languages, thus increasing the potential audience of the content.
* Bandwidth selection: Authors can express that a media object such as an audio track is available in different versions, each having been encoded for a different transmission bandwidth. This guarantees that presentations can be played even when only low-bandwidth access is available.

To understand the utility of SMIL we can analyze television news broadcast as an example, large parts of the screen contain text, still images, and graphical elements with full-motion video occupying only a small part of the screen real estate. These media types can all be included on a Web page today. However, the Web lacks a simple way to express synchronization over time such as "play audio file A in parallel with video file B" or "show image C after audio file A has finished playing." SMIL enables this type of information to be expressed easily, allowing television-like content to be created on the Web.

SMIL avoids having to swamp the Internet with high-bandwidth video if you want to create television-like content, said *Hoschka*. When rewritten in SMIL, many of today's television news broadcasts would require far less bandwidth, eliminating the need to convert low-bandwidth media types such as text and images into high-bandwidth video. Till 1998

RealNetworks and Allaire Corp. have been the only major vendors to announce significant SMIL-supporting products.

SMIL Tools: Prime Versions

SMIL 1.0:

SMIL 1.0 is the W3C Recommendation (standard) for Web-based multimedia first implemented by RealNetworks with the advent of RealSystem G2 in June of 1998. RealNetworks co-authored the SMIL 1.0 specification. SMIL 1.0 enables the delivery of long format, Web-based multimedia to a broad range of audiences, from modems to T3 Internet connections. As an open XML-based language, SMIL enables a wide range of audio-visual presentation authoring environments, ranging from simple text editors to graphical editing tools such as RealNetworks RealSlideshow.

SMIL 1.0 enables authors to bring TV-like content to the Web, avoiding the limitations of traditional television and lowering the required Internet bandwidth for this type of content. With SMIL, producing audio-visual presentations for the Web is easy, since it can be done using a simple text editor, and does not require learning a programming language.

SMIL Boston:

Next version of XML-based multimedia language features reusable modules, generic animation, improved interactivity and TV integration Leading the Web to its full potential. SMIL Boston builds upon the W3C SMIL 1.0 Recommendation, and adds important extensions, including reusable modules, generic animation, improved interactivity, and TV integration, all written in the Extensible Markup Language (XML).

The SMIL Boston Working Draft proposes several extensions to SMIL 1.0, such as integration with TV broadcasts, animation functionality, improved support for navigation of timed presentations, and the ability to integrate SMIL markup in other XML-based languages. These extensions are based on the feedback received from authors, implementers and others using the SMIL 1.0 infrastructure existing today.

SMIL Boston Modules Enable Integration with other XML-based Languages Designing the syntax and semantics of a markup language requires significant time and effort. Fortunately, designers of other XML-based languages are able take •full advantage of SMIL Boston, as it is designed as a set of reusable modules. With SMIL Boston, language designers can for example add timing information to Extensible HyperText Markup Language (XHTML) and Scalable Vector Graphics (SVG), simply by importing the SMIL Boston Timing and Synchronization module, rather than building timing models and syntax from scratch.

SMIL Boston Enables Creation of Animations in XML Animation is a popular approach to create compelling Web content while reducing the download time for a presentation. While the most popular form of animation on the Web today is animated GIF, it has several limitations. As the animation is encoded in binary format, one needs special editing tools to create it. Further, only *GIF* images can be used in the animation one cannot include a *JPEG* image, or an XHTML headline, or an SVG vector graphics object.

The SMIL Boston animation module eliminates the limitations found of the animated GIF format. Since SMIL Boston modulesnare based on XML, animations can be written using a simple text editor. It enables animation of any media format, such as JPEG images, PNG images, even video clips. The SMIL Boston animation module can also be used to add animation capabilities to other XML-based languages, such as XHTML, SVG or an XML-based 3D language.

One of the benefits of SMIL presentations over traditional TV content is that users can navigate within the presentation, thereby focusing on the parts of the presentation that interests them most. This can be achieved by providing a table of contents of the presentation.

Using SMIL Boston, the table of contents and the content itself can be contained in the same SMIL file, rather than being split over several files. This simplifies authoring, and reduces delays when users navigate through the presentation.

Another benefit over traditional TV content is that SMIL allows authors to include additional content (e.g. background information) on the topic of the presentation. In SMIL Boston, optional parts can be contained in the same SMIL file as the main presentation. This allows the user to access optional content without interrupting the main presentation.

Future digital television broadcasts are to use very similar techniques as today's SMIL presentations. Rather than broadcasting audio and video signals only, digital TV broadcasts may consist of a combination of images, text and other media objects that are synchronized at the receiver. Some of the capabilities of SMIL Bostan are:

* New Transitions module describing transitions within SMIL and other XML-based documents
* Improved control for runtime content choices
* New Metadata module for better description of SMIL documents published on the Web
* Improved interactivity
* Improved hyper navigation
* Improved integration into other XML-based languages
* Tighter integration with multimedia protocols such as RTP and RTSP

SMIL Boston modularizes SMIL functionality, providing standards based integration of SMIL functionality with other XML based languages and applications. Content authors and application developers both benefit from this flexibility: application developers can integrate needed functionality while content authors are able to build on their existing knowledge base.

SMIL 2.0:

SMIL has grown substantially from its first incarnation. SMIL 2.0 describes modules for timing, animation, layout, linking, media objects, transitions, and more. The basic media types supported are animation, audio, image, text, text stream, and video. Some tag names from the 1.0 release have been updated or deprecated to make SMIL 2.0 compatible with the document object model.

So why should anyone give a heap of beans about SMIL? SMIL makes for compelling content. Video presentations on the Web basically stink today. A two-inch video popup, for example, has little visual impact. Animation files, a la Macromedia Flash, on the other hand, can generate impact and motion. Integrate the two techniques within a single presentation and you are getting somewhere.

Both animation and video suffer from some key problems, however. Imagine internationalizing a video. You might have to dub the video in six languages and make it available in three bandwidth-optimized versions. Eighteen files just to support a video clip. If you want to add optional captions for the hearing impaired, the number will increase up to 36 files.

With the SMIL approach, the video, audio, and text components can be treated as individual synchronized streams. The video object can self-select the appropriate bandwidth version. The language for the audio and text stream can be chosen dynamically from user preferences as the SMIL page is composed. Thirty-six files have now been reduced to no more than 15 simpler files. More importantly, if there is a problem with a caption, it can be fixed in a text editor without impacting the other files.

SMIL: Important Documents

SMIL 2.0

* W3C Recommendation: Synchronized Multimedia

Integration Language (SMIL 2.0) <http://www.w3.org/TR/smil20>

* Translations </AudioVideo/SMIL/translations> of SMIL 2.0
* W3C Note "XHTML+SMIL Profile" <http://www.w3.org/TR/XHTMLplusSMIL/>
* SMIL 2.0 Testsuite <http://www.w3.org/2001/SMIL20/testsuite/>
* Implementation Results from SMIL2.0 Test suite <http://www.w3.org/2001/05/23/SMIL-Implementation-result.html>
* For SMIL profile used in 3GPP MMS <http://www.mobilemms.com/mmsfaq.asp> (Multimedia Messaging Service) and Streaming Service

SMIL 1.0

* W3C Recommendation: Synchronized Multimedia Integration Language (SMIL) 1.0 Specification </TR/REC-smil>
* Translations </AudioVideo/SMIL/translations> of SMIL 1.0
* SMIL 1.0 Player Testcases <http://smil.nist.gov/Testcase.html> and
* SMIL Player Feature List <http://smil.nist.gov/Feature.html>

SMIL: Players

SMIL 2.0

* RealOne Platform <http://www.realnetworks.com/solutions/ecosystem/realone.html?src=rnhmfs> by RealNetworks with full support for the SMIL 2.0 Language profile.
* GRiNS for SMIL-2.0 <http://www.oratrix.com/GRiNS/

SMIL-2.0/> by Oratrix provides a SMIL 2.0 player which supports SMIL 2.0 syntax and semantics.

* SMIL Player by InterObject <http://www.inobject.com/mmplay.htm>. The player supports SMIL 2.0 Basic Profile. The player runs on PC with Windows NT/2000/XP and handheld devices with Pocket PC, such as Compaq iPAQ. Refer to product specifications
* Internet Explorer 6.0 <http://www.microsoft.com/windows/ie/preview/default.asp> by Microsoft includes implementation of XHTML+SMIL Profile
* Internet Explorer 5.5 <http://www.microsoft.com/windows/ie/default.htm> by Microsoft supports many of the SMIL 2.0 draft modules including Timing and Synchronization, BasicAnimation, SplineAnimation, BasicMedia, MediaClipping, and BasicContentControl.
* NetFront v3.0 <http://k-tai.impress.co.jp/cda/article/news_toppage/13103.html> is a micro browser for PDA/mobile phone/information appliances. It claims to support HTML 4.01/XHTML 1.0/ SMIL Basic/SVG Tiny.
* Pocket SMIL <http://wam.inrialpes.fr/software/pocketsmil/>, it is written in C++.
* RubiC <http://www.roxia.co.kr> is developed by Roxia Co.,Ltd. It includes an authoring tool and player, and fully supports SMIL 2.0 specification. "RubiC" is also available for mobile handset for mobile internet MMS (Multimedia Messaging Service)
* List of MMS Simulators <http://lists.w3.org/Archives/Public/www-mobile/2002Aug/0007.html>

SMIL 1.0

* Grins (SMIL1.0) <http://www.oratrix.com/GRiNS/index.html> by Oratrix
* HPAS <http://www.research.digital.com/SRC/HPAS> by Compaq

* Lp player <http://www.prodworks.com/> by Productivity Works
* QuickTime 4.1 <http://www.apple.com/quicktime/authoring/qtsmil.html> by Apple
* Realplayer 8 <http://www.real.com/> by RealNetworks
* Soja, <http://www.helio.org> a Java based SMIL player by Helio
* S2M2 <http://smil.nist.gov/player> , a Java Applet-based SMIL Player by NIST
* Schmunzel <http://www.salzburgresearch.at/suntrec/schmunzel/>, a Java player by SunTREC Salzburg.
* X-SMILES <http://www.xsmiles.org/> a Java based open browser by TML laboratory

SMIL: Authoring Tools

* Ezer <http://www.smilmedia.com> by SMIL Media
* Fluition <http://www.confluenttechnologies.com> by Confluent Technologies
* Grins <http://www.oratrix.com/GRiNS/index.html> by Oratrix
* GoLive6 <http://www.adobe.com/products/golive/overview.html> by Adobe
* HomeSite <http://www.allaire.com/products/homesite/index.cfm> by Allaire
* MAGpie <http://ncam.wgbh.org/webaccess/magpie>, a captioning tool by WGBH
* Hi-Caption <http://www.hisoftware.com/hmcc/acc4mcc.html>, a captioning tool by Hisoftware
* MovieBoard <http://www.simple.co.jp/products/10MovieBorad.htm>, for e-learning (Japanese only)
* MMS Simulators <http://lists.w3.org/Archives/Public/www-mobile/2002Aug/0007.html> list

* Perly SMIL <http://www.webiphany.com/perlysmil/>, a SMIL 1.0 Perl module
* RealSlideshow Basic <http://forms.real.com/rnforms/products/tools/slideshowbasic/index.html? key=868E21032182964> by RealNetworks
* SMIL Composer SuperToolz <http://autodownload.sausage.com> by HotSausage
* Smibase <http://smibase.com/>, a server-installed software suite
* SMIL Editor V2.0 <http://www.docomo-sys.co.jp/prod/soft/smil2.html>, by DoCoMo.
* SMILGen <http://www.smilgen.org> by RealNetworks, a SMIL (and XML) authoring tool designed to ease the process of XML.
* SMIL Scenario Creator <http://w3-mcgav.lab.kdd.co.jp/sc/indexe.html> by KDDI
* TAG Editor 2.0 - G2 release <http://tag.digital-ren.com> by Digital Renaissance
* Tagfree 2000 SMIL Editor <http://www.tagfree.com/english/product/product02.asp?menu=2>
* TransTool <http://www.psych.uiuc.edu/~kmiller/dvguide/analysis_tools.htm> - open source transcription tool
* VeonStudio <http://www.veon.com/> by Veon
* SMG <http://www.smilmedia.com.> for a PDA, a BREW, a Phone and a PC by Smilmedia
* The IBM Toolkit for MPEG-4 <http://www.alphaworks.ibm.com/tech/tk4mpeg4> creates MPEG-4 binary from content created in XMT-O (based on the SMIL 2.0 syntax and semantics).

SMIL's critics say it overlaps and even conflicts with existing standards, including HTML 4.0, Dynamic HTML, Cascading Style Sheets (CSS) and in particular, the Document Object Model (DOM).

Finally better impact, improved accessibility, and easier maintenance add up to better user and better developer experience. It is not true that SMIL will replace HTML. But it should at least displace HTML from the task of serving up unsynchronized video in pop-up windows. Whether SMIL makes its mark via standalone players such as RealPlayer and QuickTime or via browsers like IE 5.5, folks will smile when they surf to your SMIL enhanced site.

DOCUMENT OBJECT MODEL (DOM):

The Document Object Model is a platform-and language-neutral interface that allow programs and scripts to dynamically access and update the content, structure and style of documents. The document can be further processed and the results of that processing can be incorporated back into the presented page.

Need of Document Object Model:

"Dynamic HTML" is a term used by some vendors to describe the combination of HTML, style sheets and scripts that allows documents to be animated. The W3C has received several submissions from members companies on the way in which the object model of HTML documents should be exposed to scripts. These submissions do not propose any new HTML tags or style sheet technology. The W3C DOM Working Group is working hard to make sure interoperable and scripting-language neutral solutions are agreed upon.

W3C's Document Object Model (DOM) is a standard Application Programming Interface (API) to the structure of documents; it aims to make it easy for programmers to access components and to delete, add, or edit their content, attributes and style. In essence, the DOM makes it possible for programmers to write applications that work properly on all browsers and servers and on all platforms. While programmers may need to use different programming languages, they do not need to change their programming model. W3C's DOM thus offers programmers a platform and language neutral program interface, which will make programming reliable across platforms with languages such as Java and ECMA Script a reality.

It is the most widely implemented XML parser interface today. DOM reproduces an XML document's data hierarchy in a programming language's native object format, giving programmers an easy and familiar way of working with the data in the document. Developers can iterate through the document's data elements and even change the document's content programmatically.

However, the DOM recommendation does not cover searching or file input/output (loading and saving XML documents). The DOM API loads the entire XML document into memory, favoring repetitive operations performed on short documents. For lengthy documents, the SAX (Simple API for XML) API is a better choice.

DOM Level 2 Brings Platform-Neutral Dynamic Content to the Web Created and developed by the W3C Document Object Model (DOM) Working Group, this specification extends the platform- and language-neutral interface to access and update dynamically a document's content, structure, and style first described by the DOM Level 1 Recommendation. The DOM Level 2 provides a standard set of objects for representing Extensible Markup Language (XML) documents and data, including namespace support, a style sheet platform which adds support for CSS 1 and 2, a standard model of how these objects may be combined, and a standard interface for accessing and manipulating them.

Leading the Web to its full potential, the World Wide Web Consortium (W3C) released the Document Object Model Level 2 specification as a W3C Recommendation. The specification reflects cross-industry agreement on a standard API (Applications Programming Interface) for manipulating documents and data through a programming language (such as Java or ECMA Script). A W3C Recommendation indicates that a specification is stable, contributes to Web interoperability, and has been reviewed by the W3C Membership, who favor its adoption by the industry.

This W3C recommendation extends the basic data representation capability of the DOM API to other programming concepts such as custom namespaces, style sheets, events, iterators, filters, and range functions. This gives developers a standardized way of expressing functions that they previously had to create on their own. For example, if you want your document to call a particular function whenever it encounters a specific event in the data, DOM Level 2 provides a simple and standard way of doing so.

The DOM Level 2 Recommendation builds on the solid work done in DOM Level 1, and gives Web authors the power to move to XML for dynamic content," says Lauren Wood of SoftQuad Software Inc., and Chair of the W3C DOM Working Group. "The DOM also provides developers with the interoperability and integration ability they need. There are now several implementations of the DOM, in different programming languages, which provide the basis of powerful systems meeting the business needs of several large organizations.

Most commercial XML processing software include support only for namespaces and style sheets, so using a product that supports DOM Level 2 will give developers a greater range of flexibility. However, because the other types of triggers are not widely supported, one could run into compatibility problems that negatively affect the portability of his project.

DOM Level 2 Delivers Interoperable Software for XML Documents with Namespace Support. DOM Level 1 was designed for HTML 4.0 and XML 1.0. With DOM Level 2, authors can take further advantage of the extensibility of XML. Simply put, anywhere you use XML, you can now use the DOM to manipulate it.

The standard DOM interface makes it possible to write software (similar to plug-ins) for processing customized tag-sets in a language- and platform-independent way. A standard API makes it easier to develop modules that can be re-used in different applications. DOM Level 2 provides support for XML namespaces, extending and improving the XML platform. As more sites move to XML for content delivery, DOM Level 2 emerges as a critical tool for developing dynamic Web content. DOM Level 2 Extends the Dynamic, Device Independent Web The DOM defines a standard API that allows authors to write programs that work without changes across tools and browsers from different vendors. But beyond this, it provides a uniform way to produce programs that work across a variety of different devices, so all may benefit from dynamically generated content.

DOM Architecture:

The DOM Architecture is divided into various modules. Each module addresses a particular domain. Domains covered by the current DOM API are XML, HTML, Cascading Style Sheets (CSS), and tree events. Future domains can be the rendered content (that is, the content displayed on the screen which might differ from the input document), user agent function, etc.

DOM Core:

The DOM Core defines a tree-like representation of the document, also referred as the DOM tree, enabling the user to traverse the hierarchy of elements accordingly.

Refer also to the DOM Range and Traversal modules to manipulate the tree elements/structure defined in the DOM Core.

DOM XML:

The XML DOM extends the Core platform for specific XML 1.0 needs, such as processing instructions, CDATA, and entities.

DOM HTML:

The HTML DOM defines a set of convenient easy to use ways to manipulate HTML documents. The initial HTML DOM only describes methods, such as how to access an identifier by name, or a particular link. The HTML DOM is sometimes referred to as DOM Level 0 but has been imported into DOM Level 1.

DOM Events:

This part defines XML-tree manipulation oriented events with tree mutation and user-oriented events such as mouse, keyboard, and HTML-specific events.

DOM Cascading Style Sheets:

The DOM CSS defines a set of convenient, easy to use ways to manipulate CSS style sheets or the formatting of documents.

DOM Load and Save:

Loading an XML document into a DOM tree or saving a DOM tree into an XML document is a fundamental need for the DOM user. This module includes a variety of options controlling load and save operations.

DOM Validation:

This module defines a set of methods to modify the DOM tree and still make it valid.

It is the most widely implemented XML parser interface today. DOM reproduces an XML document's data hierarchy in a programming language's native object format, giving programmers an easy and familiar way of working with the data in the document. Developers can iterate through the document's data elements and even change the document's content programmatically.

The DOM XPath defines a set of convenient, easy to use functions to query a DOM tree using an XPath 1.0 expression, such as evaluate.

DOM Requirements:

The DOM requirements contains all requirements for each Level, and is regularly updated to reflect the requirements of the latest Level.

The W3C DOM Working Group is a royalty-free Working Group, as defined in the Current Patent Practice Note. A list of disclosures from the Working Group participants is available in its white paper. At present the W3C is not aware of any patents that are essential to implement the DOM specifications. Therefore, it is the W3C's opinion that the DOM specifications can be implemented on a royalty-free basis.

SCALABLE VECTOR GRAPHICS (SVG):

Over the past few years, there has been a demonstrated interest in vector graphics and animation on the Web. In 1999, the *World Wide Web Consortium (W3C)* started developing an open format called Scalable Vector Graphics (SVG). The first SVG 1.0 Specification was published in September 2001.

Scalable Vector Graphics (SVG) offers Web developers a method to create and animate images through an XML programming language. Consequently, rather than being removed from their code as is often the case with proprietary technology, developers can gain finer degrees of control over the appearance of Web pages. Animation techniques can range from a simple linear movement to 3D double helix morphing effects. Web developers, once they are more aware of the possibilities, can find unprecedented levels of control.

It is open source and offers seamless database integration, server-scripting compatibility, and efficient accessibility/ localization workflow. SVG is a language for describing two-dimensional graphics in XML. SVG allows for three types of graphic objects: vector graphic shapes (e.g., paths consisting of straight lines and curves), images and text. Graphical objects can be grouped, styled, transformed and composited into previously rendered objects. Text can be in any XML namespace suitable to the applications, which enhances searchability and accessibility of the SVG graphics. The feature set includes nested transformations, clipping paths, alpha masks, filter effects, template objects and extensibility.

SVG drawings can be dynamic and interactive. The Document Object Model (DOM) for SVG, which includes the full XML DOM, allows for straightforward and efficient vector graphics animation via scripting. A rich set of event handlers such as onmouseover and onclick can be assigned to any SVG graphical object. Because of its compatibility and leveraging of other Web standards, features like scripting can be done on SVG elements and other XML elements from different namespaces simultaneously within the same Web page.

Features:

There are many advantages of using SVG as the following short feature list demonstrates:

* Compatibility with other mediums such as wireless devices
* Scalable Server Solutions
* Small file sizes for faster Web page downloads
* Unlimited color and font choices
* Zoomable graphics and images
* Scripting control for custom interactive events and animation
* Clean, crisp, high-resolution printing from Web browsers
* Bitmap-style filter effects for high-impact graphics
* Text-based format easily integrates with other Web technologies
* Built in International Language Support
* Reduced Maintenance Costs
* Easily Updated
* Rich Multimedia Capabilities

Besides these important features, one of the best features of SVG is its Human readability. From the earliest days developers have been examining existing HTML and JavaScript to learn how to write new content, to make improvements, and to develop a better Web. SVG is intentionally following the same mode. Flash designer *Joshua Davies* of Praystation.com fame releases some of his source code and developers all over the world love it (the results are delivered as a non-human, readable binary format). Intentionally, every SVG graphic has its source visible and is human readable. Power to the developers through "View Source." Not only does human readability have benefits for content creators and developers; it has enormous benefits to accessibility. The text within an SVG image is just that text. Anyone can read the text, where it is located, and how it will be rendered by simply looking at the source. An image described as four wheels, a body, some doors, and seats is probably a vehicle of some kind. Someone that has trouble seeing the image, for whatever reason, has a chance of finding the meaning by reading the source. Another example is user style sheets. Suppose users cannot view a graphic because they are color-blind. Since they can read the source, they can easily write a user style sheet to override the colors in the graphic.

Similar Web based technology, *Flash*, the Web standard for animation and vector graphics is also available but SVG is all time better than Flash. Flash and SVG are often compared because the two have similar features. The reality is that SVG has some distinct advantages over its main competitor Flash. Perhaps chief among them is the compliance with other standards. SVG can utilize CSS and the DOM, where as Flash relies on proprietary technology that is not open source, at least not in the sense that we can right click on the page and see what is happening behind the scenes. SVG by contrast is open source and developers can readily learn from other developer's efforts in this area. While SVG has not yet reached the popularity level of Flash, times are changing quickly bringing with it a sense of enthusiasm for SVG.

While discussing about the populrity and acceptability of SVG, it is important to know that Mozilla plans to fully support SVG, Microsoft has similar plans, and Adobe GoLive 5 also supports SVG. Additionally, SVG editors are now surfacing on the Web. Programs such as Jasc's WebDraw that allows for the creation of SVG in a visual format are excellent additions to the SVG paradigm. The SVG 1.0 Recommendation has significant support from industrial giants some of them are Adobe, Apple, Canon, Corel, Hewlett-Packard, Macromedia, Microsoft, Kodak, Sun and many others, who contributed to the specification. There are a large number of different SVG viewer implementations. The most popular is the Adobe browser plug-in/ActiveX control. Adobe has released its viewer on all the versions of Windows that Microsoft supports (98, 2000, Millennium, and XP), Macintosh OS versions 8.5 to X, Linux, and Solaris. It runs in Internet Explorer, Netscape, Mozilla, Opera, and many other browsers.

Drawbacks:

There are however some drawbacks in this technology, one of the major drawbacks at the moment are:

* No browser fully supports SVG currently. As a consequence, SVG has to be displayed through the use of a plug-in such as the Adobe SVG plug-in. While it is a good plug-in it does not currently support all the SVG specifications, it is a heavy download, and perhaps the biggest barrier is that it is CPU intensive. Still, despite these drawbacks it does allow for cross-browser implementation of SVG and the use of the plug-in is likely to increase dramatically in the years to come.
* The Adobe SVG Viewer relies on JavaScript for most of its dynamic and interactive features, so it will not work in Internet Explorer 5 for Macintosh. Critical bugs were found running the Adobe SVG Viewer with Netscape on both Macintosh and PC.
* The other drawback is that there is a distinct lack of online material that directly relates to understanding how SVG can be employed in developing Web sites.

After analysing various features and drawbacs it can be

concluded, as the future of SVG not only seems bright, it seems certain to play a major role on the Web in the years to come.

XFORM:

The World Wide Web Consortium (W3C) announced the release of the first Public Working Draft of the XForms Data Model in 1999. The XForms Data Model Working Draft, along with the XForms Requirements document, provide the first cross industry efforts in seven years to produce the next generation of Web-based forms. W3C is building a better Web Form when HTML Forms were introduced to the Web in 1993, they provided a means to gather information and perform transactions. The structure of forms served the needs of many users at that time, as well as the devices used to access the Web.

Seven years later, the Web is a space where hundreds of millions of users expect to use many different devices to perform increasingly complex transactions, many of which exceed the limitations of the original forms technology. The W3C HTML Working Group has a charter to develop a form architecture that provides a better match to workflow and database applications, to the proliferation of new Web-enabled devices, and to the XML-driven Web.

The XForms Subgroup has accepted the challenge and produced a form architecture that separates data modeling, logic, and presentation. The XForms Data Model has emerged as the first in a series of XForms specifications.

The current design of Web forms doesn't separate the purpose from the presentation of a form. XForms, in contrast, are comprised of separate sections that describe what the form does, and how the form looks. This allows for flexible presentation options, including classic XHTML forms, to be attached to an XML form definition. The following illustrates how a single device-independent XML form definition, called the **XForms Model**, has the apability to work with a variety of standard or proprietary user interfaces:

* The **XForms User Interface** provides a standard set of visual controls that are targeted toward replacing today's XHTML form controls. These form controls are directly usable inside XHTML and other XML documents, like SVG. Other groups, such as the Voice Browser Working Group, may also independently develop user interface components for XForms.
* An important concept in XForms is that forms collect data, which is expressed as XML **instance data**. Among other duties, the XForms Model describes the structure of the instance data. This is important, since like XML, forms represent a structured interchange of data. Workflow, auto-fill, and pre-fill form applications are supported through the use of instance data.

Finally, there needs to be a channel for instance data to flow to and from the XForms Processor. For this, the **XForms Submit Protocol** defines how XForms send and receive data, including the ability to suspend and resume the completion of a form.

Key Goals of Xforms:

* Support for handheld, television, and desktop browsers, plus printers and scanners
* Richer user interface to meet the needs of business, consumer and device control applications
* Decoupled data, logic and presentation
* Improved internationalization
* Support for structured form data
* Advanced forms logic
* Multiple forms per page, and pages per form
* Suspend and Resume support
* Seamless integration with other XML tag sets

XForms Data Model Separates Purpose from Presentation:

XForms aims to ease the transition of the Web from HTML to XML. As XHTML 1.0 allows HTML content authors to make a smooth entry into the XML world, XForms allow Web application authors to combine the modularity of XML with the simplicity of HTML to gain key advantages in the areas of device independence, accessibility, business-to-business and consumer e-commerce, and embedded devices.

The XForms Data Model deliberately separates the purpose of a form from its presentation. This allows the application author to rigorously define the form data, independent of how end-users interact with the application. The separation facilitates the development of Web applications with user interaction components, and provides advantages to Web application developers.

XForms Deliver Structured Data, Device Independence:

In the XForms suite of specifications, the rules for describing, validating, and submitting application data are expressed in XML, as well as the submitted data. By providing the rules and data in XML, XForms lays the foundation for combinations with other XML applications, supporting the extensible Web.

Separating purpose and presentation also makes device independence easier to achieve by allowing Web application authors to write the data model once for all devices. Because the data model is not tied to presentation, developers may customize the presentation in a way that best suits each device's user interface. Support for device independence paves the way for a Web that is accessible to all users.

The XForms Data Model is the first in a series of XForms specifications. Other XForms work focuses on the logic layer - identifying relationships and dependencies between data model fields - and on the presentation aspects.

XPATH:

XPath is the result of an effort to provide a common syntax and semantics for functionality shared between XSL Transformations and XPointer. The primary purpose of XPath is to address parts of an XML document. In support of this primary purpose, it also provides basic facilities for manipulation of strings, numbers and booleans. XPath uses a compact, non-XML syntax to facilitate use of XPath within URIs and XML attribute values. XPath operates on the abstract, logical structure of an XML document, rather than its surface syntax. XPath gets its name from its use of a path notation as in URLs for navigating through the hierarchical structure of an XML document.

In addition to its use for addressing, XPath is also designed so that it has a natural subset that can be used for matching (testing whether or not a node matches a pattern); XPath models an XML document as a tree of nodes. There are different types of nodes, including element nodes, attribute nodes and text nodes. XPath defines a way to compute a string-value for each type of node. Some types of nodes also have names. XPath fully supports XML Namespaces. Thus, the name of a node is modeled as a pair consisting of a local part and a possibly null namespace URI; this is called an expanded-name.

The primary syntactic construct in XPath is the expression. An expression is evaluated to yield an object, which has one of the following four basic types:

* node-set (an unordered collection of nodes without duplicates)
* boolean (true or false)
* number (a floating-point number)
* string (a sequence of UCS characters)

Expression evaluation occurs with respect to a context. XSLT and XPointer specify how the context is determined for XPath expressions used in XSLT and XPointer respectively. The context consists of:

* a node (the context node)
* a pair of non-zero positive integers (the context position and the context size)
* a set of variable bindings
* a function library
* the set of namespace declarations in scope for the expression

The context position is always less than or equal to the context size. The variable bindings consist of a mapping from variable names to variable values. The value of a variable is an object, which can be of any of the types that are possible for the value of an expression, and may also be of additional types not specified here.

The function library consists of a mapping from function names to functions. Each function takes zero or more arguments and returns a single result. This document defines a core function library that all XPath implementations must support. For a function in the core function library, arguments and result are of the four basic types. Both XSLT and XPointer extend XPath by defining additional functions; some of these functions operate on the four basic types; others operate on additional data types defined by XSLT and XPointer.

The namespace declarations consist of a mapping from prefixes to namespace URIs. The variable bindings, function library and namespace declarations used to evaluate a subexpression are always the same as those used to evaluate the containing expression. The context node, context position, and context size used to evaluate a subexpression are sometimes different from those used to evaluate the containing expression. Several kinds of expressions change the context node; only predicates change the context position and context size. When the evaluation of a kind of expression is described, it will always be explicitly stated if the context node, context position, and context size change for the evaluation of subexpressions; if nothing is said about the context node, context position, and context size, they remain unchanged for the evaluation of subexpressions of that kind of expression.

One important kind of expression is a location path. A location path selects a set of nodes relative to the context node. The result of evaluating an expression that is a location path is the node-set containing the nodes selected by the location path. Location paths can recursively contain expressions that are used to filter sets of nodes.

CASCADING STYLE SHEETS:

Cascading Style Sheets (CSS) is a simple mechanism for adding style (e.g. fonts, colors, spacing) to Web documents.

CSS Browsers:

The easiest way to start experimenting with style sheets is to download one of the browsers that support CSS. Not all of the browsers below implement the full specification, but releases are coming out fast so this should soon change. Various sites describe bugs and work-arounds.

* The KDE <http://www.kde.org> project released KDE 3.1, which includes the Konqueror Web browser and file manager. It has improved support for CSS 2.1, including fixed table layout and positioning.
* Opera <http://www.opera.com/> released version 7 of its browser, with some new CSS-based goodies: small-screen mode, alternative styles, etc. (Opera 6 runs on multiple platforms, version 7 is so far Windows-only, shareware).
* Apple <http://www.apple.com/> released a beta of the Safari Web browser.
* Mozilla <http://www.mozilla.org/> released version 1.1 and Netscape version 7.0, based on Mozilla 1.0.1. Both have excellent CSS support. (Mozilla is Open Source, Netscape is binary-only but free, both run on many platforms).

* The Chimera project <http://chimera.mozdev.org/> released version 0.4. Chimera is a browser for Mac OS X, based on Mozilla's Gecko layout engine.

* The X-Smiles team <http://www.x-smiles.org/> has released version 0.5 ("Oulu") of the X-Smiles XML browser, which supports, among other things, XHTML, SMIL, Xforms and the CSS Mobile Profile.

* NetClue <http://www.netcluesoft.com/> released Clue Browser v4.1.1. It supports HTML, XML/XHTML, namespaces, CSS (level 1 and part of level 2), DOM, Javascript, etc.

* Microsoft released Internet Explorer for the Mac 5.1, with bug fixes and improved performance. Supports full CSS1 and partial CSS2.

* OmniWeb 4 <http://www.omnigroup.com/applications/omniweb/> is a Web browser for the Mac (OS X) and has a built-in source editor (with HTTP PUT support).

* Galeon 1.0 <http://galeon.sourceforge.net/> is a Web browser for Gnome. It uses the Gecko rendering engine from Mozilla.

* Adobe <http://www.adobe.com/> produces an SVG plugin for browsers under Mac and Windows and for Mozilla 0.9.1 under Linux & Solaris. Supports SVG with CSS styling.

* K-Meleon <http://kmeleon.sourceforge.net/> version 0.6 has been released, a lightweight browser based on the Gecko rendering engine of Mozilla.

* Espial's <http://www.espial.com> Escape 4.7 browser implements CSS support for HTML, XML and XHTML. Written in Java for the embedded software market.

* iCab <http://www.icab.de>, a browser for the Mac, is starting to support CSS. The preview release of version 2.5 reportedly supports most of CSS1.

* Openwave's <http://www.openwave.com/> mobile browser.

* Nokia <http://www.nokia.com/> started selling mobile phones that support XHTML and CSS during 2001.
* The Arachne WWW browser <http://www.arachne.cz/> for DOS and Linux supports CSS1 since version 1.70.
* CSIRO <http://www.cmis.csiro.au/> released the CSIRO SVG Toolkit, with a viewer for SVG + CSS and other utilities.
* IONIC <http://www.ionicsoft.com/index.html> offers the Ionic SVG toolkit, with a viewer for SVG + CSS and other tools.
* The Koala team wrote Jackaroo <http://koala.ilog.fr/jackaroo/>, an SVG + CSS viewer.
* Microsoft <http://www.microsoft.com> shipped Internet Explorer 5 for the Macintosh. It apparently supports full CSS1, the first browser to do so.
* Closure <http://www.uni-karlsruhe.de/~unk6/closure/> is a Web browser written in Common Lisp; supports CSS1.
* ICE Soft <http://www.icesoft.com/> released v.5 of their two embeddable browsers.
* Microsoft has released Internet Explorer 5.0 for Windows, Solaris and HP-UX
* Silicon Graphics has an embeddable CSS-enhanced web browser that is used in a number of applications and their desktop.
* Arena <http://www.yggdrasil.com/Products/Arena/>, previously W3C's testbed browser, is now being developed by Yggdrasil. It has a partial implementation of CSS1.

CSS Specifications:

Cascading Style Sheets, level 1 (CSS1) became a W3C Recommendation in December 1996. It describes the CSS language as well as a simple visual formatting model. CSS2, which became a W3C Recommendation in May 1998, builds on CSS1 and adds support for media-specific style sheets (e.g.

printers and aural devices), downloadable fonts, element positioning and tables. The CSS Mobile Profile specification became a W3C Candidate Recommendation in Oct 2001. CSS3 is currently under development. Progress may be checked as new drafts published. Translations into some languages are available from the CSS1 translations page and the CSS2 translations page.

EXTENSIBLE STYLE LANGUAGE (XSL):

The World Wide Web Consortium (W3C) has published the first working draft of its Extensible Style Language (XSL) 1.0 in 1998. XML brought new features which were unavailable in HTML without necessarily making HTML obsolete. The idea is that web authors should have various tools to hand for each job, one simple to learn and straightforward to use, the other perhaps less simple but with greater functionality and extensibility so as to be readily customizable. HTML and CSS are the basic tools, with XML and XSL intended as their industrial-strength cousins. The W3C goes on the say that CSS, already a mature standard, and XSL are to be based on a single formatting model. The two will share the same underlying concepts and use the same terminology as far as is possible. It can handle tree transformations as well as document transformations, it permits XML documents to be displayed in different ways in response to different user queries, and it can support many languages, including historical texts like ancient Greek and Aztec. Ian Jacobs of W3C explains"It's also designed to be used for print a little bit more than CSS". In addition, where CSS works with HTML or XML, XSL is optimized for use with XML. It does seem odd, though, that the W3C is out pushing a new stylesheet language when the newly formed Web Standards Group (CI No 3,471) is complaining that browser vendors aren't adhering closely enough to existing web standards.Microsoft has posted Extensible Style Sheet Language (XSL) tools on its Web site to enable users to experiment with the technology as it works its way through the standards process.

With the addition of a robust XSL Editor, Whitehill (xsl) Composer provides the user with the ability to import and edit existing XSL, as well as providing an Absolute Positioning feature, which allows users to position and align fragments in relation to the page layout or to other fragments. This functionality significantly increases the speed at which users create the presentation of their XML data while leveraging any pre-existing investment in XSL.

The World Wide Web Consortium (W3C) has issued the Extensible Stylesheet Language (XSL) 1.0 as a W3C Recommendation, representing cross-industry agreement on an XML-based language that specifies how XML documents may be formatted. It works in concert with XSL Transformations (XSLT), an XML language that performs transformations of structured documents.

XSL 1.0 brings Structured Styling to XML Documents:

For document-driven industries, the Extensible Markup Language (XML) has held great promise, but also presented some limitations. While XML has proven an effective format for structured data, it had yet to provide the advanced levels of formatting and structural transformation common to proprietary publishing tools.

XSLT 1.0, the XML language which performs transformations on XML data and documents, has been a W3C Recommendation since November 1999, and already enjoys significant usage in both developer communities and in commercial products. XSL 1.0 builds on XSLT 1.0, and provides users with the ability to describe how XML data and documents are to be formatted. XSL 1.0 does this by defining "formatting objects," such as footnotes, headers, columns, and other features common to paged media.

Designers would use XSL 1.0 stylesheets to indicate rendering preferences for a type of XML document, including how it is styled, laid out, and paginated onto a presentation medium such as a browser window, a pamphlet, or a book. An XSL engine would take the XML document and the XSL stylesheet, and would produce a rendering of the document. XSLT 1.0 makes it possible to significantly change the original structure of an XML document (automatic generation of tables of contents, cross-references, indexes, etc.), while XSL 1.0 makes complex document formatting possible through the use of formatting objects and properties.

XSL 1.0 enriches XML Documents and Data with Professional Printing Capabilities:

As XSL 1.0 is focused on the formatting of paged media, it makes it possible for professional printing capabilities and functions to perform with XML documents today. XSL 1.0 and XSLT make it possible for the needs of Web and print-based media formatting to be met. Now, one can have documents and data stored in XML, specify how to format and render them, and produce versions for both Web rendering and for print media.

XSL 1.0 Complements CSS Technologies:

The Cascading Style Sheet language (CSS), both levels 1 and 2 has long been recognized as the style language of choice for HTML and XHTML documents. CSS may still be used for XML formatting, and in cases where structural transformations are not needed, suit the needs of Web designers.

XSL Benefits from Industry Support and XML experts participated in the creation of both the transformation and formatting components of XSL, including (in alphabetical order) Adobe, Antenna House, Arbortext, Bitstream, Enigma, IBM, James Clark, Microsoft, Oracle, RivCom, SoftQuad, Software AG, Sun Microsystems, University of Edinburgh, and Xerox. Implementation commitments are significant, and are included in the testimonials for XSL 1.0.

URI, URL and URN

The Web is an information space. Human beings have a

lot of mental machinery for manipulating, imagining, and finding their way in spaces. URIs are the points in that space. Unlike web data formats, where HTML is an important one, but not the only one, and web protocols, where HTTP has a similar status, there is only one Web naming/addressing technology: URIs.

URI (Uniform Resource Identifiers):

URIs, URLs are short strings that identify resources in the web: documents, images, downloadable files, services, electronic mailboxes, and other resources. They make resources available under a variety of naming schemes and access methods such as HTTP, FTP, and Internet mail addressable in the same simple way. They reduce the tedium of "log in to this server, then issue this magic command ..." down to a single click.

It is an extensible technology: there are a number of existing addressing, and more may be incorporated over time.

URL (Uniform Resource Locator):

An informal term (no longer used in technical specifications) associated with popular URI schemes: http, ftp, mailto, etc.

URN (Uniform Resource Name):

An URI that has an institutional commitment to persistence, availability, etc. Note that this sort of URI may also be a URL. See, for example PURLs. A particular scheme, URN, specified by RFC2141 and related documents, intended to serve as persistent, location-independent, resource identifiers. Engelbart also identified the need for a library system, including catalog numbers for documents. Catalog numbers are a long-standing tradition in publishing and library science. The technology behind Uniform Resource Identifiers is suitable for use as catalog numbers, given sufficient socioeconomic infrastructure: rights management, payment assurance, privacy, digital signatures, etc.

ACTIVE SERVER PAGE (ASP):

To search and display dynamic and live information, such

as that found in locally produced relational databases, requires the addition of other languages. In such case the systems should use Active Server Pages (ASP). Before discussing it is necessory to know about dynamic web page and the static web page.

Static Web Pages:

It is easy to create Web pages to display static data from a database table. Most systems, such as Microsoft Access, include a "Save As HTML" feature to do just that. However, pages created in this way are a "snapshot in time"; they do not change as the database is changed. It is essential to re-create the pages each time changes are made to the data. Publishing and maintaining a large number of static web page's maintenance is worse, users cannot search the database or choose particular items of data; they can only see what it is previously saved in HTML format.

Dynamic Web Pages:

Dynamic Web pages allow the user to connect to up-to-the-minute data, search it, and display it in different ways. It contains following features:

Client-side processing:

There are two ways of incorporating processing into a Web page: *client-side processing* and *server-side processing*. In client-side processing, the server sends a Web page containing both code and data back to the client (user's computer). The browser gets the whole thing and proceeds to call up programs on the user's computer to process the data. The user's computer does all the work; the server just supplies the code and data.

Client-side processing has traditionally been characterized by programs, or scripts, written in languages such as Java, JavaScript, or Visual Basic Scripting Edition (VBScript). Microsoft's VBScript is a subset of the Visual Basic language which is used in both client-side and server-side processing.

Access 2000 has a new object and method for creating client-side access to its databases. It is called a "data access page", and automates all the programming to convert Access tables into dynamic Web pages. The disadvantage is that it imbeds an Access program into the Web page and the user must have a significant amount of software on his or her computer to make use of it (Viescas, 1999).

Server-side processing:

The other way is to use server-side processing. Here, the server calls up programs residing on the server. The programs process the data and send the processed data back to the user's browser as HTML for display. This puts the processing load on the server, and it must have necessary programs installed. The server does all the work.

Common Gateway Interface (CGI):

An early method of *server-side processing*, still widely used, is CGI, or Common Gateway Interface. It is a standard against which to write programs for Web access. Programs written according the CGI standard take requests from a Web page, retrieve and process data from a database, and send the processed data back to the user's browser.

CGI programs may be written in almost any language that can be compiled: Visual Basic (not VBScript), C, Perl, and so on. A complete CGI setup usually includes a requesting HTML page, a CGI program, and a response HTML page to display the data. The CGI program searches and manipulates the database then creates lines of HTML code in which data are embedded. The program finally writes a file of HTML code to be sent to the browser. The file is read by the browser as a regular Web page.

Since CGI programs reside on the server, not on the user's computer, you may have to jump through hoops to get the network administrator to install a CGI program. For security reasons, some administrators will not permit CGI programs to be used at all.

Active Server Pages:

A simpler method is to use *Active Server Pages (ASP)*.

ASP is Microsoft's method of providing server-side processing for use by Web browsers. ASP imbeds scripting statements directly into the Web page, rather than by using a separate program. ASP differs from CGI in the following ways:

* ASP is proprietary to Microsoft and CGI is not. ASP requires the use of Microsoft server software, and works best in a complete Microsoft environment; CGI can be used on most any computer platform, and is widely used on UNIX servers.
* ASP usually uses VBScript whereas CGI programs may be written in any language that can be compiled. Although VBScript may be used in client-side processing, it is always server-side in an ASP context.
* ASP imbeds the script within the Web page, while CGI programs stand alone, separate from the Web page that calls them.
* Unless you are a programmer, it is much easier to use ASP than CGI.

For most applications, CGI is slower than ASP.

ASP uses ActiveX Data Objects (ADO), which is a Microsoft-developed technology for working with databases on the Internet. They are pre-packaged programming libraries that are built into the Web server and called upon to do some work when it needs to be done. ADO relieves the programmer from writing code for every little thing that he/she wants to do. Not much useful work would get done if a painter must first grab a camel, pluck its hairs, make a brush, fashion a bucket out of tin, and construct a ladder each time he/she wanted to paint a wall. Instead, he/she grabs the tools and materials off the shelf and concentrates on the painting project. ASP programmers can reach into a set of pre-built tools (ADO) and concentrate on the larger picture of working with data.

ASP technology has many uses, but this article will

concentrate on using it to search and retrieve data from a Microsoft Access database. Other texts and Web tutorials describe non-database ASP applications. Typically, the browser requests an AS page from the server, either by URL or through the use of a Web form. The server sees the .asp extension, and sends the AS page to the ASP engine on the server. The engine reads the file, which usually contains a mixture of server side scripting and HTML. As the ASP engine reads the file, whenever it comes to server-side script, it executes it. Whenever it comes to HTML, it outputs it back to the server.

Access has a built-in utility for exporting an Access table, query, form, or report as an Active Server Page. It is limited in its functionality, although it may be a good place to start. This article will discuss creating ASP from scratch. The benefit of ASP is that the full power of a relational database is available to the user, with the Web providing the interface. The user needs nothing more than a browser. Typically, the user points his or her browser to a menu on your Web site which links to various AS pages that work with the database.

LIBWWW- THE W3C PROTOCOL LIBRARY:

Libwww is a highly modular, general-purpose client side Web API written in C for Unix and Windows. It is well suited for both small and large applications, like browser/editors, robots, batch tools, etc. Pluggable modules provided with libwww include complete HTTP/1.1 (with caching, pipelining, PUT, POST, Digest Authentication, deflate, etc), MySQL logging, FTP, HTML/4, XML, RDF, WebDAV, and much more. The purpose of libwww is to serve as a testbed for protocol experiments.

Rough consensus and running code is the main idea behind libwww. As for all W3C OpenSource code, the purpose of libwww is to provide an environment for experimenting with extensions and new features. The focus of libwww is performance, modularity, and extensibility. It contains highly efficient code for HTTP and URIs but also for many other parts of the Web, primarily for client side applications like robots, browsers, GUI apps, and automated tools.

Designed and implemented libwww from version 2.17 up to version 5.2.8, Tim Berners-Lee and Jean-Francois Groff, Who brought up with the initial design and implementation of libwww. Libwww has been part of the World Wide Web almost from the beginning. *Tim Berners-Lee* designed and implemented the first version back in November 1992 as part of demonstrating the potential of the Web. Many people have picked up libwww and used it in a variety of contexts. Applications such as Lou Montulli's Lynx character based client, Mosaic Web browser by Marc Andreesen and Eric Bena, and the CERN server by Ari Luotonen were all using later versions of libwww. Later on, applications like the Arena browser by Dave Raggett and Håkon W. Lie have been added to the list.

Libwww was free from the very start and was released on a regular basis to the Web Community. When CERN stopped being the center of the Web in late 1994, libwww moved from CERN which continued its development. In May 1998, the code base was made even more available in that people now can check it out directly from CVS codebase. Today, libwww is freely available under W3C Copyright for use by anyone and has a growing OpenSource community helping maintaining it. Along with the core library comes set of sample applications that demonstrate how to use libwww but at the same time can perform useful tasks in their own right.

MULTI MODAL INTERACTION:

Through the web pages one can speak to, a new class of mobile devices that support multiple modes of interaction. And which contains following features:

* Adapting the Web to allow multiple modes of interaction:
    * GUI, Speech, Vision, Pen, Gestures, Haptic interfaces
* Augmenting human to computer and human to human interaction

* Communication services involving multiple devices and multiple people
* Anywhere, Any device, Any time
* Services that adapt to the device, user preferences and environmental conditions
* Accessible to all

The Multimodal Interaction Activity is extending the web user interface to allow multiple modes of interaction, offering users the choice of using their voice, or an input device such as a key pad, keyboard, mouse or other input device. For output, users will be able to listen to spoken prompts and audio, and to view information on graphical displays. The Working Group is developing markup specifications for synchronization across multiple modalities and devices with a wide range of capabilities.

The Multimodal Interaction Activity was chartered in February 2002 as a royalty free group under W3C's *Current Patent Practice (CPP)* Note. Organizations are currently participating in the Working Group are Alcatel, Apple, AT&T, Avaya, Canon, Cisco, Comverse, Corel, EDS, Ericsson, France Telecom, Hewlett-Packard, IBM, Intel, IWA/HWG, Kirusa, Loquendo, Microsoft, Mitsubishi Electric, Motorola, NEC, Nokia, Nortel Networks, Nuance Communications, OnMobile Systems, Opera Software, Openstream, Oracle, Panasonic, PipeBeach, ScanSoft, Siemens, SnowShore Networks, SpeechWorks International, Sun Microsystems, T-Online International, Toyohashi University of Technology, V-Enable, VoiceGenie, and Voxeo, etc.

All participating organizations are required to make a patent disclosure statement as set out in the *CPP* Note. A separate page is being maintained for patent disclosures for the Multimodal Interaction Activity. The Working Group is obliged by its charter to produce a specification which relies only on intellectual property available on a royalty-free basis.

Desktop systems have proven to be highly effective for

accessing the World Wide Web. The high resolution displays, pointing devices and full size keyboards make it easy to interact efficiently with large amounts of information. When you are on the move, you need a small lightweight device that fits easily into your pocket or purse. Cell phones are extremely popular, but their small size limits the amount of information they can display, as well as the number and kinds of keys they can feature.

Mobile profiles have emerged for a number of W3C specifications: XHTML, CSS, SMIL and SVG. Mobile access to the web is now becoming a reality. The small keypads make it difficult to enter search strings or web addresses, especially for ideographic languages with many thousands of characters. Recent years have also seen a tremendous growth of interest in using speech as a means to interact with Web-based services over the telephone. W3C responded to this by establishing the Voice Browser Activity which is developing requirements and specifications for the W3C Speech Interface Framework.

Spoken interfaces based upon VoiceXML prompt users with pre-recorded or synthetic speech and understand simple words or phrases. As the technology improves we can look forward to richer natural language conversations. There is now an emerging interest in combining speech interaction with other modes of interaction. Multimodal interaction will enable the user to speak, write and type, as well as hear and see using a more natural user interface than today's single mode browsers.

Multimodal Access:

The different modalities may be supported on a single device or on separate devices working in tandem, for example, you could be talking into your cell phone and seeing the results on a PDA. Voice may also be offered as an adjunct to browsers with high resolution graphical displays, providing an accessible alternative to using the keyboard or screen. This can be especially important in automobiles or other situations where hands and eyes free operation is essential. Voice interaction can escape the physical limitations on keypads and displays as mobile devices become ever smaller. It is much easier to say a few words than it is to thumb them in on a keypad where multiple key presses may be needed for each character. Complementing speech, ink entered with a stylus or imaging device can be used for handwriting, gestures, drawings, and specific notations for mathematics, music, chemistry and other fields. Ink is expected to be popular for instant messaging.

Mobile devices working in isolation generally lack the power to recognize more than a few hundred spoken commands. The storage limitations restrict the use of prerecorded speech prompts. Small speech synthesizers are possible, but tend to produce robotic sounding speech that many users find tiring to listen. A solution is to process speech recognition and synthesis remotely on more powerful platforms. A similar case holds for complex voice dialogs with rich natural language understanding. Simple dialogs could be handled locally, but for richer interaction, it will be necessary to couple the device with a remote dialog engine.

Multimodal applications should be able to adapt to changing device capabilities, user preferences and environmental conditions. For instance, users should be able to disable speech input and output when this would be distracting to nearby people. It should be easy for developers to tailor applications to dynamically adapt to such changes, making best use of the available modes of interaction at any given time. In addition, developers should be able to create applications involving multiple devices and multiple users, augmenting human to computer and human-to-human interaction.

The Multimodal Interaction Working Group is chartered to work on developing standards for synchronization across modes and devices, building on top of W3C's existing specifications, for instance, combining XHTML, SMIL and XForms with markup for speech synthesis and speech recognition. Alternatively it can provide mechanisms for loosely coupling visual interaction with voice dialogs represented in VoiceXML. Additional work will focus on a means to provide the ink component of Web-based, multimodal applications.

Extensible Multimodal Annotation Markup Language (EMMA):

EMMA is being developed as a data format for the interface between input processors and interaction management systems. It will define the means for recognizers to annotate application specific data with information such as confidence scores, time stamps, input mode (e.g. key strokes, speech or pen), alternative recognition hypotheses, and partial recognition results etc. EMMA is a target data format for the semantic interpretation specification being developed in the Voice Browser Activity, and which describes annotations to speech grammars for extracting application specific data as a result of speech recognition. EMMA supercedes earlier work on the natural language semantics markup language in the Voice Browser Activity.

Pen input:

This work item sets out to define an XML data format for ink entered with an electronic pen or stylus as part of a multimodal system. This will enable the capture and server-side processing of handwriting, gestures, drawings, and specific notations for mathematics, music, chemistry and other fields. The starting point for this work is a specification contributed by IBM, Intel, the International Unipen Foundation and Motorola. This will be reviewed with respect to the requirements for ink in the context of multimodal applications.

Functions:

It helps in interpreting and representing the user's input. Simple natural language processing is needed to transform natural language input (whether from speech, pen or keystrokes) so that it can be used to fill in forms, follow hypertext links, shift the focus of interaction and so on. Simple natural language processing is also useful for dynamically generating tailored visual and aural responses. One approach to implementing this is to combine XHTML with markup for prompts, grammars and the means to bind results to actions. XHTML defines various kinds of events, for example, when the document is loaded or unloaded, when a form field gets or loses the input focus, and when a field's value is changed. These events can in principle be used to trigger aural prompts, and to activate recognition grammars. This would allow a welcome message to start playing when the page is loaded. When you set the focus to a given field, a prompt could be played to encourage the user to respond via speech rather than via keystrokes. Page grammars could be used for navigation and for switching tasks. Grammars are not restricted to speech, and ink grammars could be used for recognizing gestures and characters entered with a stylus.

It supports collaborative processing between local and network devices. Cell phones are expected to include support for an increasing number of specs i.e. XHTML, CSS, SMIL, SVG, SyncML, ECMAScript, Java, JPEG, MP3, and more. At the same time, the costs must be held down to a low enough level to make the phones affordable to people from all walks of life. This together with battery considerations constrains the available memory and processor speed. This motivates looking at an architecture where the speech and natural language processing is done in the network. In addition, this will encourage innovation, for example on richer natural language capabilities, without the need for everyone to upgrade their phones to enjoy the benefits.

The *IETF Speech Services Control (SpeechSC) working group* is developing protocols to support distributed speech recognition, speech synthesis and speaker verification services, and expects to take advantage of W3C's work on the *Speech Recognition Grammar Specification (SRGS)*, the *Speech Synthesis Markup Language (SSML)*, *Semantic Interpretation (SI)* and *Extensible Multimodal Markup Annotations (EMMA)*.

Another idea is to couple a local graphical user interface

with a remote voice dialog engine, perhaps based upon VoiceXML. Here the idea is to allow events to be passed between the device and the remote dialog engine. To the application developer, these events would look just the same whether they originated locally or remotely. The IETF SIP working group is developing a means for pass such events over *SIP (Session Initiation Protocol)*. In this model, events can carry data, and can thus be used to initiate a range of actions, for instance, changing the focus of interaction, setting the value of a form field, loading a new page, or altering the current page via the DOM. SIP can also be used to synchronize several devices, for instance to update the display on a PDA, automotive or desktop system in concert with the much smaller display on a cell phone. When it comes to setting up a session that potentially involves multiple devices and servers, SIP looks like it will provide an effective solution together with server-side scripts.

PLATFORM FOR INTERNET CONTENT SELECTION (PICS):

The PICS specification enables labels (metadata) to be associated with Internet content. It was originally designed to help parents and teachers control what children access on the Internet, but it also facilitates other uses for labels, including code signing and privacy. The PICS platform is one on which other rating services and filtering software have been built.

In August of 1995, leading members of the Internet community came together to begin the development of technical specifications that would enable users to easily find appropriate content and avoid content that they consider inappropriate or unwanted, either for themselves or their children. These specifications were designed to ease the creation of, and access to, labeling schemes (and associated content selection and filtering mechanisms), allowing various people or organizations to label Web content in ways that best suit their different viewpoints. The PICS specifications were not intended to be limited to applications regarding potentially offensive content. Rather, it was hoped that PICS would be used for many purposes, such as third-party ratings on the timeliness and technical accuracy of a site's content.

Technical specifications were completed in early 1996. Since then PICS has been incorporated into a number of products, a variety of PICS-based rating services have been (and continue to be) developed for the web, and a number of stand-alone filtering tools are PICS-compatible.

Many who were involved in the creation of PICS recognized that the World Wide Web provides access to an extraordinary range of content, some of which some people consider either inappropriate, unwanted, or harmful for some users, especially children. The global nature of the Web, and the fact that it serves numerous communities with a great diversity of values, suggested that national, or even international laws restricting certain kinds of speech on the Web would neither be effective nor necessarily desirable for the Web. Instead, PICS was developed to accommodate a wide range of communities online.

The original PICS proposers based their work on a general set of principles, detailed below. In the time since PICS and other content selections tools have been deployed on the web, much has been learned about the use of PICS-based techniques. This note builds on those Principles a set of functional guidelines for implementing PICS-based components of the Web infrastructure, PICS rating services, and PICS-based content selection tools to assure that they are designed in a manner that comports with the original PICS principles and the free flow of information on the web.

PICS Statement of Principles:

PICS is a cross-industry working group whose goal is to facilitate the development of technologies to give users of interactive media, such as the Internet, control over the kinds of material to which they and their children have access. PICS members believe that individuals, groups and businesses should have easy access to the widest possible range of content selection products, and a diversity of voluntary rating systems. In order to advance its goals, PICS will devise a set of standards that facilitate the following:

Self-rating:

Enable content providers to voluntarily label the content they create and distribute.

Third-party rating:

Enable multiple, independent labeling services to associate additional labels with content created and distributed by others. Services may devise their own labeling systems, and the same content may receive different labels from different services.

Ease-of-use:

Enable parents and teachers to use ratings and labels from a diversity of sources to control the information that children under their supervision receive.

PICS members believe that an open labeling platform which incorporates these features provides the best way to preserve and enhance the vibrancy and diversity of the Internet. Easy access to technology which enables first- and third-party rating of content will give users maximum control over the content they receive without requiring new restrictions on content providers.

Membership in PICS includes a broad cross-section of companies from the computer, communications, and content industries, as well as trade associations and public interest groups. PICS member will deploy products and services based on these standards.

Guidelines for the Usage of PICS:

In addition to the principles above, some of the systems

and services based on PICS ought to be implemented with the following guidelines in mind. These guidelines promote the principles of diversity, disclosure, control, and transparency.

Using PICS Rating Systems and Services:

- The Web, through PICS implementations, ought to support access to a variety of labeling systems that reflect the diversity of moral and cultural values held by those that use the net.
- No single rating system and service can perfectly meet the needs of all the communities on the web.
- The ability of multiple organizations to use PICS to create lists of suggested content is an encouraged means of using PICS. These lists may be distributed through label bureaus and be used for searching, or as "white" lists of materials that should be permitted even if they would otherwise be blocked.
- Filtration and labeling schemes should be designed such that the combined effect does not lead to a chilling of expression or the creation of significant barriers to diverse opinion and content. Small and non-commercial sites should continue to be a part of the web available to all users.

Creating Labeled Content:

- The creation of content that is labeled should be done in a way so as to maximize the transparency and integrity of the Web.
- PICS-based systems should facilitate disclosure of the criteria used to rate content.
- Content rating should be as simple as possible for authors and content providers who wish to label content.
- The decision to self-label should be at the discretion of content creators and publishers.

- If a content creator is concerned about the accuracy of a third party rating, she should be able to investigate how her materials are rated and have some means of requesting a change in the ratings where they do not match the stated criteria of the rating service.

Using Labeled Content:

- Users should have the ability to understand and control the choices made in the selection of content in an easy and transparent manner.
- Users of PICS-based content selection systems should have easy access to information about the filtering criteria, the values or principles underlying them, and to the configuration of the content selection systems. This can be accomplished by providing the following information in the product documentation or at the Service URL:
- a clear statement of the methodology used to create the labels;
- a contact (both physical and virtual) for questions or concerns.

When access to a particular URL is blocked through an implementation of PICS, error conditions or other user interface functions ought to specifically indicate that the URL is not accessible because of blocking by a content selection tool. Relevant information could include:

- the rating system whose value is out of range (if more than one is being used) and which variable and value led to the blocking of a URL.
- some indication of where the blocking occurred.(i.e. is it part of the browser and under local control, or is it a proxy and if so who owns and/or operates the proxy.)
- It should be as easy as possible for an authorized user to install and modify filters.

– In particular, a filtering software have the ability to import filtering preferences that are specified using the PICSRules language.

Resources for Labeling Service Developers:

To start a new labeling service, it is needed to take the following steps:

* Decide who will assign labels.
  – Web site operators who self-label and/or
  – A panel of raters that you recruit and/or
  – A computer program that analyzes the contents of materials and assigns labels
* Decide the labeling vocabulary and criteria

Express the labeling vocabulary and criteria according to the format specified in the technical specification. One can create this file from scratch, or you can fill out web forms at the PICS application incubator and the file will be created for the person.

* Create the labels
* Arrange for distribution of your labels
  – Give your labels to someone else who is running a PICS label bureau and/or
  – Run your own PICS label bureau and/or
  – Convince web site operators to distribute the labels for their own pages, either by putting them into HTML META tags or sending them along with web pages.

The PICS Application Incubator project at the University of Michigan School of Information will provide a limited amount of free technical consulting to organizations that are considering establishing new labeling services.

PICS Capabilities:

PICS Can be used for more than just content filtering:

While the motivation for PICS was concern over children

accessing inappropriate materials, it is a general "meta-data" system, meaning that labels can provide any kind of descriptive information about Internet materials. For example, a labeling vocabulary could indicate the literary quality of an item rather than its appropriateness for children. Most immediately, PICS labels could help in finding particularly desirable and this is the main motivation for the ongoing work on a next generation label format that can include arbitrary text strings. More generally, the W3C is working to extend Web meta-data capabilities generally and is applying them specifically in the following projects:

* *Digital Signature Project* coupling the ability to make assertions with a cryptographic signature block that ensures integrity and authenticity.
* Intellectual Property Rights Management using a meta-data system to label Web resources with respect to their authors, owners, and rights management information.
* Privacy (P3) using a meta-data system to allow sites to make assertions about their privacy practices, and for users to express their preferences for the type of interaction they want to have with those sites.

Regardless of content control, meta-data systems such as PICS are going to be an important part of the Web, because they enable more sophisticated commerce (build and manage trust relationships), communication, indexing, and searching services.

The promise of digital commerce is that it will allow you to use the Internet to purchase the services of the best organic gardening advisors or mad cow disease specialists, whether they live in New Delhi or New York. To do this, you need to do more than verify that the person at the other end of the wire is who he says he is. You need to assess competence, reliability, judgment. In other words, you need a system of branding, but applied much more widely for highly specialized and hard-to-evaluate services and products. You need value-added services that will not only lead you to the right product or service but also rate its quality or otherwise vouch for it.

PICS enables censorship:

This seemingly straightforward question, upon closer inspection, turns out to be many different questions when asked by different people. Many people are concerned about governments assuming one or more of the roles described in the answer to the previous question. Others are concerned about employers setting filtering rules, abuse of power by independent labelers, or a chilling effect on speech even if speech is not banned outright. People also employ different definitions of censorship. The most expansive definition is, "any action by one person that makes otherwise available information unavailable to another person." Under this expansive definition, even a parent setting filtering rules for a child would count as censorship. PICS documents have adopted the more restrictive definition of censorship as actions that limit what an individual can distribute, and use the term "access controls" for restrictions on what individuals can receive. But the distinction blurs if a central authority restricts access for a set of people. Finally, people have different definitions of "enable." Some would say that PICS enables any application that uses PICS-compatible components, while we reserve the term "enables" for applications that can easily be implemented with PICS-compatible components but could not be easily implemented otherwise.

PICS makes it easier or harder for governments to do so:

A government could try to assume any or all of the six roles described above, although some controls might be harder than others to enforce. As described below, governments could assume some of these roles even without PICS, while other roles would be harder to assume if PICS had not been introduced. It's important to note that W3C does not endorse any particular government policy. Potential government policies:

– **Set labeling vocabulary and criteria.** A government could impose a labeling vocabulary and require all publishers (in the government's jurisdiction) to label their own materials according to that vocabulary. Alternatively, a government might try to achieve the same effect by encouraging an industry self-policing organization to choose a vocabulary and require subscribers to label their own materials. Civil liberties advocates in Australia are especially concerned about this (see The Net Labeling Delusion <http://www.pobox.com/~rene/liberty/label.html>). PICS makes it somewhat easier for a government to impose a self-labeling requirement: without PICS, a government would have to specify a technical format for the labels, in addition to specifying the vocabulary and criteria, and there might not be any filtering software available that could easily process such labels.

- **Assign labels.** A government could assign labels to materials that are illegal or harmful. This option is most likely to be combined with government requirements that such materials be filtered but it need not be; a government could merely provide such labels as an advisory service to consumers, who would be free to set their own rules, or ignore the labels entirely. If a government merely wants to label, and not impose any filtering criteria, then PICS again provides some assistance because it enables a separation of labeling from filtering. On the other hand, a government that wishes to require filtering of items it labels as illegal gets little benefit from PICS as compared to prior technologies, as discussed below in the question about national firewalls.

- **Distribute labels.** A government could operate or finance operation of a Web server to distribute labels (a PICS label bureau); the labels themselves might be provided by authors or independent third parties. Taken on its own, this would actually contribute to freedom of expression, since it would make it easier for independent organizations to express their opinions (in the form of labels) and make those opinions heard. Consumers would be free to ignore any labels they disagreed with. Again, since PICS separates labeling from filtering, it enables a government to assist in label distribution without necessarily imposing filters. If combined with mandatory filtering, however, a government-operated or financed label bureau could contribute to restrictions on intellectual freedom.

– **Write filtering software.** It's unlikely that a government would write filtering software rather than buying it; the supplier of filtering software probably has little impact on intellectual freedom.

– **Set filtering criteria.** A government could try to impose filtering criteria in several ways, including government-operated proxy servers (a national intranet), mandatory filtering by service providers or public institutions (e.g., schools and libraries), or liability for possession of materials that have been labeled a particular way. In some ways, by enabling independent entities to take on all the other roles, PICS highlights this as the primary political battleground. Each national and local jurisdiction will rely on its political and legal process to answer difficult policy questions: Should there be any government-imposed controls on what can be received in private or public spaces? If so, what should those controls be? Most kinds of mandatory filters could be implemented without PICS. A government could express its required filtering criteria in the form of a PICSRule that everyone would be required to install and run, but without PICSRules a government could express its requirements in less technical form. One potential policy, however, mandatory filtering based on labels provided by non-government sources, would have been difficult to impose without PICS.

Install/run filters. A Government could require that filtering software be made available to consumers, without mandating any filtering rules. For example, a government could require that all Internet Service Providers make filtering software available to its customers, or that all PC browsers or operating systems include such software. Absent PICS, governments could have imposed such requirements anyway, since proprietary products such as SurfWatch and NetNanny are available.

Some other controls:

PICS encourages individual controls rather than government controls:

For example, a national proxy-server/firewall combination that blocks access to a government-provided list of prohibited sites does not depend on interoperability of labels and filters provided by different organizations. While such a setup could use PICS-compatible technology, a proprietary technology provided by a single vendor would be just as effective. Other controls, based on individual or local choices, benefit more from mixing and matching filtering software and labels that come from different sources, which PICS enables. Thus, there should be some substitution of individual or local controls for centralized controls, although it is not obvious how strong this substitution effect will be. In Europe initial calls for centralized controls gave way to government reports calling for greater reliance on individual recipient controls; the end results of these political processes, however, are yet to be determined.

Labeling

It matters whether labels are applied to IP addresses or to URLs, an IP address identifies the location of a computer on the Internet. A URL identifies the location of a document. To simplify a little, a URL has the form http://<domain-name>/<filename>. A web browser first resolves (translates) the domain-name into an IP address. It then contacts the computer at that address and asks it to send the particular filename. Thus, a label that applies to an IP address is a very broad label: it applies to every document that can be retrieved from that machine. Labeling of URLs permits more flexibility: different documents or directories of documents can be given different labels.

This difference of granularity will, naturally, have an impact on filtering. Filters based on IP addresses will be cruder: if some but not all of the documents available at a particular IP address are undesirable, the filter will have to either block all or none of those documents. PICS, by contrast, permits labeling of individual URLs, and hence permits finer grain filters as well.

Self-labeling

PICS makes author self-labeling more effective. Without a common format for labels, authors could not label themselves in a way that filtering programs could make use of. PICS provides that format.

PICS makes a government requirement of self-labeling more practical to implement. It enables such a requirement to have more impact. A government requirement of self-labeling would have little impact if the labels were not usable by filtering programs. PICS provides the common format so that filtering software from one source can use labels provided by other sources (authors in this case).

Self-labeling depend on universal agreement on a labeling vocabulary and criteria for assigning labels to material. Although universal agreement is not necessary, there does need to be some harmonization of vocabulary and labeling criteria, so that labels provided by different authors can be meaningfully compared.

PICS makes it easier for governments to cooperate in imposing self-labeling requirements. PICS provides a language-independent format for expressing labels. If governments agreed on a common set of criteria for assigning labels, the criteria could be expressed in multiple languages, yet still be used to generate labels that can be compared to each other.

It is effective for authors to label their own materials as inappropriate for minors. What about labeling appropriate materials? Both kinds of labeling could be effective, but only if a high percentage of the materials of a particular type are labeled. If the inappropriate materials are labeled, then a filter can block access to the labeled items. If the appropriate materials are labeled, then a filter can block access to all the unlabeled items.

Third-party labeling

Anyone can create a PICS label that describes any URL, and then distribute that label to anyone who wants to use that label. This is analogous to someone publishing a review of your web site in a newspaper or magazine.

Isn't there a danger of abuse if a third-party labeler gets too powerful? If a lot of people use a particular organization's labels for filtering, that organization will indeed wield a lot of power. Such an organization could, for example, arbitrarily assign negative labels to materials from its commercial or political competitors. The most effective way to combat this danger is to carefully monitor the practices of labeling services, and to ensure diversity in the marketplace for such services, so that consumers can stop using services that abuse their power.

Why did PICS use the term "label", with all of its negative associations? PICS documents use the term "label" broadly to refer to any machine-readable information that describes other information. Even information that merely classifies materials by topic or author (traditional card catalog information) would qualify as labels if expressed in a machine-readable format. The PICS developers recognized that the term "label" has a narrower meaning, with negative connotations, for librarians and some other audiences, but it was the most generic term the PICS creators could find without reverting to technical jargon like "*metadata*."

In media with centralized distribution channels, such as movies, labeling and filtering are not easily separated. For example, unrated movies are simply not shown in many theaters in the USA. In addition to its technical contribution, PICS makes an intellectual contribution by more clearly separating the ideas of labeling and filtering. Many of the negative connotations associated with "labeling" really should be associated with centralized filtering instead. There are, however, some subtle questions about the impact of labeling itself, as articulated in the next two questions.

There will always be a tradeoff, however, between speed of decision-making and the ability to take into account subtleties and context. When a large number of decisions need to be made in a short time, some will have to be made based on less than full information. The challenge for society, then, will be to choose carefully which decisions merit full discussion, in which case labels should be irrelevant, and which decisions can be left to the imperfect summary information that a label can provide.

Filtering through PICSRules

PICSRules is a language for expressing filtering rules (profiles) that allow or block access to URLs based on PICS labels that describe those URLs. The purposes for a common profile-specification language are:

Sharing and installation of profiles:

Sophisticated profiles may be difficult for end-users to specify, even through well-crafted user interfaces. An organization can create a recommended profile for children of a certain age. Users who trust that organization can install the profile rather than specifying one from scratch. It will be easy to change the active profile on a single computer, or to carry a profile to a new computer.

Communication to agents, search engines, proxies, or other servers:

Servers of various kinds may wish to tailor their output to better meet users' preferences, as expressed in a profile. For example, a search service can return only links that match a user's profile, which may specify criteria based on quality, privacy, age suitability, or the safety of downloadable code.

Portability betwen filtering products:

The same profile will work with any PICSRules-compatible product.

Role of PICS as a firewall:

PICS does not make national firewalls easier to implement, but an effective national firewall would make it possible for a government to impose PICS-based filtering rules (or non PICS-based filtering rules) on its citizens. A firewall partitions a network into two components and imposes rules about what information flow between the two components. The goal of a national firewall is to put all the computers in the country into one component, and all computers outside the country into the other component. This is difficult to do, especially if people deliberately try to find out connections (e.g., telephone lines) between computers inside the country and those outside the country. Given a successful partition, however, PICS could be used to implement the filtering rules for a firewall. In particular, the government could identify prohibited sites outside the country that people inside the country could not access; such a filtering could be implemented based on PICS-formatted labels or, without relying on PICS-compatible technology, with a simple list of prohibited URLs.

Implementation of firewall through PICS:

PICSRules can provide a way to express filtering preferences, but has no impact on the ability of a government to partition the computers inside a country from those outside the country.

PICS enables ISP compliance with government requirements that they prohibit access to specific URLs:

ISP compliance with government prohibition lists is already practical, even without PICS. It would also be possible to comply using PICS-based technologies. PICS does make it easier for ISPs to comply with a government requirement to block access to sites labeled by non-governmental entities (including those that are self-labeled by the authors of the sites).

PICSRules enables ISP compliance with government requirements that they prohibit access to specific URLs:

Governments can make such requirements with or without PICSRules. PICSRules does make it possible for governments to precisely state filtering requirements, and perhaps simplify ISP compliance with changing government requirements, if the ISP implements a general interpreter for the PICSRules language.

Compatibility of proxy-server based implementations of PICS filters with the principle of individual controls:

PICS enables mixing and matching of the five roles. In particular, a service provider could install and run filtering software on a proxy server, but allow individuals to choose what filtering rules will be executed for each account. AOL already offers a primitive version of this idea, not based on PICS; parents can turn the preset filtering rules on or off for each member of the family.

Usability of client based implementations of PICS filters for individual controls:

Governments could require the use of filters on clients. In case of USA the city of Boston, requires public schools to install a client-based filtering product on all computers with Internet access, and requires public libraries to install a client-based filtering product on all computers designated for children.

Does any country have a right to filter what is available on web?

W3C leaves this question to the political and legal processes of each country. Some people argue that unrestricted access to information is a fundamental human rights question that transcends national sovereignty.

PICS Technical Specifications:

Completed Specifications for PICS-1.1

These are official W3C recommendations. They are stable. The normative specifications are in English. Translations of some of these are available.

Service descriptions: It specifies the format for describing a rating service's vocabulary and scales; analogous to a database schema.

Label format and distribution: It specifies the format of labels and methods for distributing both self-labels and third-party labels.

PICSRules: It specifies an interchange format for filtering preferences, so that preferences can be easily installed or sent to search engines.

PICS Signed Labels (DSig) 1.0 Specification: Specifies the syntax and semantics of digital signatures in PICS labels.

PORTABLE NETWORK GRAPHICS (PNG):

PNG is an extensible file format for the lossless, portable, well-compressed storage of raster images. PNG provides a patent-free replacement for *GIF* and can also replace many common uses of *TIFF*. Indexed-color, grayscale, and truecolor images are supported, plus an optional alpha channel for transparency. Sample depths range from 1 to 16 bits per component (up to 48bit images for RGB, or 64bit for RGBA). The PNG specification was issued as a W3C Recommendation during October 1996. It is a mature document that is considered to contribute towards realising the full potential of the Web. Viewers for PNG are available on many platforms; there are an increasing number of content creation tools available; and thus modern browsers implement support for it. The MIME type for PNG, approved in 14 October 1996.

PLATFORM FOR PRIVACY PREFERENCES (P3P):

The Platform for Privacy Preferences Project (P3P),

developed by the World Wide Web Consortium, is emerging as an industry standard providing a simple, automated way for users to gain more control over the use of personal information on Web sites they visit. At its most basic level, P3P is a standardized set of multiple-choice questions, covering all the major aspects of a Web site's privacy policies. Taken together, they present a clear snapshot of how a site handles personal information about its users. P3P-enabled Web sites make this information available in a standard, machine-readable format. P3P enabled browsers can "read" this snapshot automatically and compare it to the consumer's own set of privacy preferences. P3P enhances user control by putting privacy policies where users can find them, in a form users can understand, and, most importantly, enables users to act on what they see.

The following resources provide information on P3P-enabling a web site:

* P3P Implementation Guide <http://p3ptoolbox.org/guide/ > - Why implement P3P, how does it work, preparing for implementation, creating P3P files.
* P3P Deployment Guide </TR/p3pdeployment> - Contains more technical details on deployment and server configuration than the Implementation Guide.
* How to Create and Publish Your Company's P3P Policy (in 6 Easy Steps) - A very brief overview.
* P3PToolbox.org <http://www.p3ptoolbox.org/> Features more information about P3P, P3P software, and upcoming P3P implementation workshops.
* W3C P3P Validator- To make sure your P3P enabled web site is working properly.

Current Specifications, Working Drafts and Notes:

* **Platform for Privacy Preferences (P3P1.0):** These are W3C Recommendations edited by Massimo Marchiori, normative specification of the Platform for Privacy

Preferences (P3P). This document, along with its normative references, includes all the specification necessary for the implementation of interoperable P3P applications.

* **A P3P Preference Exchange Language 1.0 (APPEL1.0):** W3C Working Draft edited by Marc Langheinrich, this is the latest public draft of the language for exchanging privacy preferences. This document complements the P3P1.0 specification (P3P10) by specifying a language for describing collections of preferences regarding P3P policies between P3P agents.
* **The Platform for Privacy Preferences 1.0 Deployment Guide:** W3C Note (Martin Presler-Marshall, editor). This is a guide to help site operators deploy the Platform for Privacy Preferences (P3P) on their site. It provides information on the tasks required, and gives guidance on how to best complete them.
* **A P3P Assurance Signature Profile:** W3C Note (Joseph Reagle, editor). This is not a normative specification. Instead, it captures the authors' thoughts on how applications might use the XML Signature specification to meet their requirements (defining signature semantics and algorithm profile); the example application is P3P. This is not a product or deliverable of any Working Group, nor does it reflect a consensus on how to use XML Signature's SignatureProperty. Instead this document presents a possible use of SignatureProperty, as permitted (but not required) by the XML Signature specification, for further exploration/discussion.
* **An RDF Schema for P3P:** W3C Note (Brian McBride, Rigo Wenning and Lorrie Cranor, editors). This document describes an RDF Schema for P3P.

QUALITY ASSURANCE ACTIVITY:

W3C creates the technical specifications regarded by the Web community at large as Web standards. In order for these standards to permit full interoperability and access to all, it is very important that the quality of implementation be given as much attention as standards development. There has always been and still is a strong demand from the Web community, including end users, Web agencies, organizations, and software developers, for better support and better implementation of W3C specifications in both commercial and non-commercial products.

As of November 2002, W3C has published about 46 recommendations. As our family of specifications gets more complex, their acceptance and deployment on the market becomes an ongoing challenge. Past experience with HTML, CSS and more recently SMIL, all implemented with various degrees of conformance by vendors, were strong incentives to start the QA Activity with due diligence.

The Quality Assurance (QA) Activity at W3C has a dual focus: to solidify and extend current quality practices, and to educate by sharing our understanding of coordination, certification, funding, and tracking of the quality of products and services related to W3C technologies. The mission of the QA Team is to improve the quality of W3C specification implementation in the field. In order to achieve that end, the QA Activity:

* Works on the quality of the specs themselves.
* Promotes the development of good validators, test tools and harnesses for implementors and end users.
* Thinks ahead in terms of what additional steps could be taken to achieve QA goals more efficiently, including certification, education, and communication.

W3C creates the technical specifications regarded by the web community at large as "Web standards", but to lead the web to its full potential, it must ensure that its deliverables, W3C recommendations are implemented correctly. W3C has decided to take a new lead in improving the quality of implementation for W3C technologies. The Quality Assurance Activity gathers and formalizes QA efforts for the various languages and protocols.

QA Activity has published two W3C Notes: (CHIPs and CUAP)

The QA Activity has released two W3C Notes.

* **CHIPs:** It is a set of good practices to improve implementations of HTTP and related standards as well as their use. It explains a few basic concepts, points out common mistakes and misbehaviors, and suggests "best practices".
* **CUAP:** It explains some common mistakes in user agents due to incorrect or incomplete implementation of specifications, and suggests remedies. It also suggests some "good behavior" where specifications themselves do not specify any particular behavior (e.g., in the face of error conditions). This document is not a complete set of guidelines for good user agent behavior.

Role of W3C:

Several W3C Working Groups, as well as individuals from the W3C Team and the Web community have started to assemble test suites, produce validation tools and follow good QA practices. In addition, external organizations such as NIST and OASIS, and individuals have been active in the field of conformance and testing of W3C technologies, with varying degrees of W3C Working Group coordination.

These existing efforts are important and serve as a basis for future work as we move forward in the life cycle of our QA Activity at W3C. In order to be really effective, however, QA work for W3C technologies must be driven from inside W3C and must coordinate with all W3C Activities.

QA is absolutely necessary in order to ensure interoperability and usability and also to have consistency between the specifications W3C produces. The Web community, industry, and Members will benefit from the QA Activity as a guarantee of interoperable products, which is the core mission of W3C.

Current Situation:

The QA Working Group is mainly working on a framework of documents to help W3C Working Groups and external bodies achieve quality with regards to our specifications. The list of the seven Framework Documents is available and updated regularly.

* QA Framework: Introduction </TR/qaframe-intro>
* QA Framework: Operational Guidelines </TR/qaframe-ops>
* QA Framework: Operational Examples and Techniques <http://www.w3.org/QA/WG/qaframe-ops-extech>
* QA Framework: Specification Guidelines </TR/qaframe-spec>
* QA Framework: Specification Examples and Techniques </QA/WG/qaframe-spec-extech>
* QA Framework: Test Suite Guidelines </TR/qaframe-test>

The QA Working Group is working on the publication of new drafts for the entire QA Framework, and has has started to review materials and organization of other W3C Working Groups to improve its own material and to help Working Groups define a better QA strategy. The QA Team and the QA Interest Group are working on resources and tools (like MUTAT, a test framework) to help people who want to promote best practices. The HTML Validator has been taken under the responsibility of the QA Team.

TIMED-TEXT:

The Timed-Text specification should cover all necessary aspects of timed text on the web. Typical applications of timed text are the real time subtitling of foreign language movies on the web, captioning for people lacking audio devices or having hearing impairments, karaoke, scrolling news items or teleprompter applications. The issue of developing an interoperable timed text format came up during the development of the SMIL 2.0 specification. Today, there are a number of incompatible formats for captioning, subtitling and other forms of timed text used on the web. This means that when creating a SMIL presentation, the text portion often needs to be targeted to one particular playback environment. This poses an issue for creating interoperable SMIL presentations. Moreover, the accessibility community relies heavily on captioning to make audiovisual content accessible to a hearing-impaired audience. The lack of an interoperable format adds a significant additional cost to the costs of captioning web content, which are already high.

Timed Text will enrich the user experience for services involving timed text, and is seen as an important stimulus for instance in the usage of captioning and subtitling. The organizations willing to work on Timed Text include vendors of streaming multimedia technology, web browser companies, representatives of the accessibility community, caption content producers and consumer electronics companies.

VALIDATORS:

Log Validator:

Log Validator is a web server log analysis tool which finds the N most popular documents matching a particular criteria. Thanks to a modular, extensible design, the criteria can be chosen and modified arbitrarily. The Log Validator was first written with Validation (HTML, etc.) in mind, it can thus help web content managers find and fix the most frequently accessed invalid documents on their web site, acting as a comprehensive validation tool.

The first HTML validator service has been a way to check the validity of one's web page with regards to web standards (HTML, CSS, etc.). Other services, like HTML Tidy allows to (semi-) automatically fix invalid documents. This tool is here to make your life as a webmaster, web designer, web developer even easier, by telling you which documents you should fix in priority. It has first been developed by Gerald Oskoboiny as an internal W3C tool to check the HTML validity of the web pages on the W3C website.

In 2002, the Quality Assurance team at W3C decided to re-write it as a modular, portable, and easy-to-use tool for webmasters. This tool takes a web server's last logs and processes it through validation modules. Those validation modules check the most popular documents' validity for a certain technology.

The (X)HTML validation module, for example, helps you find, among the most popular pages on your site, which are invalid, and thus tell you which (invalid) pages you should fix first. This is a step-by-step process, you can set up this tool to run every week, and painlessly fix only a few documents at the time. Eventually, you will have fixed your whole site, or at least the most important parts of it.

MUTAT:

MUTAT is a simple cgi script to demonstrate possible uses of EARL and also use of RDF to configure a Quality Assurance helper application. Quality Assurance experts have come up with a variety of solutions to handle entry and retrieval of the data they need - sometimes little more than a paper and pencil. The idea behind MUTAT was to demonstrate automating the process for human-centered testing, and output the results in EARL. The script presents the user with a series of questions: first a page of fill-in information on their identity and testing environment, and then the actual tests. The tests can be formatted either as a single page of text-based questions and links or a succession of framed HTML pages, with form inputs for the results. Both the initial information questions and the test questions are configured using an RDF file. There is also a feature that allows filtering of test questions.

You can go straight to the bare front page of the testing

tool with this link <bin/mutat>, but that probably won't be very interesting without the URI of a file containing tests. There are two existing examples of test files that show off different features in the script. The links show how one can use GET-style URIs to set values in the test and customize the opening page.

VOICE BROWSER:

W3C is working to expand access to the Web to allow people to interact via keypads, spoken commands, listening to prerecorded speech, synthetic speech and music. This will allow any telephone to be used to access appropriately designed Web-based services, and will be a boon to people with visual impairments or needing Web access while keeping their hands and eyes free for other things. It will also allow effective interaction with display-based Web content in the cases where the mouse and keyboard may be missing or inconvenient.

To fulfill this goal, the W3C Voice Browser Working Group is defining a suite of markup languages covering dialog, speech synthesis, speech recognition, call control and other aspects of interactive voice response applications. Specifications such as the Speech Synthesis Markup Language, Speech Recognition Grammar Specification, and Call Control XML are core technologies for describing speech synthesis, recognition grammars, and call control constructs respectively. VoiceXML is a dialog markup language that leverages the other specifications for creating dialogs that feature synthesized speech, digitized audio, recognition of spoken and DTMF key (touch tone) input, recording of spoken input, telephony, and mixed initiative conversations.

These specifications bring the advantages of web-based development and content delivery to interactive voice response applications. Further work is anticipated on enabling their use with other W3C markup languages such as XHTML, XForms and SMIL. This will be done in conjunction with other W3C Working Groups, including the Multimodal Interaction Activity.

Applications:

Some possible applications include:

* Accessing business information, including the corporate "front desk" asking callers who or what they want, automated telephone ordering services, support desks, order tracking, airline arrival and departure information, cinema and theater booking services, and home banking services.
* Accessing public information, including community information such as weather, traffic conditions, school closures, directions and events; local, national and international news; national and international stock market information; and business and e-commerce transactions.
* Accessing personal information, including calendars, address and telephone lists, to do lists, shopping lists, and calorie counters.
* Assisting the user to communicate with other people via sending and receiving voice mail and email messages.

W3C's work on voice browsers originally started in the context of making the Web accessible to more of us, more of the time. In October 1998, W3C organized a workshop on "Voice Browsers". The workshop brought together people involved in developing voice browsers for accessing Web based services. The workshop concluded that the time was ripe for W3C to bring together interested parties to collaborate on the development of joint specifications for voice browsers. As a response, an activity proposal and charter were written to establish a W3C "Voice Browser" Activity.

Speech Recognition Grammar (SRGS):

The speech recognition grammar specification covers both speech and DTMF (touch-tone) input. DTMF is valuable in noisy conditions or when the social context makes it awkward to speak. Grammars can be specified in either an XML or an equivalent augmented BNF (ABNF) syntax, which some authors may find easier to deal with. Speech recognition is an inherently uncertain process. Some speech engines may be able to ignore "um's" and "aah's", and to perform partial matches. Recognizers may report confidence values. If the utterance has several possible parses, the recognizer may be able to report the most likely alternatives (n-best results).

Speech Synthesis (SSML):

The Speech Synthesis specification defines a markup language for prompting users via a combination of prerecorded speech, synthetic speech and music. You can select voice characteristics (name, gender and age) and the speed, volume, pitch, and emphasis. There is also provision for overriding the synthesis engine's default pronunciation.

Semantic Interpretation:

The semantic interpretation specification describes annotations to grammar rules for extracting the semantic results from recognition. The annotations are expressed in a syntax based upon a subset of ECMAScript, and when evaluated, yield a result represented either as XML or as a value that can be held in an ECMAScript variable. The target for the XML output is EMMA (Extensible Multimodal Annotation Markup Language) which is being developed in the Multimodal Interaction activity.

Call Control (CCXML):

W3C is working on markup to enable fine-grained control of speech (signal processing) resources and telephony resources in a VoiceXML telephony platform. The scope of these language features is for controlling resources in a platform on the network edge, not for building network-based call processing applications in a telephone switching system, or for controlling an entire telecom network. These components are designed to integrate naturally with existing language elements for defining applications which run in a voice browser framework. This will enable application developers to use markup to perform call screening, whisper call waiting, call transfer, and more. Users can be offered the ability to place outbound calls, conditionally answer calls, and to initiate or receive outbound communications such as another call.

The purpose of the next major version of the dialog markup language (code named "V3") is to provide powerful dialog capabilities which can be used to build advanced speech applications, and to provide these dialog capabilities in a form which can be easily and cleanly integrated with other W3C languages. For example, the Multimodal Interaction Activity would be able to combine this dialog language with markup languages for other modalities to build multimodal applications.

Work started in early 2003 on collecting detailed requirements for this dialog markup language. The requirements will be drawn from sources including deferred change requests on VoiceXML 2.0, other activities within the Voice Browser group (especially Call Control), external contributions such as SALT 1.0 and XHTML+Voice Profiles, and other interested working groups within W3C especially Multimodal, XHTML, and WAI. It is intended that the first working draft of this dialog language will be published in the 2004.

WEB COMPUTER GRAPHICS METAFILE:

CGM (Computer Graphics Metafile) has been an ISO standard for vector and composite vector/raster picture definition since 1987. CGM has a significant following in technical illustration, interactive electronic documentation, geophysical data visualization, amongst other application areas and is widely used in the fields of automotive engineering, aeronautics, and the defence industry.

WebCGM is a profile for the effective application of CGM in Web electronic documents. WebCGM has been a joint effort of the CGM Open Consortium, in collaboration with W3C staff and supported by the European Commission Esprit project. It represents an important interoperability agreement amongst major users and implementors of CGM, and thereby unifies current diverse approaches to CGM utilization in Web document applications. WebCGM's clear and unambiguous conformance requirements will enhance interoperability of implementations, and it should be possible to leverage existing CGM validation tools, test suites, and the product certification testing services for application to WebCGM .

While WebCGM is a binary file format and is not "stylable", nevertheless WebCGM follows published W3C requirements for a scalable graphics format where such are applicable. The design criteria for the graphical content of WebCGM aimed at a balance between graphical expressive power on the one hand, and simplicity and implementability on the other. A small but powerful set of metadata elements is standardized in WebCGM, to support the functionalities of: hyperlinking and document navigation; picture structuring and layering; and, search and query on WebCGM picture content.

Status:

The WebCGM Profile specification was issued as a W3C Recommendation on 21st January 1999. This means it is a mature document that is considered to contribute towards realising the full potential of the Web. Viewers for CGM are available on many platforms and are being adapted to support the WebCGM Profile specification.

MIME type:

CGM has been a registered MIME type since 1995. The MIME type for CGM is unusual in that it requires two parameters - the CGM version, and the CGM Profile in use. This is because, without Profiles, it is very difficult to achieve interoperability with CGM (which is why W3C issued a WebCGM Profile). It also means that the MIME type does not need to be re-registered whenever there is a new profile.

6
METADATA

Introduction:

Metadata can be defined literally as "data about data," to "information about the data that helps in optimization and management of that data". But the term is normally understood to mean structured data about digital (and non-digital) resources that can be used to help support a wide range of operations. These might include, for example, resource description and discovery, the management of information resources (including rights management) and their long-term preservation.

While the first use of 'metadata' originated in contexts related to digital information (chiefly with regard to databases), the general understanding of the term has since broadened to include any kind of standardised descriptive information about resources, including non-digital ones. So, for example, library catalogues, abstracting and indexing services, archival finding aids and museum documentation might all be seen as containing metadata. The advantages of this are twofold. Firstly, it allows librarians, archivists and museum documentation specialists to co-operate usefully across professional boundaries. Secondly, it enables the cultural heritage professions to communicate more effectively with those domains that also have an interest in metadata: e.g., software developers, publishers, the recording industry, television companies, the producers of digital educational content and those concerned with geographical and satellite-based information. If metadata is useful in managing a collection of data and locating specific data objects, it stands to reason that more metadata would make these tasks easier. However, extensive metadata requirements place an extra burden on data suppliers and system resources, and may not provide much added value to end users. Proper metadata generation should involve both the data producer and the consumer, taking into account the user's needs and the producer's availability to provide that metadata. Metadata is useful in several aspects of a data system, including data access, data management, and data analysis. We being informational professional concentrate on the data access aspect in deriving our information architecture guidelines and to apply these guidelines for specially data management.

Metadata standards and applications

One consequence of this wide range of communities having an interest in metadata is that there are a bewildering number of standards and formats in existence or under development. The library world, for example, has developed the MARC formats as a means of encoding metadata defined in cataloguing rules and has also defined descriptive standards in the International Standard Bibliographic Description (ISBD) series. Other domains have defined metadata standards based on implementations of the Standard Generalised Markup Language (SGML) or the Extensible Markup Language (XML). Examples of these are the Encoded Archival Description (EAD) and the CIMI Document Type Definition (DTD); an SGML DTD developed by the *CIMI consortium.*

As it is clear that metadata is not only used for resource description and discovery purposes. For example, metadata can be used to help administer and manage resources, e.g. to record information about their location and acquisition. It can also be used to record any intellectual property rights vested in resources and to help manage user access to them. Other metadata might be technical in nature, documenting how resources relate to particular software and hardware environments or for recording digitisation parameters. The creation and maintenance of metadata is also seen as an important factor in the long-term preservation management of digital resources and for helping to preserve the context and authenticity of resources. Examples of these 'richer' understandings of metadata are the development of an *Australian Recordkeeping Metadata Schema (RKMS)*, the MPEG-7 Multimedia Content Description Interface standard for audio-visual resources and the NISO draft definition of technical metadata for digital still images.

Popular metadata standards include *Dublin Core, USMARC, Federal Geographic Data Committee (FGDC), Global/Government Information Locator Service (GILS), Directory Interchange Format (DIF), Inter-University Consortium for Political* and *Social Research (ICPSR), and Survey Design and Statistical Methodology (SDSM), Consortium for the Computer Interchange of Museum Information (CIMI),* and the *Information Resource Dictionary System (IRDS) Content Model Standard.*

One thing they have in common is a means to access that data—a search and order system. The amount of metadata available in the system is immaterial "if it isn't organized in a manner to add value"; specifically, to turn the data into "actionable information". This actionable information can be defined by viewing the search and order system from the viewpoint of the different people that will interact with it in different ways. Such data systems vary greatly, and while their metadata requirements are necessarily domain-specific, there are some general guidelines that can be followed in the information architecture design to insure that the appropriate type of metadata is captured.

End-users of a search system may ask any of the following questions:

* which data do I need?
* what does this object contain?
* who generated these data?
* when and where were these data collected?
* how should this data set be used?

Thus, search metadata answers age old interrogative questions from the end user's viewpoint. Considering these questions from the database administrator's perspective helps define metadata requirements for data management.

The Dublin Core:

The Dublin Core is a metadata specification devised to enhance existing network catalogs of electronic documents. In an effort begun in March 1995, the initial goal was "to advance the state of the art in the development of resource description (or metadata) records for networked electronic information objects". At the *Second Dublin Core Workshop* the report restated the goal "to define a small, universally understood set of metadata elements that would allow authors and information providers to describe their work and to facilitate interoperability among resource discovery tools". Dublin Core developers found that existing catalogs which automatically generate indexes used by locator services provide too little information while manually generated records are too costly to create and maintain for the large number of electronic documents currently available on the Internet. The Dublin Core's purpose is to provide a system that is between the two extremes and allows mapping to more extensive complex record systems. Dublin Core principles specify that the metadata elements be optional, repeatable, and extensible. One of the specific purposes of DC is to support cross-domain resource discovery; i.e. to serve as an intermediary between the numerous community-specific formats being developed. It has already been used in this way in the service developed by the EU-funded *EULER project* and by the UK Arts and Humanities Data Service (AHDS) catalogue. The Dublin Core element set is also used by a number of Internet subject gateway services and in services that broker access to multiple gateways, e.g. the broker service being developed by the EU-funded *Renardus project*.

Dublin Core developers also struggle to balance quality and quantity of required metadata. They began with 13 metadata elements, but at the second workshop a minimal effort approach suggested 8 elements for inclusion in HTML documents. The list was finalized in 1996 with the 15 core elements shown here:

* Title
* Creator (Author)
* Subject
* Description
* Publisher
* Contributors
* Date
* Resource Type
* Format
* Resource Identifier
* Source
* Language
* Relation (to other resources)
* Coverage (spatial, temporal)
* Rights (e.g., copyright notice)

Once again the higher number the elements of metadata, the more descriptive it is, and thus, higher quality, but a smaller number of "core" elements promotes interoperability, flexibility, and maintainability.

Resource Description Framework (RDF):

If the resource identified by a URL is unavailable, the URL is nearly úseless. Reliability of URLs is currently subject to a number of single points of failure. As the number of users of the Web increases, and as the Web is increasingly used in mission-critical applications, it becomes clear that redundancy at all points is a requirement.

With each level of indirection and redundancy comes the possibility of version skew, forgery, and corruption. Information providers and consumers should be able to select from a number of authentication mechanisms to balance between integrity, speed, and convenience. It is expected to be able to address robustness (reliability and authenticity) through the use of RDF.

The Resource Description Framework (RDF) integrates a variety of applications from library catalogs and world-wide directories to syndication and aggregation of news, software, and content to personal collections of music, photos, and events using XML as an interchange syntax. The RDF specifications provide a lightweight ontology system to support the exchange of knowledge on the Web.

One of the major issues of the World Wide Web as it exists today is that it is really hard to automate any tasks which one has to perform on the web. So far, the web is mainly built as a forum for human interaction; because most web documents are written for human consumption, the only available form of searching on the web (for example) is to simply match words or sentences contained in documents. Anyone who has used a web search service like AltaVista or *HotBot* knows that typing in a few keywords and receiving a couple of thousand "hits" is not necessarily very useful. A lot of manual "weeding" of information has to happen after that; it may also happen that the keywords for which you are searching are not prominent in the relevant document itself.

A possible solution for the search problem - and for the general issue of letting automated "agents" roam the web performing useful tasks - is to provide a mechanism which allows a more precise description of things on the web. This, in turn, could elevate the status of the web from machine-readable to something we might call machine-understandable.

Standardisation Efforts at W3C:

One could say that the history of metadata at W3C begins with PICS or Platform for Internet Content Selection. PICS is a mechanism for communicating ratings of web pages from a server to clients; these ratings, or rating labels, contain information about the content of web pages: for example, whether a particular page contains a peer-reviewed research article, or was authored by an accredited researcher, or contains sex, nudity, violence, foul language etc. Instead of being a fixed set of criteria, PICS introduced a general mechanism for creating rating systems. Different organizations could rate content based on their own objectives and values, and users - for example, parents worried about their children's web usage - could set their browser to filter out any web pages not matching their own criteria. Development of PICS was motivated by the anticipation of restrictions on the Internet such as some recent US legislation (the Communications Decency Act and its subsequent overruling by the Federal Supreme Court).

PICS is a restricted metadata framework. It allows certain things to be expressed very precisely about web pages; in particular, PICS is useful when all the possible data values can be known in advance. The development of RDF as a general metadata framework - and in a way as a general knowledge representation mechanism for the web was heavily inspired by PICS.

RDF - the Resource Description Framework, as our proposed mechanism is called is a foundation for processing metadata; it provides interoperability between applications that exchange machine-understandable information on the Web. RDF emphasizes facilities to enable automated processing of Web resources. RDF metadata can be used in a variety of application areas; for example: in resource discovery to provide better search engine capabilities; in cataloging for describing the content and content relationships available at a particular Web site, page, or digital library; by intelligent software agents to facilitate knowledge sharing and exchange; in content rating; in describing collections of pages that represent a single logical "document"; for describing intellectual property rights of Web pages, and in many others. RDF with digital signatures will be key to building the "Web of Trust" for electronic commerce, collaboration, and other applications.

RDF encourages the view of "metadata being data" by using XML (the eXtensible Markup Language) as its encoding syntax. The resources being described by RDF are, in general, anything that can be named via a URI (Uniform Resource Identifier). The broad goal of RDF is to define a mechanism for describing resources that makes no assumptions about a particular application domain, nor defines the semantics of any application domain. The definition of the mechanism should be domain neutral, yet the mechanism should be suitable for describing information about any domain.

The recently published document about RDF introduces a model for representing metadata and one possible syntax for expressing and transporting this metadata in a manner that maximizes the interoperability of independently developed web servers and clients. This document is to be followed by others addressing issues such as how to define schemata (classes) for metadata, how to write queries, etc.

At the core, RDF data consists of nodes and attached attribute/value pairs. Nodes can be any web resources (pages, servers, basically anything for which you can give a URI), even other instances of metadata. Attributes are named properties of the nodes, and their values are either atomic (text strings, numbers, etc.) or other resources or metadata instances. In short, this mechanism allows us to build labeled directed graphs.

The essence of RDF is the model of nodes, attributes, and their values. In order to store instances of this model into files or to communicate these instances from one agent to another, we need a graph serialization syntax. The particular language we use is XML (XML being W3C's work-in-progress to define a richer Web syntax for a variety of applications). RDF and XML are complementary; there will be alternate ways to represent the same RDF data model, some more suitable for direct human authoring.

RDF in itself does not contain any predefined vocabularies for authoring metadata. We do, however, expect that standard vocabularies will emerge, after all this is a core requirement for large-scale interoperability. Some of the vocabularies in the foreseeable future are a PICS-like rating architecture, a digital library vocabulary (currently referred to as "Dublin Core"), and a vocabulary for expressing digital signatures. Anyone can design a new vocabulary, the only requirement for using it is that a designating URI is included in the metadata instances using this vocabulary. This use of URIs to name vocabularies is an important design feature of RDF: many previous metadata standardization efforts in other areas have foundered on the issue of establishing a central attribute registry. RDF permits a central registry but does not require one.

Future of Metadata on the Web:

The RDF working group - the W3C vehicle for crafting new standards - includes representatives from key companies and organizations: Netscape, Microsoft, IBM, Nokia, OCLC, etc. The interest from the large web browser vendors gives us hope that large scale deployment of tools which understand about RDF will take place; this in turn should lead to the widespread adoption of RDF on the web.

Once the web has been sufficiently "populated" with rich metadata, what can we expect? First, searching on the web will become easier as search engines have more information available, and thus searching can be more focused. Doors will also be opened for automated software agents to roam the web, looking for information for us or transacting business on our behalf. The web of today, the vast unstructured mass of information, may in the future be transformed into something more manageable - and thus something far more useful.

Dublin Core, Open Directory, and General Purpose Catalogs:

- *Dublin Core Metadata Initiative*

The Dublin Core Metadata Initiative is an open forum engaged in the development of interoperable online metadata standards that support a broad range of purposes and business models. DCMI's activities include consensus-driven working groups, global workshops, conferences, standards liaison, and educational efforts to promote widespread acceptance of metadata standards and practices.

* *OCLC Connexion* (formally CORC - Cooperative Online Resource Catalog): CORC became a production service in July 2000; it started as a research project exploring the cooperative creation and sharing of metadata by libraries.
* *Open Directory Project*- The Open Directory Project is the largest, most comprehensive human-edited directory of the Web. It is constructed and maintained by a vast, global community of volunteer editors.
* RDF dumps of the are available. These dumps don't quite conform to the final RDF specification but rather to an earlier working draft.
* *xmlTree* - An index of XML content providers. The index is served in both RDF form and presented for human readability.
* *DSpace* - A newly developed digital repository created to capture, distribute and preserve the intellectual output of MIT. The dspace component of Semantic Web Advanced Development aims to survey existing RDF data stores and examine effective techniques for storing complex metadata in a variety of systems.
* *TAP* - TAP's goals are to enable the Semantic Web by providing some simple tools that make the web a giant distributed Database. TAP is open source development effort by R.V. Guha (IBM) and Rob McCool (Stanford) which provide a set of protocols and conventions that create a coherent whole of independantly produced bits of information, and a simple API to navigate the graph. Local,

independantly managed knowledge bases can be aggegated to form selected centers of knowledge useful for particular applications.

Perl Developers:

* The RDFStore Perl RDF API <http://rdfstore.sourceforge.net/> by Alberto Reggiori is a system for managing RDF models in Perl and includes a Perl version of the Stanford Java RDF API, the RDQL query language and persistent storage.

Python Developers:

* The Redfoot RDF framework by James Tauber and Dan Krech provides a system for building distributed data-driven web applications with RDF and Python. It includes an RDF database, query API, template language, module architecture, editor all with web interface, sample applications and the beginnings of P2P support.
* The W3C Semantic Web Area for Play by Tim Berners-Lee and Dan Connolly contains lots of small Python tools for RDF and beyond-RDF research tools including the Closed World Machine (CWM) data manipulator, rules processor and query system mostly using using the Notation 3 textual RDF syntax. Available under W3C open source license.
* The 4Suite 4RDF Python library provides open source tools for manipulating and querying RDF data, including inference capabilities.

C Developers:

* The Redland RDF Application Framework library by Dave Beckett, Institute for Learning and Research Technology, University of Bristol is a portable C library that provides a high-level, object based interface for RDF allowing the model to be stored persistently, queried and manipulated. Includes the Raptor RDF Parser Toolkit for handling RDF/

XML and other syntaxes and also provides Perl, Python, Tcl and Java interfaces. Available under open source / free software licenses (LGPL, GPL, MPL).

* RDFDB is a database that supports the RDF data model directly. It can load data from files or data can be inserted using the database API. It also supports an SQL-like query language. RDFDB is a very scalable and very fast triple store by R.V. Guha

Tcl/Tk Developers

* The XWMF - An eXtensible Web Modeling Framework project by Alexander Block and Reinhold Klapsing contains various tools in Tcl including a parser, data model query tool and graphical editor. Available under open source and/or LGPL licenses.

PHP Developers

* RAP RDF API for PHP by Chris Bizer. A pure PHP package for manipulating RDF models and parsing/ serializing the RDF/XML syntax. See also the documentation and online demo. GPL License. Version 0.3 with new rdf:nodeID and rdf:datatype support announced 13 January 2003.

Other Related Technolologies:

Conceptual Graphs

* **Corese(A COnceptual REsource Search Engine):** The Corese platform implements an RDF/RDFS processor based on Conceptual Graphs (CG). Corese enables the processing of RDF Schemas and RDF statements within the CG formalism. The graph matching algorithm, called projection, enables to retrieve RDF statements according to a query and hence implements a search engine.

DESCRIBING AND RETRIEVING PHOTOS USING RDF AND HTTP:

Describing & retrieving (digitized) photos with Resource Description Format (RDF) metadata describes the RDF schemas, a data-entry program for quickly entering metadata for large numbers of photos, a way to serve the photos and the metadata over HTTP. The data-entry program has been implemented in Java, a specific Jigsaw frame has been done to retrieve the RDF from the image through HTTP. The RDF schema uses the Dublin Core schema as well as additional schemas for technical data.

Diagram of the parts of the photo-RDF system. Top left: the pictures are digitized and stored as JPEG images. Bottom left: metadata is written into the pictures with the data-entry program (and can also be edited if corrections are necessary). Right: requests from the Web are served by Jigsaw, by sending either the picture or the metadata, depending on the form of the request.

The system comprises the following, largely independent, pieces:

* Scanning the photos and storing them in JPEG format. Negatives are good for scanning the best quality, but any process that yields JPEG could be used, including digital cameras.
* A data-entry program that allows easy entry/editing of the metadata for each photos and stores the data in RDF form inside the JPEG file.
* A module for the Jigsaw server that can serve either the JPEG image data or the RDF description that is stored in it, using HTTP content negotiation to determine which of the two a client wants.

Some digital cameras are already producing information about the picture, which may be read and reformatted in RDF by scripts. The RDF data is expressed in three separate schemas, one of which is the Dublin Core schema. The other two deal with technical data of the photo and with subject categories. The reason for using three schemas is solely to allow each of them to be used in other projects, to the users of the data-entry program the actual RDF is completely hidden.

The data-entry program "rdfpic":

Screen dump of **rdfpic**, the metadata editor, showing the screen to enter technical data. The data-entry program is very simple. It has been designed to enable quick entry of metadata for lots of photos, under the assumption that the photos will usually be from one or a few series. Most fields therefore show by default the value that was entered for the previous photo, and give quick access to the values entered for the last few photos. Typically, only very few fields will have to be changed from one photo to the next and the amount of typing will be minimized.

The program is written in Java, but the user interface is in fact generated at run-time directly from a machine-readable version of the schemas (currently not the RDF syntax, but a transformation of it, with equivalent information). This means that the program does not need to be changed when we change the RDF schemas.

The RDF data is stored in the JPEG file in comment blocks (blocks of type "COM", as defined by ISO DIS 10918-1). According to the JPEG standard, a comment block can contain arbitrary text. There is no way to assign a type to the text. It is a matter to rely on the fact that RDF can easily be distinguished from plain text by heuristics. JPEG limits each comment block to 64K, but there can be as many blocks as necessary, so arbitrary amounts of text can be added. In practice, the descriptions generated by the rdfpic program are typically only a few hundred bytes long.

Jigsaw extension:

To serve either the RDF version or the complete image using existing browsers and tools, the best way is to use Content Negotiation. It doesn't exclude the use of other techniques, such as HTTP extensions, to be able to retrieve and store metadata in a better way.

Using Content Negotiation it will provide following benefits:

* It will work right away with all text-based browsers (lynx, emacs with emacsspeak, etc.) and
* The output can be rendered directly by selecting, e.g., the title or the description from the RDF.
* An RDF crawler will be able to get all the descriptions of a collection of photos to create a knowledge database, just by asking for the right MIME type.

In Jigsaw, a frame has been created, to simulate two different resources under the same URI, the one of the image itself. Those two resources have their own set of HTTP values, such as ETags, Content-Length and others and the result is sent out using the classic Content Negotiation of HTTP. The RDF can be also be fetched directly without doing Content Negotiation, by just adding the wanted MIME type after a semicoln (;) e.g.: foo.jpg;application%2Frdf+xml ("%2F" is "/", escaped for occurrence in a URL.)

RDF schemas:

The metadata is separated into three different schemas:

Dublin Core schema: The Dublin Core schema is a general schema for identifying original works, typically books and articles, but also films, paintings or photos. It contains such properties as creator, editor, title, date of publishing and publisher. The Dublin Core Metadata Initiative is developing it and the version of our interest is the RDF-format of version.

Technical schema: This schema captures technical data about the photo and the camera, such as the type of camera, the type of film, and the date the film was developed and the scanner and software used for digitizing.

Content schema: This schema is used to categorize the subject of the photo by means of a controlled vocabulary. This schema allows photos to be retrieved based on such characteristics as portrait, group portrait, landscape, architecture, sport, animals, etc.

All the properties are optional. The more properties are given values, the better the photo will be described and the easier it will be to find it, but leaving properties undefined doesn't make the metadata invalid. There are no dependencies between the properties, each property can be given a value independent of whether any other property has a value. The values are also independent, except for restrictions of common sense.

Dublin Core Schema:

Here is an interpretation of the Dublin Core properties, applied to photo material. In parentheses the label that is shown in the user interface of rdfpic, if it is different from the property name.

title

a short description of the photo. Example: Marian climbs on the "elephant"

subject

a set of keywords to describe the photo. See the content schema below for the list of keywords. Example: portrait, landscape

description

a longer description of the photo. Example: Marian attempts to climb on the granite rock that is nicknamed "the elephant"

creator ("author/creator")

the photographer, as a URL that can be further described with other schemas. Example: http://www.example.org/People/Bos

publisher

the person or institution making the photo available, often the same as the creator. Example: http://www.example.org/People/Bos

contributor

a person who contributed in some way, e.g., the person who digitized the photo; may be a URL or a name. date

the date and time the photo was taken, conforming to ISO format [*ISOdate*]. The year is required, everything else can be omitted: yyyy[-mm[-dd[Thh:mm[:ss[.sTZD]]]]]. The default time zone is UTC. Example: 1999-10-01

type

always "image" (see the Dublin Core's List of Resource Types <http://dublincore.org/documents/2000/07/11/dcmi-type-vocabulary/>)

format

always "image/jpeg"

identifier ("number")

a number for the photo that is meaningful to the publisher. This is not the URL of the photo and it does not have to be globally unique.

source

not used.

language

not used.

relation

identifies a series: the event or topic for a series of photographs. Can be a URL or a string. Example: Marian in Le Sidobre.

coverage ("location")

the location shown on the photo. (Note that we only use

the "spatial coverage," not the "temporal coverage," since we assume that a photo is instantaneous and thus the date field is enough.). Example: Le Sidobre (Tarn)

rights

copyright statement, or the URL for one. Example: http://www.example.org/People/Lafon/Copyright?1998

Technical Schema:

The technical schema is defined by this RDF schema:

camera

the brand and type of the camera, or a URL for the camera. If the latter, the URL identifies one actual camera, not all cameras of that type. Example: http://www.example.org/People/Lafon/FooCamera8000i

film

the brand and type of film. In contrast to the camera property, this is not an individual roll of film, but identifies all films of the same type. (We assume films of the same type are sufficiently similar; except for fabrication errors, they are interchangeable.) The value may be a string or a URL that is further described elsewhere. As a convention, digital cameras should be considered as "digital" film. Example: Ilfoo HP5

lens

a definition of the lens used, maybe a URI describing it, a URI pointing to the camera for compact cameras, or just plain text description. Example: FooLens AF:70-210

devel-date

date on which the film was developed. The date must be in the same form as the date property. Example: 1998-08-04

content schema:

The content schema contains the keywords we use in the "subject" property of the Dublin Core schema. That property should contain as many of the following keywords as are applicable. The keywords have the following meaning:

Portrait

The photo contains a portrait of one person.

Group-portrait

The photo contains a portrait of a group of people.

Landscape

The photo contains a landscape or skyline.

Baby

The photo contains a baby.

Architecture

The photo contains interesting buildings.

Wedding

The photo contains scenes from a wedding.

Macro

The photo contains an extreme close-up and would, when viewed under normal circumstances, be larger than life-size.

Graphic

The photo contains a pattern, texture or design, that is interesting for its abstract, graphic quality.

Panorama

The photo contains a wide-angle view of a landscape or skyline.

Animal

The photo contains an animal.

PART IV : DIGITAL APPLICATIONS AND LIBRARIES

7
ARTIFICIAL INTELLIGENCE AND EXPERT SYSTEM

Introduction and Historical Developments:

Artificial intelligence began to emerge a separate field of study during the 1940s and 1950s when the computer became a commercial reality. Prior to this time, a number of important areas of research that would later help to shape early artificial intelligence work were beginning to mature. These developments all began to converge during this period. First there was the work of logicians such as Alonz Church, Kurt Godel, Emil Post and Alan Turing. They were carrying on earlier work in initiated by Whitehead and Russel, Tarski and Kleene. This work began in earnest during the 1920s and 1930s. It helped to produce formalized method for reasoning the form of logic known as prepositional and predicate calculus. It demonstrated that facts and ideas from a language such as English could be formally described and manipulated mechanically in meaningful ways. Turing, sometimes regarded as the father of artificial intelligence, also demonstrated, as early as 1936, that a simple computer processor (later named as Turing machine) could manipulate symbols as well as numbers.

The new field of cybernetics, a name coined by Nobert Wiener, brought together many parallels between human and machine cybernetics, the study of communication in human and machine, become an active area of research during the 1940s and 1950s. It combined concepts from information theory, feedback control system (both biological and machine), and electronic computers. In the early 1900s new development being made in formal grammars, which helped to provide new approaches to language theories in the general field of linguistics.

Of course artificial intelligence is not just the product of this century. Early researchers dating back several hundred years had laid much groundwork. Names like Aristotle, Leibnitz, Babbage, Hollerith and many others also played important roles in building a foundation that eventually led to what we now know as artificial intelligence.

The mid 1950s are generally recognized as the official birth period of artificial intelligence, when a summer workshop sponsored by IBM was held at dartmount College. Between 1956 and 1957 the logic theorist, one of the first programs for automatic theorem proving, was complete by Newell, Shaw and Simon. As part of this development, the first list- processing language called IPL (Information Processing Language) was also completed. Between 1955 and 1957, *Noam Chomsky* worked out the theory of generative grammars. Chomsky's work had a strong influence on artificial intelligence in the area of computational linguistics or natural language processing.

Important events of the late 1950s were centered on pattern recognition and self-adapting systems. During this period Rosenblatt's perceptions are types of pattern recognition devices that have a simple learning ability based linear threshold logic. This same period (1958) marked the beginning of the development of LISP by *John McCarthy*, the recognized programming languages of artificial intelligence.

Some significant events related to artificial intelligence during the 1960s include the following:

1961-65 *A. L. Samuel* developed a program that learned to play checkers at a master's level.

1965 *R. A. Robinson* introduced resolution as an inference method in logic.

1965 Work on DENDRAL was begun at Standford University by J. Ledgerberg, Edward Feigerbaum and Carl Djerassi. DENDRAL is an expert system that discovers molecular structures given only information of the constituents of the compound and mass spectra data. DENDRAL was the first knowledge based expert system to be developed.

1968 Work on MACSYMA was initiated at Massachusetts Institute of Technology (MIT) by Carl Engleman, William Martin and Joel Moses. MACSYMA is a large interactive program, which solves numerous types of mathematical problems written in LISP, MACSYMA was a continuation of earlier work on SIN, an integration-solving program.

Importance of Artificial Intelligence:

Artificial intelligence may be one of the most important developments of this century. It will affect the lives of most of the individuals in civilized countries by the end of the century. Countries leading in the development of artificia! intelligence by then will emerge as the dominant economic powers of the world.

The importance of artificial intelligence became apparent to many of the world leading countries during the late 1970s. Leaders in those countries who recognized the potential for artificial intelligence were willing to seek approval for long-term commitments for the resources needed to fund intensive research programs in artificial intelligence. The Japanese were first to demonstrate their commitment. They launched a very ambitious program in artificial intelligence research and development known as the fifth generation, this plan was officially announced in October 1981. It calls for the implementation of a ten-year plan to develop intelligent supercomputers. It is a cooperative effort between government and private companies having an interest in the manufacture of the computer products, robotics and related fields.

Following the Japanese, other leading countries of the world have announced plans for some form of artificial intelligence program. The British initiated a plan called the Alvey Project with a respectable budget. The European common market countries have jointly initiated a separate cooperative plan named the *ESPRIT program*. Other countries including Canada, the Soviet Union, Italy, Austria, Irish Republic and Singapore have made some commitments in funded research and development.

The DARPA (Development of Defence Advanced Research Project Agency) has increased its funding for research in artificial intelligence, including development support in three significant programs:

1) Development of an Autonomous Land Vehicle (ALV), a driver less military vehicle.
2) The development of a pilot's associate (an expert system which provides assistance to fighter pilots), and
3) The strategic computing program (an artificial intelligence based military super computer project).

One thing is clear that the future of the country is closely tied to the commitment it is willing to make in funding research programs in artificial intelligence.

Artificial Intelligence in related fields:

Fields which are closely related to artificial intelligence and overlap somewhat include engineering, particularly electrical and mechanical engineering, linguistics, psychology, cognitive science and philosophy. Some researchers also regard robotics as a branch of artificial intelligence, but this view is not common. Many researchers consider robotics as a separate interdisciplinary field which combines concepts and techniques from artificial intelligence, electrical, mechanical and optical engineering.

Psychologists are concerned with the working of the mind, the mental and emotional processes that drive human behaviour. During the past twenty years artificial intelligence has adopted models of thinking and learning from psychology, while psychologists in turn have patterned. Many of their question based experiments were first raised by artificial intelligence researchers. It has been claimed that artificial intelligence researchers think less like computer scientists then they do psychologists and philosophers. As a consequence, researchers from artificial intelligence and psychology have joined together at some universities to form a separate discipline known as cognitive science.

Artificial intelligence also has much in common with engineering, particularly electrical and mechanical engineering. Artificial intelligence and electrical engineering are both interested in computational processes and systems, and how they relate to the senses of perception such as vision and speech. Mechanical engineering and artificial intelligence share common interests in their desire to build intelligent robots. Their goal is to build robot that can see and move on ground, perform mechanical tasks, and understand human speech.

The field of linguistics shares an interest in the theory of grammars and languages with artificial intelligence. Both field have a desire to build a well-founded theory, and to see the development of systems that understand natural language, that can synthesize speech, and that are capable of language translation.

Finally, Artificial intelligence has some overlap with almost all fields in that it offers the potential for broad applications. Applications have already been proven in such areas as medicine, law, manufacturing, economics, banking, biology, chemistry, defence, civil engineering and aerospace to name a few.

ARTIFICIAL INTELLIGENCE:

Artificial intelligence is a branch of computer science concerned with the study and creation of computer systems that exhibit some form of intelligence. System that learn new concepts and tasks, systems that can reason and draw useful conclusions about the world around us, system that can understand a natural language or perceive and comprehend a visual sense, systems that perform other types of feats that require human types of intelligence.

In artificial intelligence the goal is to develop working computer systems that are truly capable of performing tasks that require high level of intelligence. Intelligence is the integrated sum of those feats that gives us the ability to remember a face not seen for thirty or more years, or to build and send rockets to the moon. The food for this intelligence is knowledge.

Systems here already been developed to perform many types of intelligent tasks, and expectations are high for near term development of even more impressive systems. We now have systems that can learn from examples from being told, from past-related experiences, and through reasoning. We have systems which can solve complex problems in mathematics, in scheduling many diverse tasks, in finding optimal system configurations, in planning complex strategies for military and for business, in diagnosing medical diseases and other complex systems to name a few. We have systems that can "understand" large parts of natural languages. We have systems that can see well enough to "recognize" objects from photographs, video cameras and other sensors. We have systems that can reason with incomplete and uncertain facts.

In spite of these impressive achievements, we still have not been able to produce coordinated autonomous systems, which possess some of the basic abilities of a three-year-old child. These include the ability to recognize and remember numerous diverse objects in a scene, to learn new sounds and associate them with objects and concepts, and to adapt readily too many diverse new situations. These are the challenges now facing researchers in artificial intelligence and they are not easy ones.

Component areas of Artificial Intelligence:

The component areas of artificial intelligence includes:

* Robotics
* Memory organization
* Knowledge representation
* Storage and recall
* Learning models
* Inference techniques
* Commonsense reasoning
* Dealing with uncertainty in reasoning and division making
* Understanding natural languages
* Pattern recognition m/c vision methods
* Search and matching
* Speech recognition and synthesis and variety of artificial intelligence tools.

Tools to build knowledge in Artificial Intelligence:

A family of personal consultant expert system shells was developed by Texas Instruments, Inc. in the early 1980s. These shells are rule based building tools palterned after the Mycin system architecture and developed to run on a PC as well as larger systems such as +I explorer. The largest and most versatile of these is:

Personal Consultant Plus:

It permits the use of structures called frames to organize functionally related production rules into sub problem groups. The frames are hierarchically linked into a tree structure that is traversed during a user consultation; for example, a home electrical appliance diagnostic system might have sub frames of microwave cooker, iron, blender and toaster.

Hierarchical File Structure of P.C. Plus

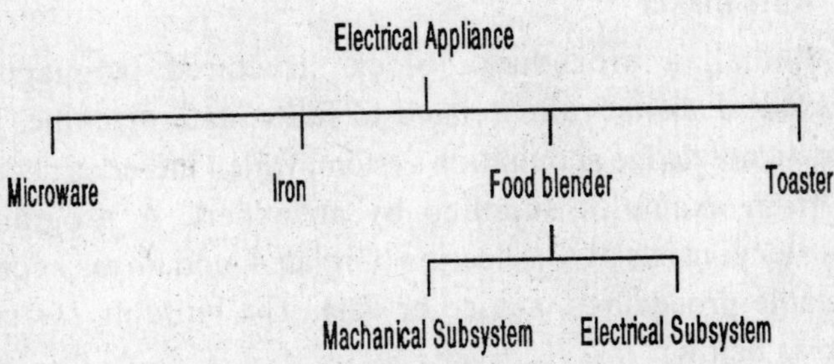

When diagnosing a problem, only the relevant frames would be matched, and the rules in each frames would address only that part of the over all problem. A feature of the frame structure is that parameter property inheritance is supported from ancestor to descendent frames.

An interactive dialog is carried out between user and system during a consultation session. The system prompts the user with English statements provided by the developers. Menu windows with selectable colors provide the user parameter value selections. A help facility is also available so the developer can provide explanations and give general assistance to the user during a consultation session.

A system editor provides a number of helpful facilities to build, store and print a knowledge base parameter and property values, textual prompts, help messages and debug traces are all provided through the editor. In addition, user defined functions written in LISP may be provided by a developer as part of rule's conditions and/or actions. The system also provides access to other sources of information, such as dBASE II and dBASE III.

Radian Rulemaster:

It was developed in early 1980s by the Radian Corporation. It was written in 'c' language to run on a variety of mini and microcomputer systems. Rulemaster is rule-based building tool, which consists of two main components

- Radial
- Rule maker

Radial, a procedural, block structured language for expressing decision rules related to finite state machine. Rule maker, a knowledge acquisition system, which includes decision trees from examples supplied by an expert. A program in rulemaster consists of a collection of related module may contain executable procedures, advice or data. The building system is shown as below:

Rulemaster's knowledge can be based on partial certainty using Fuzzy logic or heuristic methods defined by the developer. User can define their own data types or abstract types as provided in Pascal. An explanation facility is provided to explain its chain of reasoning. Programs in other languages can also be called from Rulemaster.

One of the unique features of Rulemaster is the Rulemaster component, which has the ability to induce rules from examples. Experts are known to have difficulty in directly expressing rules related to their decision processes.

Knowledge Engineering Environment (KEE):

It is one of the most powerful building tools for the development of large-scale systems developed by Intellicorp. This system employs sophisticated representation schemes structured around frames called units. The frames are made up of slots and facets, which contain object attribute, values, rules, methods, logical assertions, text or even other frames. The frames are organized into one or more knowledge bases in the form of hierarchical structures, which permits multiple inheritance down hierarchical paths, rules, procedures and object oriented representation methods are also supported. Inference is carried out through inheritance, forward chaining, backward chaining or a mixture of these methods. A form of hypothetical reasoning is also provided through different viewpoints, which may be explored concurrently.

KEE's support environment includes, a graphic-oriented debugging package, flexible end-user interface using windows, menus and an explanation capability with graphic displays, which show inference chain. A graphic based simulation package called Simkit may be provided at additional cost.

KEE has been used for the development of intelligent user interfaces, genetics, diagnosis and monitoring of complicated systems, planning, design, process control, scheduling and simulation. The system is based on LISP and developed for operations on systems such as symbolis machine, Xerox 1100s or TI explorers, systems can also be ported to open architecture machines which support common LISP without extensive modification.

OPS 5 System:

The OPS and other OPS building tools were developed at Carnegie Mellon University in conjunction with DEC during the late 1970s. This system was developed to build the RI/Xcon expert system, which configures Vax, and other DEC minicomputer systems, which are forward chaining in the interference process. The system was written in 'c' language to run on the DEC Vax and other minicomputers. It was a sophisticated method of indexing rules to reduce the matching times during the match-select-execute cycle.

EXPERT SYSTEM:

Expert systems are the recent product of artificial intelligence. It began to emerge as a university research system during the early 1970s. They have now become one of the most important innovations of artificial intelligence since they have been shown to be successful commercial products as well as interesting research tools.

Expert systems have been proven to be effective in a number of problem domains, which normally require any kind of intelligence possessed by a human expert. The areas of application are almost end less wherever human expertise is needed to solve problems; expert systems are favorable candidates for application. Application domains include law, chemistry, biology, engineering, manufacturing, aerospace, military operations, finance, banking, meteorology, geophysics and more.

An expert system is a set of programs that manipulate encoded knowledge to solve problems in a specialized domain that normally require human expertise. An expert system's knowledge is obtained from expert sources and coded in a form suitable for the system to use in its inference or reasoning processes.

Characteristics of Expert Systems:

It differs from the conventional computer system in several important ways, as

* It use knowledge rather then data to control the solution process.
* The knowledge is encoded and maintained as an entity separate from the control program.
* Expert systems are capable of explaining how a particular conclusion was reached, and why requested information is needed during a consultation. This is important as it gives the user a chance to asses and understand the system's reasoning ability, thereby improving the user's confidence in the system.
* Expert systems use the symbolic representations for knowledge (rules, networks, or frames) and perform their inference through symbolic computation that closely resembles manipulation of natural language.
* Expert systems often reason with meta-knowledge, that is they reason with knowledge about themselves, and their own knowledge and capabilities.

Background History:

It was emerged from the research laboratories of a few leading U.S. universities during the 1960s and 1970s.

- The first expert system to be completed was DENDRAL, developed at Standford University in the late 1960s. This system was capable of determining the structure of the chemical compounds given a specification of the compounds constituent elements and mass spectrometry data obtained from samples of the compound DENDRAL used heuristic knowledge obtained from experienced chemists to help constrain the problem and thereby reduce the search space.
- Shortly after DENDRAL was completed, the development of MYCIN began at the Standford University. MYCIN is an expert system, which diagnoses infectious blood diseases and determines a recommended list of therapies for the patient. The initial MYCIN knowledge base contained about only 200 rules. This number was gradually increased to more than 600 rules by the early 1980s.
- PROSPECTOR, an expert system that assists geologists in the discovery of mineral deposits.
- RI, an expert system, used by the Digital Equipment Corporation to select and configure components of complex computer systems.

Applications:

Application can now be found in almost all areas of business and government. They include such as

- Different types of medical diagnosis.
- Diagnosis of complex electronic and electromechanical system.
- Diagnosis of diesel electric locomotive systems.
- Diagnosis of software development projects.

- Planning experiments in biology, chemistry and molecular genetics.
- Forecasting crop damage.
- Identification of chemical compound structures and chemical compounds.
- Location of faults in computer and communication system.
- Scheduling of customer orders, job shop production and various manufacturing tasks.
- Evaluation of loan applicants for lending institutions.
- Planning curricula for students
- Teaching students specialized tasks (like trouble shooting equipment faults)

Importance of Expert System:

The value of expert systems was well established by the early 1980s. a number of successful applications had been completed by then and they proved to be cost effective.

Rule based system architecture:

The most common form of architecture used in expert and other types of knowledge based systems is the production system, also called the rule based system. This type of system uses knowledge encoded in the form of production rules, that is, if-then rules. Rules have an antecedent or condition part, the left hand side, and a conclusion or action part, the right hand side.

If : Condition I and Condition II and Condition III.

Then : Taken Action IV.

If : The temperature is greater than 200°C and the water level is low.

Then : Open the safety valve.

Each rule represents a small chunk of knowledge relating to the given domain of expertise. A number of related rules collectively may correspond to a chain of inferences which lead from some initially known facts to some useful conclusions.

When the known facts support the conditions in the rules left side, the conclusion or action part of the rules is then accepted as known.

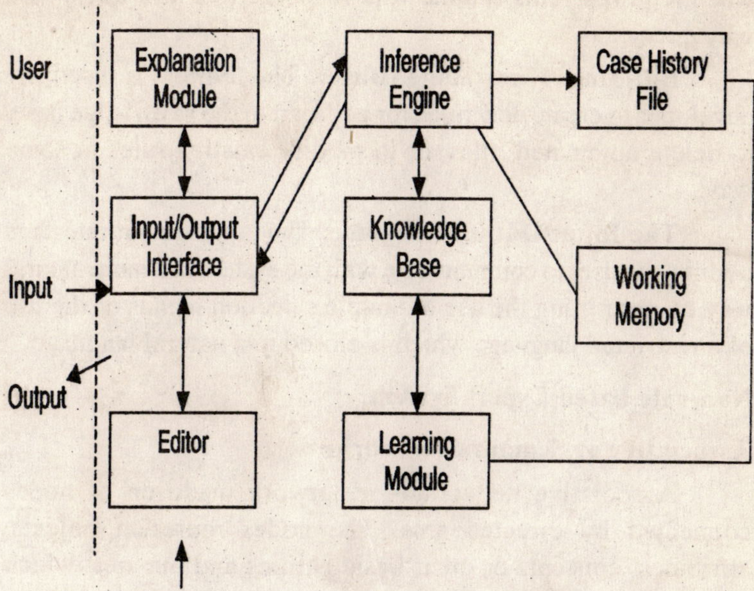

Components of a typical Expert System

Knowledge Base : The knowledge base contains facts and rules about some specialized knowledge domain.

Inference Process: The inference engine accepts user input queries and responses to questions through the I/O interface and uses this dynamic information together with the static knowledge.

The inferring process is carried out recursively in three stages:

1. Match
2. Select and
3. Execute.

During the match stage, the contents of working memory are composed to facts and rules contained in the knowledge base.

Explanation how and why : The explanation module provides the user with an explanation of the reasoning process, when required. This is done with response to a how query or a why query.

Building Knowledge Base: The editor is used by developer to create new rules for addition to the knowledge base, to delete automated rules, or to modify existing rules in some way.

The Input/Output Interface: The input-output interface permits the user to communicate with the system in a more natural way by permitting the use of simple selection menus or the use of a restricted language which is closed to a natural language.

Non-rule based Expert System:

Associative or Semantic Network:

Associative network is a network made up of nodes connected by directed arcs. The nodes represent objects, attributes, concepts or other basic entities and the arcs, which are labeled, describe the relationship between the two nodes they connect.

It is especially useful in depicting hierarchical knowledge structure, where property inheritance is common. It is not popular form of representation for standard expert systems.

One expert system is based on the use of an associative network representation is CASNET (Casual Associational Network), which was developed at Rutgers University during the early 1970s, it is used to diagnose and recommend treatment for Glaucoma, the leading cause for blindness.

While discussing about the CASNET, it is divided into three planes or types of knowledge. These different knowledge types are:

* Patient Observations (Tests, Symptoms, other signs)
* Pathophysiological States
* Disease Categories

Patient observations are provided by the user during an interactive session with the system. The system permits menu type queries, and the user selects one of the several possible choices. These observations help to establish an abnormal condition caused by a disease process. The condition is established through the casual network model as part of the cause and effect relationship relating symptoms and other signs to disease.

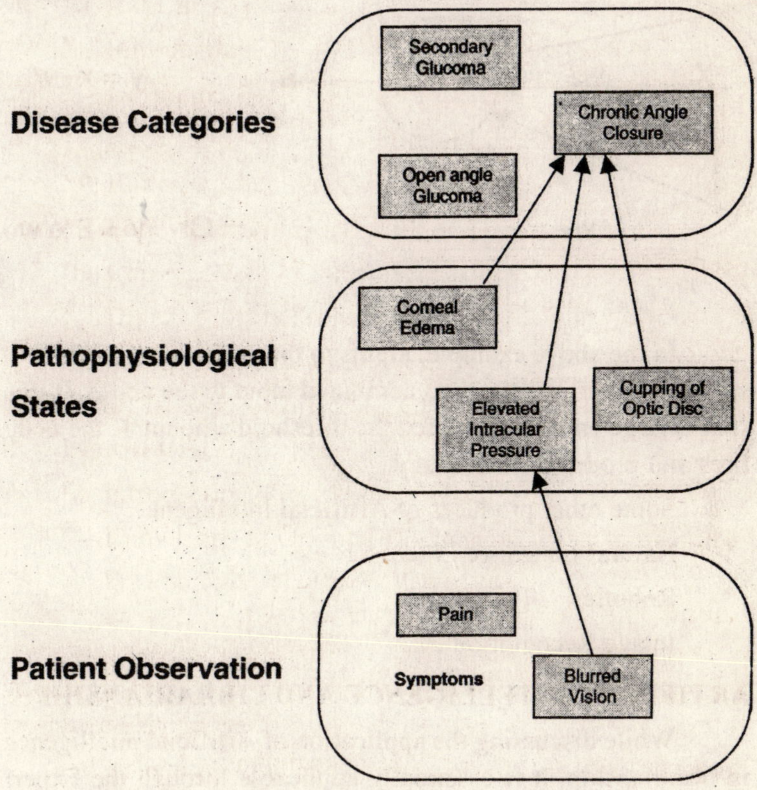

Neural Network Architecture: Neural networks were originally inspired as being model of the human nervous system. The knowledge in the neural network is distributed throughout the network in the form of inter node connections and weighted links which form the inputs to the nodes. The link weights serve to enhance or inhibit the input stimuli values which are then added together at the nodes. If the sum of all inputs to a node exceeds some threshold value T, the node executes and produces an output which is passed on to other nodes or is used to produce some output response. In the simplest case no output is produced if the total input is less then T.

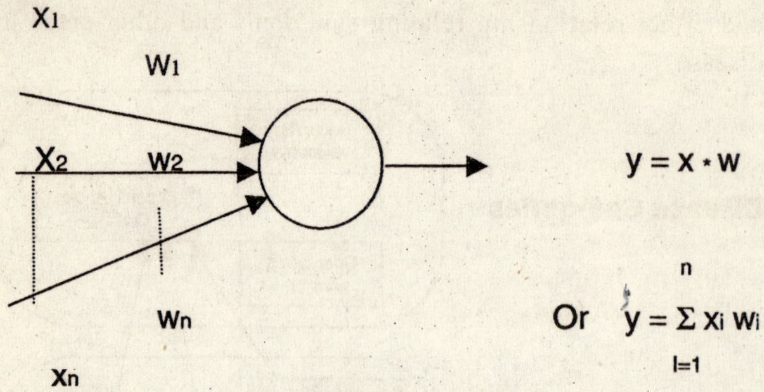

In the above example, inputs to the nodes are x1, x2,—— xn and weights are the total combined input to the nodes. If this sum is large enough to exceed the threshold amount T, the node fires and produces an output y.

Some other produces of Artificial Intelligence:

* Natural Language Processor
* Robotics
* Image Recognition etc.

ARTIFICIAL INTELLIGENCE AND LIBRARIANSHIP:

While discussing the application of Artificial intelligence in librarianship, it is essentially applicable through the Expert System, application tool of artificial intelligence. Expert Systems are a branch of artificial intelligence devoted to developing computer systems designed to perform a limited range of tasks. For some time many researchers have been considering possible uses for expert systems in the library and information science fields. Accordingly, much research and development work is now proceeding toward the production of devices that will allow computers to undertake many of the intellectual tasks now performed by librarians. This is proving to be an interesting challenge for librarianship.

There are many competing definitions of expert system. Typically the term denotes some variety of machine intelligence or a knowledge-based system. One general definition by Lancaster is, a system that performs some of the tasks of a human expert in some areas. According to Fenly, these are computer programs have been developed which exhibit human-like reasoning, which may be able to learn from their mistakes, and which quickly and cleverly perform tasks normally done by scarce and expensive human experts.

According to Yang another definition of an expert system is a computerized advisory program that attempts to imitate or substitute the reasoning processes and knowledge of experts in solving specific types of problems. Similarly, an ES works on real-world problems and should be able to reach the same conclusions as a human expert under the same circumstances. The primary objective of an expert system is the dissemination of expertise by transferring expertise from experts to a computer system and then to non-experts.

The best-known use of expert systems in librarianship is in reference work and information retrieval. The systems can be used as guides to provide overviews of library services and resources. However, they can also be used for recommending databases.

Accordingly, expert systems can be used to provide advice and guidance to library users in many of the knowledge-rich domains of librarianship. For example, much information must be interpreted, modified, translated, transformed or reformulated or otherwise processed in some fashion before it is presented to the user. Librarians often do this work. Expert systems can help reference librarians when the retrieval of information requires complex skills or expertise. For example, expert or knowledge-based systems can be developed to recommend information sources to library patrons.

EELIAS at Mônash University in Australia is an example of a library expert system that provides instruction in finding information in one discipline. It is an instructional expert system that guides users to information sources in electrical and computer systems engineering. It outlines the basic library information-seeking process and guides the user to appropriate book sources, journals, and other forms of literature. It also provides users references, subject areas, call numbers and descriptions. This form of expert system helps the user to both understand and locate materials in the library. It functions as a Pathfinder, teaching aid and a reference tool.

Expert system assistance for electronic database selection is another interesting application for library reference and information retrieval. It is often increasingly difficult for librarians to fully utilize their electronic collections due to the rapid growth of electronic databases. This abundance of electronic resources can be confusing, challenging and problematic. It can also lead to information overload.

Although most of the expert systems developed for library work have been for reference services, there have been some systems developed for technical services. Expert systems in technical services offer some notable advantages. Expert systems can assist technical service librarians just as they assist reference librarians. A system can eliminate such common human problems as fatigue, boredom, and forgetfulness, and it can free human time for more complex tasks. An expert system can also spread expertise across space and time. Cataloging is a likely area for expert system implementation because machine automation can aid in making newly acquired materials available to patrons quicker. The three basic activities of cataloging that an expert system would need to master are: describing the item and choosing access points for names and titles, assigning classification numbers, and assigning subject headings. An example of an expert system used for cataloging is the OCLC *Automated Title Page Project*. This system was developed to produce bibliographic descriptions in accordance with AACR2. Expert systems can also be used for acquisitions and serials control. The *Monograph Acquisitions Consultant* is an example of an expert system used for acquisitions. It is designed to guide the monograph selection process. Elements of the process the system address include selecting vendors or suppliers, determining what types of orders to send to particular vendors, and determining what special policies or procedures apply. Penn State University also has an expert system for acquisitions. It determines if a title requested for order would otherwise be received on an approval plan. Most of the work in expert systems in acquisitions and serials control has focused on monographic vendor selection and approval plan receipts. Expert systems have also been developed for collection management and development. There have been systems developed for this purpose. An example is the *Journal Expert Selector (JES)* at the National Library of Medicine. It attempts to capture the expertise of human journal selectors. The major criteria for the JES include the composition of the journal, producers of the journal, information in articles, and the authors of articles.

At last we can say that the Artificial Intelligence has revolutionized all of the fields by utilizing the computer skills. It has not left librarianship untouched. Its major application, Expert System has switched over the scene in libraries from huge staff based to computer based intelligent services. These Expert Systems have their unique applications in all tasks of librarianship. Nevertheless, expert systems do have some limitations. First of all, they are only as good as the designers and developers make them. If the data entered is poor or the knowledge base is insufficient for the task, an expert system will not be of much use. Also, expert systems do not offer a human touch. They cannot do many things librarians can, such as focus on the patron, interpret, read body language and give encouragement. But these are the best-known products in librarianship for providing more efficient, quick and qualitative user based services.

8
DATA MINING

Introduction:

The past two decades has seen a dramatic increase in the amount of information or data being stored in electronic format. This accumulation of data has taken place at an explosive rate. It has been estimated that the amount of information in the world doubles every 20 months and the size and number of databases are increasing even faster. Data storage became easier as the availability of large amounts of computing power at low cost. There was also the introduction of new machine learning methods for knowledge representation based on logic programming etc. in addition to traditional statistical analysis of data. The new methods tend to be computationally intensive hence a demand for more processing power.

While accumulating a big amount of data, the information scientists faced the problem as what to do with this valuable resource? It is cleary recognised that information is at the heart of operations may be it is a library and that decision-makers could make use of the data stored to gain valuable insight into their crucil activities. Database Management systems gave access to the data stored but this was only a small part of what could be gained from the data. Traditional on-line transaction processing systems, OLTPs, are good at putting data into databases quickly, safely and efficiently but are not good at delivering meaningful analysis and result. Analysing data can provide further knowledge about any operation and this knowledge generated information may become an asset for any scholar.

Definitions:

The term data mining has been stretched beyond its limits to apply to any form of data analysis. Some of the definitions of Data Mining are:

According to *William J Frawley*, *Gregory Piatetsky-Shapiro* and *Christopher J Math* "Data Mining, or Knowledge Discovery in Databases (KDD) as it is also known, is the nontrivial extraction of implicit, previously unknown, and potentially useful information from data. This encompasses a number of different technical approaches, such as clustering, data summarization, learning classification rules, finding dependency net works, analysing changes, and detecting anomalies."

According to *Marcel Holshemier* and *Arno Siebes* "Data mining is the search for relationships and global patterns that exist in large databases but are 'hidden' among the vast amount of data, such as a relationship between patient data and their medical diagnosis. These relationships represent valuable knowledge about the database and the objects in the database and, if the database is a faithful mirror, of the real world registered by the database."

Clementine User Guide, a data mining toolkit refers it as "using a variety of techniques to identify nuggets of information or decision-making knowledge in bodies of data, and extracting these in such a way that they can be put to use in the areas such as decision support, prediction, forecasting and estimation. The data is often voluminous, but as it stands of low value as no direct use can be made of it; it is the hidden information in the data that is useful"

By analysing all these definitions we can say that data mining is concerned with the analysis of data and the use of software techniques for finding patterns and regularities in sets of data. It is the computer which is responsible for finding the patterns by identifying the underlying rules and features in the data. Data mining analysis tends to work from the data up and the best techniques are those developed with an orientation towards large volumes of data, making use of as much of the collected data as possible to arrive at reliable conclusions and decisions. The analysis process starts with a set of data, uses a methodology to develop an optimal representation of the structure of the data during which time knowledge is acquired. Once knowledge has been acquired this can be extended to larger sets of data working on the assumption that the larger data set has a structure similar to the sample data. Again this is analogous to a mining operation where large amounts of low grade materials are sifted through in order to find something of value.

The data mining process starts with the raw data and finishs with the extracted knowledge which was acquired as a result of the following stages:

* **Selection** - selecting or segmenting the data according to some criteria e.g. all those people who are having telephone connection, in this way subsets of the data can be determined.
* **Preprocessing** - this is the data cleansing stage where certain information is removed which is deemed unnecessary and may slow down queries for example unnecessary to note the sex of a patient when studying pregnancy. Also the data is reconfigured to ensure a consistent format as there is a possibility of inconsistent formats because the data is drawn from several sources e.g. sex may recorded as f or m and also as 1 or 0.
* **Transformation** - the data is not merely transferred across but transformed in that overlays may added such as the demographic overlays commonly used in market research. The data is made useable and navigable.
* **Data mining** - this stage is concerned with the extraction of patterns from the data. A pattern can be defined as given a set of facts(data) F, a language L, and some measure of certainty C a pattern is a statement S in L that describes

relationships among a subset *Fs* of *F* with a certainty *c* such that *S* is simpler in some sense than the enumeration of all the facts in *Fs*.

* **Interpretation and evaluation** - the patterns identified by the system are interpreted into knowledge which can then be used to support human decision-making e.g. prediction and classification tasks, summarizing the contents of a database or explaining observed phenomena.

Data mining background:

Data mining research has drawn on a number of other fields such as inductive learning, machine learning and statistics etc.

Inductive learning:

Induction is the inference of information from data and inductive learning is the model building process where the environment i.e. database is analysed with a view to finding patterns. Similar objects are grouped in classes and rules formulated whereby it is possible to predict the class of unseen objects. This process of classification identifies classes such that each class has a unique pattern of values which forms the class description. The nature of the environment is dynamic hence the model must be adaptive i.e. should be able learn.

Generally it is only possible to use a small number of properties to characterise objects so we make abstractions in that objects which satisfy the same subset of properties are mapped to the same internal representation. Inductive learning where the system infers knowledge itself from observing its environment has two main strategies:

* **supervised learning** - this is learning from examples where a teacher helps the system construct a model by defining classes and supplying examples of each class. The system has to find a description of each class i.e. the common properties in the examples. Once the description has been formulated the description and the class form a classification rule which can be used to predict the class

of previously unseen objects. This is similar to discriminate analysis as in statistics.

* **unsupervised learning** - this is learning from observation and discovery. The data mine system is supplied with objects but no classes are defined so it has to observe the examples and recognise patterns (i.e. class description) by itself. This system results in a set of class descriptions, one for each class discovered in the environment. Again this similar to cluster analysis as in statistics.

Induction is therefore the extraction of patterns. The quality of the model produced by inductive learning methods is such that the model could be used to predict the outcome of future situations in other words not only for states encountered but rather for unseen states that could occur. The problem is that most environments have different states, i.e. changes within, and it is not always possible to verify a model by checking it for all possible situations.

Given a set of examples the system can construct multiple models some of which will be simpler than others. The simpler models are more likely to be correct if we adhere to Ockhams razor, which states that if there are multiple explanations for a particular phenomena it makes sense to choose the simplest because it is more likely to capture the nature of the phenomenon.

Statistics:

Statistics has a solid theoretical foundation but the results from statistics can be overwhelming and difficult to interpret as they require user guidance as to where and how to analyse the data. Data mining however allows the expert's knowledge of the data and the advanced analysis techniques of the computer to work together.

Statistical analysis systems such as SAS and SPSS have been used by analysts to detect unusual patterns and explain patterns using statistical models such as linear models. Statistics have a role to play and data mining will not replace such analyses but rather they can act upon more directed analyses based on the results of data mining. For example statistical induction is something like the average rate of library use/visit.

Machine Learning:

Machine learning is the automation of a learning process and learning is tantamount to the construction of rules based on observations of environmental states and transitions. This is a broad field which includes not only learning from examples, but also reinforcement learning, learning with teacher, etc. A learning algorithm takes the data set and its accompanying information as input and returns a statement e.g. a concept representing the results of learning as output. Machine learning examines previous examples and their outcomes and learns how to reproduce these and make generalisations about new cases.

Generally a machine learning system does not use single observations of its environment but an entire finite set called the training set at once. This set contains examples i.e. observations coded in some machine readable form.

Differences between Data Mining and Machine Learning:

Knowledge Discovery in Databases (KDD) or Data Mining, and the part of Machine Learning (ML) dealing with learning from examples overlap in the algorithms used and the problems addressed.

The main differences are:

* KDD is concerned with finding understandable knowledge, while ML is concerned with improving performance of an agent. So training a neural network to balance a pole is part of ML, but not of KDD. However, there are efforts to extract knowledge from neural networks which are very relevant for KDD.
* KDD is concerned with very large, real-world databases, while ML typically (but not always) looks at smaller data sets. So efficiency questions are much more important for KDD.

* ML is a broader field which includes not only learning from examples, but also reinforcement learning, learning with teacher, etc.

KDD is that part of ML which is concerned with finding understandable knowledge in large sets of real-world examples. When integrating machine learning techniques into database systems to implement KDD some of the databases require:

* more efficient learning algorithms because realistic databases are normally very large and noisy. It is usual that the database is often designed for purposes different from data mining and so properties or attributes that would simplify the learning task are not present nor can they be requested from the real world. Databases are usually contaminated by errors so the data mining algorithm has to cope with noise whereas ML has laboratory type examples i.e. as near perfect as possible.
* more expressive representations for both data, e.g. tuples in relational databases, which represent instances of a problem domain, and knowledge, e.g. rules in a rule-based system, which can be used to solve users' problems in the domain, and the semantic information contained in the relational schemata.

Practical KDD systems are expected to include three interconnected phases

* Translation of standard database information into a form suitable for use by learning facilities;
* Using machine learning techniques to produce knowledge bases from databases; and
* Interpreting the knowledge produced to solve users' problems and/or reduce data spaces. Data spaces being the number of examples.

DATA MINING MODELS:

IBM have identified two types of model or modes of

operation which may be used to unearth information of interest to the user.

Verification Model:

The verification model takes an hypothesis from the user and tests the validity of it against the data. The emphasis is with the user who is responsible for formulating the hypothesis and issuing the query on the data to affirm or negate the hypothesis.

The problem with this model is the fact that no new information is created in the retrieval process but rather the queries will always return records to verify or negate the hypothesis. The search process here is iterative in that the output is reviewed, a new set of questions or hypothesis formulated to refine the search and the whole process repeated. The user is discovering the facts about the data using a variety of techniques such as queries, multidimensional analysis and visualization to guide the exploration of the data being inspected.

Discovery Model:

The discovery model differs in its emphasis in that it is the system automatically discovering important information hidden in the data. The data is sifted in search of frequently occurring patterns, trends and generalisations about the data without intervention or guidance from the user. The discovery or data mining tools aim to reveal a large number of facts about the data in as short a time as possible.

An example of such a model is a bank database which is mined to discover the many groups of customers to target for a mailing campaign. The data is searched with no hypothesis in mind other than for the system to group the customers according to the common characteristics found.

DATA MINING PROBLEMS/ISSUES:

Data mining systems rely on databases to supply the raw data for input and this raises problems in that databases tend be dynamic, incomplete, noisy, and large. Other problems arise as a result of the adequacy and relevance of the information stored.

Limited Information:

A database is often designed for purposes different from data mining and sometimes the properties or attributes that would simplify the learning task are not present nor can they be requested from the real world. Inconclusive data causes problems because if some attributes essential to knowledge about the application domain are not present in the data it may be impossible to discover significant knowledge about a given domain. For example cannot diagnose malaria from a patient database if that database does not contain the patients red blood cell count.

Noise and missing values:

Databases are usually contaminated by errors so it cannot be assumed that the data they contain is entirely correct. Attributes which rely on subjective or measurement judgements can give rise to errors such that some examples may even be mis-classified. Error in either the values of attributes or class information are known as noise. Obviously where possible it is desirable to eliminate noise from the classification information as this affects the overall accuracy of the generated rules.

Missing data can be treated by discovery systems in a number of ways such as;

* simply disregard missing values
* omit the corresponding records
* infer missing values from known values
* treat missing data as a special value to be included additionally in the attribute domain
* or average over the missing values using Bayesian techniques.

Noisy data in the sense of being imprecise is characteristic of all data collection and typically fit a regular statistical distribution such as Gaussian while wrong values are data entry errors. Statistical methods can treat problems of noisy data, and separate different types of noise.

Uncertainty:

Uncertainty refers to the severity of the error and the degree of noise in the data. Data precision is an important consideration in a discovery system.

Size, updates, and irrelevant fields:

Databases tend to be large and dynamic in that their contents are ever-changing as information is added, modified or removed. The problem with this from the data mining perspective is how to ensure that the rules are up-to-date and consistent with the most current information. Also the learning system has to be time-sensitive as some data values vary over time and the discovery system is affected by the 'timeliness' of the data.

Another issue is the relevance or irrelevance of the fields in the database to the current focus of discovery for example post codes are fundamental to any studies trying to establish a geographical connection to an item of interest such as the sales of a product.

POTENTIAL APPLICATIONS:

Data mining has many and varied fields of application some of which are listed below.

Marketing:

* Identify buying patterns from customers
* Find associations among customer demographic characteristics
* Predict response to mailing campaigns
* Market basket analysis

Banking:

* Detect patterns of fraudulent credit card use
* Identify 'loyal' customers
* Predict customers likely to change their credit card affiliation
* Determine credit card spending by customer groups

* Find hidden correlations between different financial indicators
* Identify stock trading rules from historical market data

Insurance and Health Care:

* Claims analysis - i.e which medical procedures are claimed together
* Predict which customers will buy new policies
* Identify behaviour patterns of risky customers
* Identify fraudulent behaviour

Transportation:

* Determine the distribution schedules among outlets
* Analyse loading patterns

Medicine:

* Characterise patient behaviour to predict office visits
* Identify successful medical therapies for different illnesses

DATA MINING TECHNIQUES:

Cluster Analysis:

In an unsupervised learning environment the system has to discover its own classes and one way in which it does this is to cluster the data in the database as shown in the following diagram. The first step is to discover subsets of related objects and then find descriptions e.eg D1, D2, D3 etc. which describe each of these subsets.

Clustering and segmentation basically partition the database so that each partition or group is similar according to some criteria or metric. Clustering according to similarity is a concept which appears in many disciplines. If a measure of similarity is available there are a number of techniques for forming clusters. Membership of groups can be based on the level of similarity between members and from this the rules of membership can be defined. Another approach is to build set functions that measure some property of partitions ie groups or subsets as functions of some parameter of the partition. This latter approach achieves what is known as optimal partitioning.

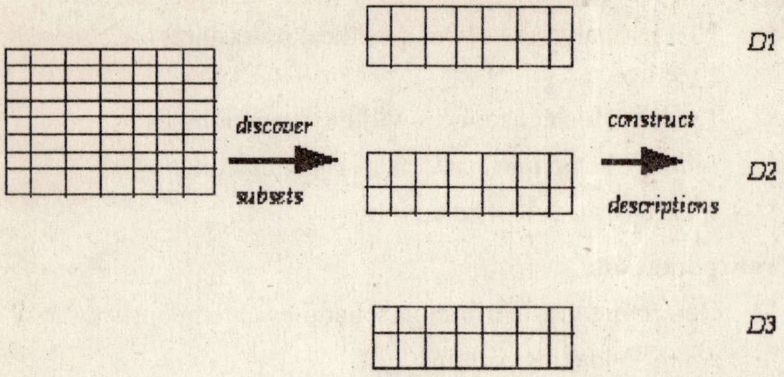

Figure: Discovering clusters and descriptions in a database

Many data mining applications make use of clustering according to similarity for example to segment a client/customer base. Clustering according to optimization of set functions is used in data analysis e.g. when setting insurance tariffs the customers can be segmented according to a number of parameters and the optimal tariff segmentation achieved.

Clustering/segmentation in databases are the processes of separating a data set into components that reflect a consistent pattern of behaviour. Once the patterns have been established they can then be used to "deconstruct" data into more understandable subsets and also they provide sub-groups of a population for further analysis or action which is important when dealing with very large databases. For example a database could be used for profile generation for target marketing where previous response to mailing campaigns can be used to generate a profile of people who responded and this can be used to predict response and filter mailing lists to achieve the best response.

imprecise data and can be used to extract patterns and detect trends that are too complex to be noticed by either humans or other computer techniques. A trained neural network can be thought of as an "expert" in the category of information it has been given to analyse. This expert can then be used to provide projections given new situations of interest and answer "what if" questions.

Neural networks have broad applicability to real world business problems and have already been successfully applied in many industries. Since neural networks are best at identifying patterns or trends in data, they are well suited for prediction or forecasting needs including:

* sales forecasting
* industrial process control
* customer research
* data validation
* risk management
* target marketing etc.

Neural networks use a set of processing elements (or nodes) analogous to neurons in the brain. These processing elements are interconnected in a network that can then identify patterns in data once it is exposed to the data, i.e the network learns from experience just as people do. This distinguishes neural networks from traditional computing programs, that simply follow instructions in a fixed sequential order.

The structure of a neural network looks something like the following:

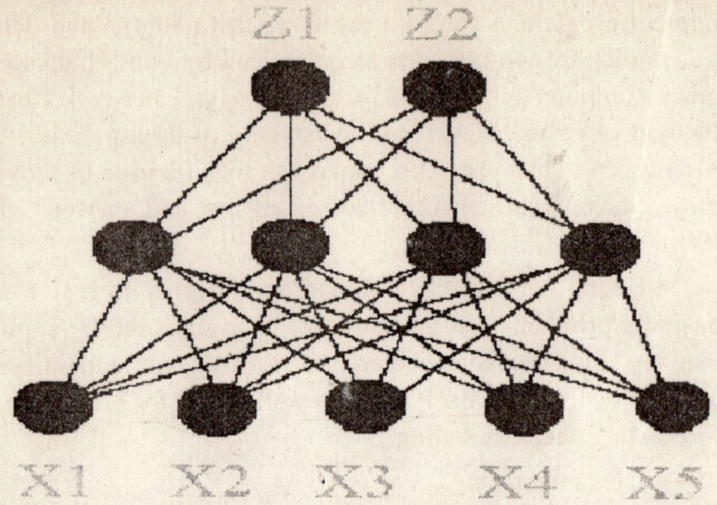

Figure: Structure of a neural network

The bottom layer represents the input layer, in this case with 5 inputs labels X1 through X5. In the middle is something called the hidden layer, with a variable number of nodes. It is the hidden layer that performs much of the work of the network. The output layer in this case has two nodes, Z1 and Z2 representing output values we are trying to determine from the inputs. For example, predict sales (output) based on past sales, price and season (input).

Each node in the hidden layer is fully connected to the inputs which means that what is learned in a hidden node is based on all the inputs taken together. Statisticians maintain that the network can pick up the interdependencies in the model. The following diagram provides some detail into what goes on inside a hidden node.

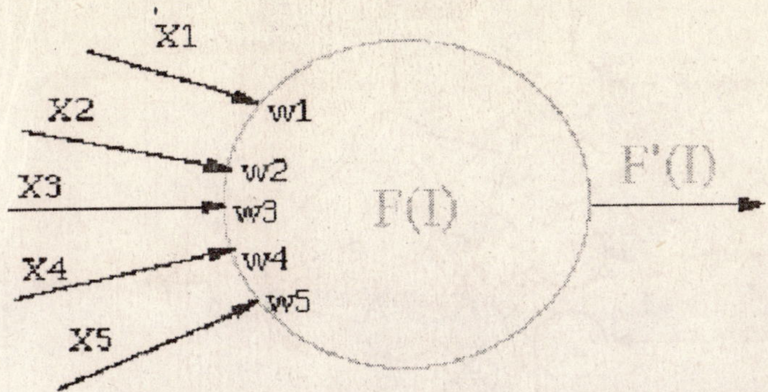

F(I)=X1*w1+X2*w2+X3*w3+X4*w4+X5*w5
F'(I)=some non-linear transformation of F(I)

Figure: Inside a Node

Simply speaking a weighted sum is performed: X1 times W1 plus X2 times W2 on through X5 and W5. This weighted sum is performed for each hidden node and each output node and is how interactions are represented in the network.

The issue of where the network get the weights from is important but suffice to say that the network learns to reduce error in it's prediction of events already known (ie, past history).

The problems of using neural networks have been summed by Arun Swami of Silicon Graphics Computer Systems. Neural networks have been used successfully for classification but suffer somewhat in that the resulting network is viewed as a black box and no explanation of the results is given. This lack of explanation inhibits confidence, acceptance and application of results. He also notes as a problem the fact that neural networks suffered from long learning times which become worse as the volume of data grows.

The Clementine User Guide has the following simple diagram to summarise a neural net trained to identify the risk of cancer from a number of factors.

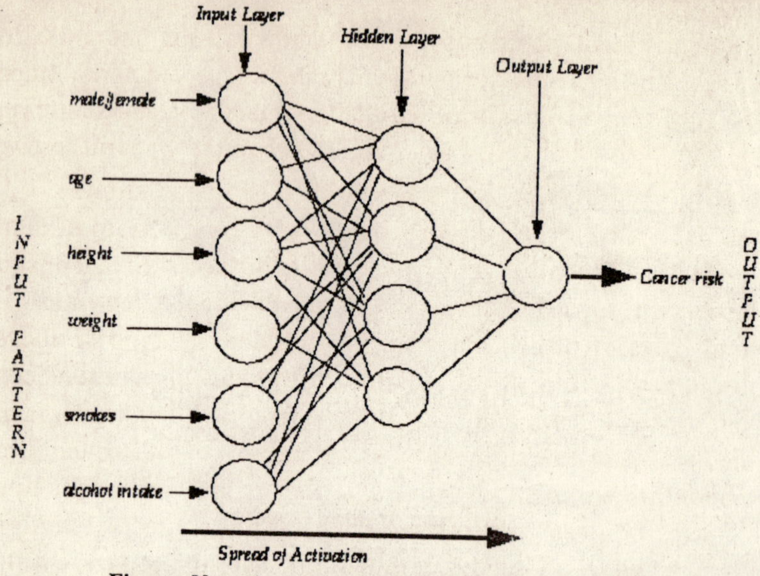

Figure: Neural network from Clementine User Guide

ON-LINE ANALYTICAL PROCESSING:

A major issue in information processing is how to process larger and larger databases, containing increasingly complex data, without sacrificing response time. The client/server architecture gives organizations the opportunity to deploy specialized servers which are optimized for handling specific data management problems. Until recently, organizations have tried to target relational database management systems (RDBMSs) for the complete spectrum of database applications. It is however apparent that there are major categories of database applications which are not suitably serviced by relational database systems. Oracle, for example, has built a totally new Media Server for handling multimedia applications. Sybase uses an *object-oriented DBMS (OODBMS)* in its Gain Momentum product which is designed to handle complex data such as images and audio. Another category of applications is that of on-line analytical processing (OLAP). OLAP was a term coined by *E F Codd* in 1993 and was defined by him as "the dynamic synthesis, analysis and consolidation of large volumes of multidimensional data."

Codd has developed several rules or requirements for an OLAP system, as

* multidimensional conceptual view
* transparency
* accessibility
* consistent reporting performance
* client/server architecture
* generic dimensionality
* dynamic sparse matrix handling
* multi-user support
* unrestricted cross dimensional operations
* intuitative data manipulation
* flexible reporting
* unlimited dimensions and aggregation levels

Comparison of OLAP and OLTP:

OLAP applications are quite different from *On-line Transaction Processing (OLTP)* applications which consist of a large number of relatively simple transactions. The transactions usually retrieve and update a small number of records that are contained in several distinct tables. The relationships between the tables are generally simple.

A typical customer order entry OLTP transaction might retrieve all of the data relating to a specific customer and then insert a new order for the customer. Information is selected from the customer, customer order, and detail line tables. Each row in each table contains a customer identification number which is used to relate the rows from the different tables. The relationships between the records are simple and only a few records are actually retrieved or updated by a single transaction.

The difference between OLAP and OLTP has been summarised as, OLTP servers handle mission-critical production data accessed through simple queries; while OLAP servers handle management-critical data accessed through an iterative analytical investigation. Both OLAP and OLTP, have specialized requirements and therefore require special optimized servers for the two types of processing. OLAP database servers use multidimensional structures to store data and relationships between data. Multidimensional structures can be best visualized as cubes of data, and cubes within cubes of data. Each side of the cube is considered a dimension.

In conclusion OLAP servers logically organize data in multiple dimensions which allows users to quickly and easily analyse complex data relationships. The database itself is physically organized in such a way that related data can be rapidly retrieved across multiple dimensions. OLAP servers are very efficient when storing and processing multidimensional data. RDBMSs have been developed and optimized to handle OLTP applications. Relational database designs concentrate on reliability and transaction processing speed, instead of decision support need. The different types of server can therefore benefit a broad range of data management applications.

9
DATA WAREHOUSING

Introduction:

Data mining potential can be enhanced if the appropriate data has been collected and stored in a data warehouse. A data warehouse is a relational database management system (RDMS) designed specifically to meet the needs of transaction processing systems. It can be loosely defined as any centralised data repository which can be queried for business benefit but this will be more clearly defined later. Data warehousing is a new powerful technique making it possible to extract archived operational data and overcome inconsistencies between different legacy data formats. As well as integrating data throughout, regardless of location, format, or communication requirements it is possible to incorporate additional or expert information. So, data warehouse provides data that is already transformed and summarized, therefore making it an appropriate environment for more efficient DSS and EIS applications.

Characteristics of a Data Warehouse:

According to Bill Inmon, the originator of the data warehousing concept, there are generally four characteristics that describe a data warehouse:

* **subject-oriented:** data are organized according to subject instead of application e.g. an insurance company using a data warehouse would organize their data by customer, premium, and claim, instead of by different products (auto, life, etc.). The data organized by subject contain only the information necessary for decision support processing.
* **integrated:** When data resides in many separate

applications in the operational environment, encoding of data is often inconsistent. For instance, in one application, gender might be coded as "m" and "f" in another by 0 and 1. When data are moved from the operational environment into the data warehouse, they assume a consistent coding convention e.g. gender data is transformed to "m" and "f".

* **time-variant:** The data warehouse contains a place for storing data that are five to 10 years old, or older, to be used for comparisons, trends, and forecasting. These data are not updated.

* **non-volatile:** Data are not updated or changed in any way once they enter the data warehouse, but are only loaded and accessed.

Processes in Data Warehousing:

The first phase in data warehousing is to "insulate" your current operational information, ie to preserve the security and integrity of mission-critical OLTP applications, while giving you access to the broadest possible base of data. The resulting database or data warehouse may consume hundreds of gigabytes - or even terabytes - of disk space, what is required then are efficient techniques for storing and retrieving massive amounts of information. Increasingly, large organizations have found that only parallel processing systems offer sufficient bandwidth.

The data warehouse thus retrieves data from a variety of heterogeneous operational databases. The data is then transformed and delivered to the data warehouse/store based on a selected model. The data transformation and movement processes are executed whenever an update to the warehouse data is required so there should some form of automation to manage and execute these functions. The information that describes the model and definition of the source data elements is called "metadata". The metadata is the means by which the end-user finds and understands the data in the warehouse and is an important part of the warehouse. The metadata should at the very least contain;

* the structure of the data;
* the algorithm used for summarization; and
* the mapping from the operational environment to the data warehouse.

Data cleansing is an important aspect of creating an efficient data warehouse in that it is the removal of certain aspects of operational data, such as low-level transaction information, which slow down the query times. The cleansing stage has to be as dynamic as possible to accommodate all types of queries even those which may require low-level information. Data should be extracted from production sources at regular intervals and pooled centrally but the cleansing process has to remove duplication and reconcile differences between various styles of data collection.

Once the data has been cleaned it is then transferred to the data warehouse which typically is a large database on a high performance box either SMP, Symmetric Multi-Processing or MPP, Massively Parallel Processing. Number-crunching power is another important aspect of data warehousing because of the complexity involved in processing ad hoc queries and because of the vast quantities of data that the organisation want to use in the warehouse. A data warehouse can be used in different ways for example it can be used as a central store against which the queries are run or it can be used to like a data mart. Data marts which are small warehouses can be established to provide subsets of the main store and summarised information depending on the requirements of a specific group/department. The central store approach generally uses very simple data structures with very little assumptions about the relationships between data whereas marts often use multidimensional databases which can speed up query processing as they can have data structures which are reflect the most likely questions.

Many vendors have products that provide one or more of the above described data warehouse functions. However, it can take a significant amount of work and specialized programming to provide the interoperability needed between products from multiple vendors to enable them to perform the required data warehouse processes. A typical implementation usually involves a mixture of products from a variety of suppliers.

Another approach to data warehousing is Parsaye's Sandwich Paradigm put forward by Dr. Kamran Parsaye, CEO of Information Discovery, Hermosa Beach, CA. This paradigm or philosophy encourages acceptance of the probability that the first iteration of a data-warehousing effort will require considerable revision. The Sandwich Paradigm advocates the following approach:

* pre-mine the data to determine what formats and data are needed to support a data-mining application;
* build a prototype mini-data warehouse i.e the meat of the sandwich, with most of the features envisaged for the end product;
* revise the strategies as necessary;
* build the final warehouse.

Data warehousing and OLTP systems:

A database which is built for on line transaction processing, OLTP, is generally regarded as unsuitable for data warehousing as they have been designed with a different set of needs in mind ie maximising transaction capacity and typically having hundreds of tables in order not to lock out users etc. Data warehouses are interested in query processing as opposed to transaction processing.

OLTP systems cannot be repositories of facts and historical data for business analysis. They cannot quickly answer ad hoc queries and rapid retrieval is almost impossible. The data is inconsistent and changing, duplicate entries exist, entries can be missing and there is an absence of historical data which is necessary to analyse trends. Basically OLTP offers large amounts of raw data which is not easily understood. The data warehouse offers the potential to retrieve and analyse information quickly and easily. Data warehouses do have similarities with OLTP like both of them are RDBMS, provides access through SQL system and provide data suitable for any business operation, etc. The data warehouse serves a different purpose from that of OLTP systems by allowing business analysis queries to be answered as opposed to "simple aggregations" such as `what is the current account balance for this customer?' Typical data warehouse queries include such things as `which product line sells best in the North Eastern part of India and how does this correlate to demographic data?'

Data Warehouse model:

Data warehousing is the process of extracting and transforming operational data into informational data and loading it into a central data store or warehouse. Once the data is loaded it is accessible via desktop query and analysis tools by the decision makers.

The data within the actual warehouse itself has a distinct structure with the emphasis on different levels of summarization as shown in the figure on next page.

The current detail data is central in importance as it:

* reflects the most recent happenings, which are usually the most interesting;
* it is voluminous as it is stored at the lowest level of granularity;
* it is always stored on disk storage which is fast to access but expensive and complex to manage.

Here Older detail data is stored on some form of mass storage, it is infrequently accessed and stored at a level detail consistent with current detailed data. Lightly summarized data is data distilled from the low level of detail found at the current detailed level and generally is stored on disk storage. When building the data warehouse have to consider what unit of time is summarization done over and also the contents or what

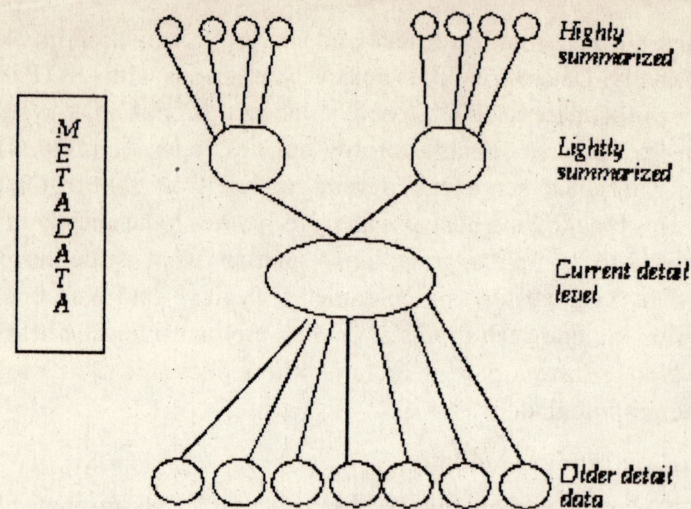

Figure: The structure of data inside the data warehouse

attributes the summarized data will contain. Highly summarized data is compact and easily accessible and can even be found outside the warehouse and Metadata is the final component of the data warehouse and is really of a different dimension in that it is not the same as data drawn from the operational environment but is used as:

* a directory to help the DSS analyst locate the contents of the data warehouse,
* a guide to the mapping of data as the data is transformed from the operational environment to the data warehouse environment,
* a guide to the algorithms used for summarization between the current detailed data and the lightly summarized data and the lightly summarized data and the highly summarized data, etc.

At the same time *Bill Inmon* fills in the details to make the presentation more alive as shown in the following diagram.

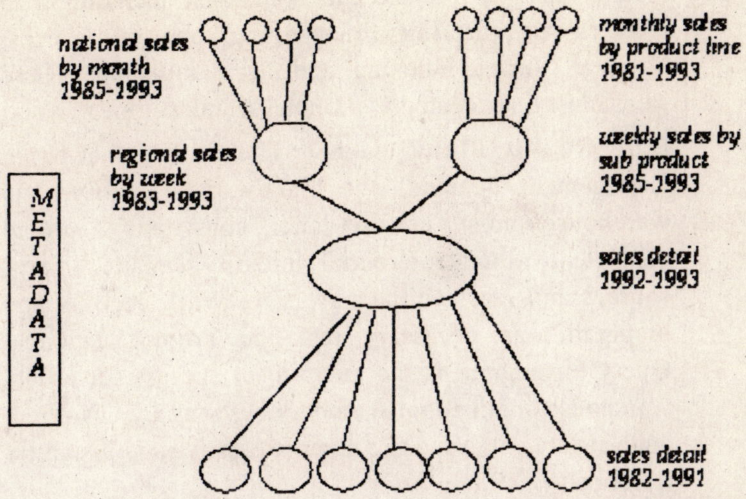

Figure: An example of levels of summarization of data inside the data warehouse

The diagram assumes the year is 1993 hence the current detail data is 1992-93. Generally sales data doesn't reach the current level of detail for 24 hours as it waits until it is no longer available to the operational system i.e. it takes 24 hours for it to get to the data warehouse. Sales details are summarized weekly by subproduct and region to produce the lightly summarized detail. Weekly sales are then summarized again to produce the highly summarized data.

Criteria for a data warehouse:

The criteria for data warehouse RDBMSs are as follows:

* **Load Performance -** Data warehouses require incremental loading of new data on a periodic basis within narrow time windows; performance of the load process should be measured in hundreds of millions of rows and gigabytes per hour and must not artificially constrain the volume of data required by the business.

* **Load Processing -** Many steps must be taken to load new or updated data into the data warehouse including data conversions, filtering, reformatting, integrity checks, physical storage, indexing, and metadata update. These steps must be executed as a single, seamless unit of work.
* **Data Quality Management -** The shift to fact-based management demands the highest data quality. The warehouse must ensure local consistency, global consistency, and referential integrity despite "dirty" sources and massive database size. While loading and preparation are necessary steps, they are not sufficient. Query throughput is the measure of success for a data warehouse application. As more questions are answered, analysts are catalysed to ask more creative and insightful questions.
* **Query Performance -** Fact-based management and ad-hoc analysis must not be slowed or inhibited by the performance of the data warehouse RDBMS; large, complex queries for key business operations must complete in seconds not days.
* **Terabyte Scalability -** Data warehouse sizes are growing at astonishing rates. Today these range from a few to hundreds of gigabytes, and terabyte-sized data warehouses are a near-term reality. The RDBMS must not have any architectural limitations. It must support modular and parallel management. It must support continued availability in the event of a point failure, and must provide a fundamentally different mechanism for recovery. It must support near-line mass storage devices such as optical disk and Hierarchical Storage Management devices. Lastly, query performance must not be dependent on the size of the database, but rather on the complexity of the query.
* **Mass User Scalability -** Access to warehouse data must no longer be limited to the elite few. The RDBMS server must support hundreds, even thousands, of concurrent users

while maintaining acceptable query performance.

* **Networked Data Warehouse** - Data warehouses rarely exist in isolation. Multiple data warehouse systems cooperate in a larger network of data warehouses. The server must include tools that coordinate the movement of subsets of data between warehouses. Users must be able to look at and work with multiple warehouses from a single client workstation. Warehouse managers have to manage and administer a network of warehouses from a single physical location.

* **Warehouse Administration** - The very large scale and time-cyclic nature of the data warehouse demands administrative ease and flexibility. The RDBMS must provide controls for implementing resource limits, chargeback accounting to allocate costs back to users, and query prioritization to address the needs of different user classes and activities. The RDBMS must also provide for workload tracking and tuning so system resources may be optimized for maximum performance and throughput. "The most visible and measurable value of implementing a data warehouse is evidenced in the uninhibited, creative access to data it provides the end user.

* **Integrated Dimensional Analysis** - The power of multidimensional views is widely accepted, and dimensional support must be inherent in the warehouse RDBMS to provide the highest performance for relational OLAP tools. The RDBMS must support fast, easy creation of precomputed summaries common in large data warehouses. It also should provide the maintenance tools to automate the creation of these precomputed aggregates. Dynamic calculation of aggregates should be consistent with the interactive performance needs.

* **Advanced Query Functionality** - End users require advanced analytic calculations, sequential and comparative analysis, and consistent access to detailed and summarized

data. Using SQL in a client/server point-and-click tool environment may sometimes be impractical or even impossible. The RDBMS must provide a complete set of analytic operations including core sequential and statistical operations.

GLOSSARY

Access strategy:

The method by which a database management system locates physical data.

Accessibility:

A design goal to make the application usable by as many users as possible including those with physical challenges. One solution is to support multiple input and output methods.

Access:

Refers to the process of obtaining data from or placing data into a disk storage device. register or RAM. (i.e. accessing a memory location).

ActiveX:

A model developed by Microsoft for writing programs so that other programs and the operating system can call them.

Alias:

A temporary name for a table or a column. Often used when you need to refer to the same table more than once as in a self-join.

ANSI:

American National Standards Institute

Application:

A complete system that performs a specific collection of tasks. It typically consists of integrated forms and reports and generally contains menus and a Help system.

Archival Image:

An image meant to have lasting utility. Archival images

are usually kept off-line on a cheaper storage medium such as CD-ROM or magnetic tape, in a secure environment. Archival images are of a higher resolution and quality than the digital image delivered to the user on-screen. The file format most often associated with archival images is TIFF, or Tagged Image File Format, as compared to on-screen viewing file formats, which are usually JPEGs and GIFs.

Archival Scans:

Digital images serve as surrogates of the original. At this point in time, there is no such thing as an Archival or Preservation scan that acts as an exact replica or replacement of the original, as it is not yet possible to record every piece of information found in the original with today's scanner technology.

Arithmetic operators:

Addition (+). subtraction (-). multiplication (*). and division (/) are arithmetic operators. They can be used with all numeric columns. Some systems also supply modulo (%). for finding the integer remainder after a division operation on two integers.

Artifacts:

Visual digital effects introduced into an image during scanning that do not correspond to the original image being scanned. Artifacts might include pixellation, dotted or straight lines, regularly repeated patterns, moire, etc.

ASCII:

American Standard Code for Information Interchange. An eight-bit code for character representation; includes seven bits plus parity.

ASP:

Active Server Pages (ASP) is used to search and display dynamic and live information, such as that found in locally produced relational databases, requires the addition of other languages. In such case the systems should use.

Asynchronous Data:

Data sent usually in parallel mode without a clock pulse. Time intervals between transmitted bits may be of unequal lengths.

Attribute:

A data value that describes one characteristic of an entity. It is also called a "field" or a "column:' A field is represented by a column within an object (entity). An object may be a table, view or report. An attribute is also associated with an SGML (HTML) tag used to further define the usage.

Authentication:

Providing a verification system to determine who actually wrote a message. Common systems use a dual-key encryption system.

Automatic Back-up of Files:

This gives a user the security to make changes to a file without worrying about accidentally destroying it; there is always another copy. One weakness of this method is that files take up twice the room on a disk.

Auxiliary Memory:

Memory other than main memory; generally a mass storage subsystem, it can include disk drives, backup tape drives, controllers and buffer memory. Typically auxiliary memory is non-volatile.

Auxiliary Storage Device:

Devices generally magnetic tapes and magnetic disks on which data can be stored for use by computer programs secondary storage.

Back End:

A back end is that part of a programming system that the user never sees. It is most commonly used to refer to the "data" part of a database system when it is separated from the user interface.

Backup:

Copying computer files from one location to another. The second location is usually a tape drive or some other media. The medium is then physically moved to a safe location away from the original computer. A backup strategy is a key part of Fault Tolerance.

Backup Device:

Disk or tape drive used with a fixed Winchester disk drive to make copies of files or other data for off line storage distribution or protection against accidental data deletion from the Winchester drive or against drive failure.

Backup File:

File copies made on another removable media device (disk. tape or sometimes a remote hard disk system) and kept to ensure recovery of data lost due to equipment failure, human errors updates disasters and the like.

Bandwidth:

Measures the data carrying capacity of a communications channel. Usually measured in bits per second (bps).

Base station:

The central radio transmitter/receiver that maintains communications with a mobile telephone. Most countries require several hundred base stations. in order to give approximated full coverage for mobile subscribers.

Baud Rate:

A variable unit of data transmission speed equal to one bit per second.

BCNF:

Boyce-codd normal form Relations are in third normal form and there are no Boyce-codd dependencies.

Benchmarking:

The process of testing a piece of hardware or software to determine its general or specific performance characteristics.

Binary data type:

A data type provided by some systems for storing bit patterns.

Binary search:

A search technique for sorted data. Start at the middle of the data. If the search value is greater than the middle value. split the following data in half. Keep reducing by half until the value is found.

Binary:

A number system like the decimal numbers. but using 2 as its base and having only the two digits a (zero) and 1 (one). It is used in computers because digital logic can only determine one of two states - "OFF" and "ON." Digital data is equivalent to a binary number.

Bit:

The smallest unit of data. Consists of a single binary digit that can take the value of 0 or 1.

Bitmap index:

A compact, high-speed indexing method where the key values are compressed to a small size that can be stored and searched rapidly.

BLOB (Binary large object):

A data domain for undefined, large chunks of data. A BLOB (or simple object) type can hold any type of data but the programmer is often responsible for displaying manipulating, and searching the data.

Block:

A group of BYTES handled, stored and accessed as a

logical data unit, such as an individual file record. Typically one block of data is stored as one physical sector of data on a disk drive.

Bluetooth:

A radio technology built around a new chip that makes it possible to transmit signals over short distances between computers and handheld devices without the use of wires. (www.bluetooth.com). Named after the Danish king Harald I Bluetooth who reigned from 940-985 A.D.

Boolean algebra:

Creating and manipulating logic queries connected with AND, OR, and NOT conditions.

Boolean expressions:

Expressions that evaluate as "true" or "false" rather than return a specific value.

Boolean operators:

The logical operators AND, OR and NOT.

Boyce-Codd dependency:

A (part of the) key being dependent on a non-key attribute.

Browser:

A software application that is used to allow users to read an HTML document in a user-friendly readable format. Two well-known browsers are Microsoft Internet Explorer and Netscape Navigator.

Buffer cache:

Memory allocated for data storage.

Buffer:

A temporary data storage area that compensates for a difference in data transfer rates and/or data processing rates between sender and receiver.

Buffered Seek:

In buffered mode head motion is postponed until a string of step pulses can be sent to the drive. These pulses represent the number of tracks that the head is to be stepped over, and are sent much faster than the heads can move. The pulses are saved or buffered and then the optimum head movement to the correct track *is* performed.

Byte:

A sequence of adjacent BINARY digits or BITS considered as a unit. 8 bits in length. One byte is sufficient to define all the alphanumeric characters. There are 8 BITS in 1 BYTE. The storage capacity of a disk drive is commonly measured in MEGABYTES, which is the total number of bits storable.

Cache Memory:

Cache Memory allows the system to load bytes of data from the hard disk to memory. The system may then refer to memory for information instead of going back to the hard disk. thereby increasing the processing speed.

Cardinality:

The number of rows in a table.

Cartesian product:

All the possible combinations of rows from the tables. Such a result is generally caused by not including all the necessary joins.

Cascade:

Propagation of an update or delete through related tables in a database.

Cascading delete:

When tables are linked by data if you delete a row in a higher-level table matching rows in other tables are deleted automatically. For example if you delete Customer 1173, all orders placed by that customer are also deleted.

CASE (Computer-aided software engineering):

Computer programs that are *designed* to support the analysis and development *of* computer systems. They make it easier to create, store, and share *diagrams* and data definitions. Some versions can analyze existing code and generate new code.

CCD Array:

Charge-Coupled Device array. Light sensitive diodes used in scanners and digital cameras that sweep across an image during capture and, when exposed to light, generate a series of digital signals that are converted into pixel values.

CDMA (Code Division Multiple Access):

A technology for digital transmission of radio signals between, for example, a mobile telephone and a base station. The system uses the same frequency to allow multiple conversations. Each conversation is cut into snippets and then remodulated and reassembled in the other end.

CGI (Common gateway interface):

With Web servers, CGI is a predefined system for transferring data across the Internet. Current scripting languages hide the details, so you can simply retrieve data, as it is needed.

Character:

An information symbol used to denote a number, letter, symbol or punctuation mark stored by a computer. In a computer a character can be represented in one (1) byte or eight (8) bits *of* data. There are 256 different one-byte binary numbers, sufficient for 26 lower case alphas, 26 upper case alphas, 10 decimal digits, control codes and error checks.

Client/Server architecture:

A 'networked' environment where a smaller system such as a PC interacts with a larger, faster system. This allows the processing to be performed on the larger system, which frees the user's Pc. The larger system is able to connect and disconnect from the clients in order to process the data more efficiently.

Client/server:

A technique for organizing systems where a few computers hold most *of* the data, which is retrieved by individuals using personal computer clients.

Client:

A software application on your computer, which is used to extract or download some application, data or service from a host system.

Client-server system:

A multi-user system in which a central processor (the server) is connected to multiple intelligent user workstations (the clients).

Clustered index:

An index in which the bottom, or leaf level is the data itself. A table can have only one clustered index.

Code:

A set of unambiguous rules specifying the way in which digital data is represented physically, as magnetized bits, on a disk drive. One of the objectives of coding is to add timing data for use in data reading.

Column:

A component of a table that holds a single attribute of the table; also called a "field."

Command:

1) An instruction sent by the central processing unit (CPU) to a controller for execution.
2) English-like commands entered by users to select computer programs or functions.
3) A CPU command, which is a single instruction such as: "add two binary numbers" or "output a byte to the display screen".

Commit:

Decision to proceed with the actual posting of a change to the database.

Comparison operators:

Operators used for comparing one expression to another in a WHERE or HAVING clause. Comparison operators include equal to (=), greater than (», less than «), greater than or equal to (>=), less than or equal to «+), and not equal to 0= or <».

Composite indexes:

Indexes based on more than one column in a table.

Composite key:

A key-whether primary, unique or foreign-consisting of more than one column. Sometimes known as concatenated key.

Comprehensive data sub-language:

A single language that handles all communications with the database.

Compression/Decompression:

The reduction of image file size for processing, storage, and transmission. The quality of the image may be affected by the compression techniques used and the level of compression applied. Decompression is the process of retrieving compressed data and reassembling it so that it resembles its original form before compression. There are two types of compression:

Lossless compression is a process that reduces the storage space needed for an image file without loss of data. If an image has undergone lossless compression, it will be identical to the image before it was compressed. Primarily used with bitonal images. **Lossy** compression is another process that reduces the storage space needed for an image file, but it discards information (information that is "redundant" and not perceptible to the human eye). If an image that has undergone lossy compression is decompressed, it will differ form the image before it was compressed, even though the difference may be difficult for the human eye to detect.

There are both standard and non-standard compression techniques available. In general, it is better to employ a compression technique that is supported by standards, non-proprietary, and maintained over time. In selecting a compression technique, it is necessary to consider the attributes of the original. Some compression techniques are designed to compress text, others are designed to compress pictures.

Computed attribute:

An attribute for which the value is calculated from other attributes. While computed attributes may be stored in relations, they are not usually done so. Most often they are produced as needed in the resolution of a query.

Concurrency control:

Strategies such as locking that prevent two or more users from changing the same piece of data concurrently.

Concurrent access:

Performing two (or more) operations on the same data at the same time. The DBMS must sequence the operations so that some of the changes are not lost.

Connection column:

A column that participates in a join, allowing one table to link with another or with itself. Connecting columns are columns from one or more tables that contain similar values.

Consistency:

The goal of making an application easier to use by using the same features, colors, and commands throughout. Modern applications also strive for consistency with a common design guide.

Constraint:

A restriction placed on a form, table, field or other objects to either force an action to happen in a certain way, or to prevent an action from happening all together. Constraints enforce referential integrity, and promote fault tolerance.

Crash:

A malfunction in the computer hardware or software, usually causing loss of data.

CSS:

Cascading Style Sheets (CSS) is a simple mechanism for adding style (e.g. fonts, colors, spacing) to Web documents.

Cyclic-Redundancy-Check (CRC):

Used 10 verify data block integrity. In a typical scheme 2 CRC bytes are added to each user data block. The 2 bytes are computed from the user data. by digital logical chips. The mathematical model is polynomials with binary coefficients. When reading back data the CRC bytes are read and compared to new CRC bytes computed from the read back block to detect a read error. The read back error-check process is mathematically equivalent to dividing the read block including its CRC by a binomial polynomial. If the division remainder is zero the data is error free.

DAO (Data Access Objects):

Microsoft's cursor-level programming for tracking through a table one row at a time. You retrieve and alter data using predefined methods and properties of the objects.

Data cache:

The area of memory allocated for data storage.

Data definition:

The process of creating (or removing) a database and its objects. Data dictionary - The system tables that contain descriptions of the database objects and how they are structured.

Data Directory:

A collection of definitions, rules and advisories of data, designed to be used as a guide or reference with the data warehouse. The directory includes definitions, examples relations, functions and equivalents in other environments, such as ISIS. IFIS, PPS and DSE.

Data independence:

Separates the data from the programs, which often enables the data definition to be changed without altering the program.

Data:

Information processed by a computer, stored in memory, or fed into a computer.

Data integrity:

Keeping accurate data, which means few errors and means that the data reflect the true state of the business. A DBMS enables you to specify constraints or rules that help maintain integrity, such as prices must always be greater than O.

Data mining:

Searching databases for unknown patterns and information. Tools include statistical analysis, pattern-matching techniques, and data segmentation analysis.

Data Processing:

The process of computer handling manipulating and modifying data such as arithmetic calculation file lookup and updating or word processing.

Data redundancy:

Having the same data stored in more than one place in a database.

Data replication:

In a distributed system, placing duplicate copies of data on several servers to reduce overall transmission time and costs.

Data retrieval:

Finding and displaying data in the database via queries.

Data warehouse:

A specialized database that is optimized for management queries. Data is extracted from online transaction processing systems. The data is cleaned and optimized for searching and analysis.

Database Administrator (DBA):

The person ultimately responsible for the functionality, integrity and safety of a database.

Database design:

The process of setting up the objects in the database (principally, but not exclusively, tables and their columns).

Database device:

The physical or logical device on which a database is stored.

Database manager:

The person with primary responsibility for the design, construction and maintenance of a database.

Database:

A collection of related tables containing data and definitions of database objects.

DBA (Database Administrator):

Person in charge of the technical and operational support for a database or all databases for an organization.

DBMS (Database management system):

Special software to create and maintain a database and enable individual library applications to extract the data they need without having to create separate files or data definitions in their computer programs must generally be supported by a data administrator.

DDL (Data definition language):

Component of a database management system that defines each data element as it appears in the database.

Deadlock:

A situation that exists when two (or more) processes each have a lock on a piece of data that the other one needs.

DECT (Digital Enhanced Cordless Telecommunications):

A standard for cordless telephony.

Default:

A value entered by the system for specified columns when the user supplies no explicit value.

Derived Image (Derivative Image):

An image that has been created from another image through some kind of automated process, usually involving a loss of information. Techniques used to create derived images include sampling to a lower resolution, using lossy compression techniques, or altering an image using image processing techniques.

DES (Data encryption standard):

A standard method for encrypting data. It is a single-key technique.

DHTML (Dynamic HTML):

A way of describing web pages that can change according to user input without having to send requests back to the server.

Digital Camera:

Copystand scanners that resemble microfilming stands. The digital camera directly captures an image without the use of film. Source material is placed on the stand and the camera is moved up or down in order to fit the material into its field of view, which allows for the scanning of a range of differently-sized materials. Resolution of digital cameras is usually fixed and is expressed as a pixel ratio.

Digital Image:

An electronic photograph scanned from an original document, made up of a set of picture elements ("pixels"). Each pixel is assigned a tonal value (black, white, a shade of gray, or color) and is represented digitally in binary code (zeros and ones). The term "image" does not imply solely visual materials as source material; rather, a digital image is simply a representation of whatever is being scanned, whether it be manuscripts, text, photographs, maps, drawings, blueprints, halftones, musical scores, 3-D objects, etc.

Digital Library:

Definitions of the digital library range from narrow to broad, with some disagreement on the actual function of a digital library. Clifford Lynch defines the digital library as "an electronic information access system that offers the user a coherent view of an organized, selected, and managed body of information." This definition recognizes the more traditional role of a library in the digital world: at the very least, a digital library should offer services along with information, such as indexing or cataloging. Users of digital library resources may come to expect (and already do expect) more sophisticated fuctions, such as information and knowledge management services, resource discovery mechanisms, and personalization of access and monitoring of new and existing digital resources.

Digital:

Any system that processes digital binary signals having only the values of a 1 or O. An example of a non-digital signal is an analog signal that continuously varies.

Diodes:

Light-sensitive electronic components used by the scanner during image capture. Diodes sense the presence or absence of light and create a digital signal that the computer then converts into pixel values.

Direct Access:

Generally refers to an auxiliary memory device having all data online. A tape drive without a tape mounted is not direct access but a Winchester Drive is direct access.

DirectX:

DirectX is a Microsoft standard that provides programmers a way to gain access to hardware under Windows. DirectX is used mostly for games, computer based training and multimedia programs.

Distributed data processing:

A system in which data is distributed across multiple servers.

Distributed database:

Multiple independent databases that operate on two or more computers that are connected and share data over a network. The databases are usually in different physical locations. Each database is controlled by an independent DBMS.

DML (Data manipulation language):

Language associated with a database management system, which is used by end users and programmers to retrieve modify and/or store data in the database.

Domain:

The collection of all possible values of an attribute. The domain of an attribute may be finite or infinite.

DOM:

Document Object Model is a platform- and language-neutral interface that will allow programs and scripts to dynamically access and update the content, structure and style of documents.

Dots per inch (dpi):

A measurement of the scanning resolution of an image or the quality of an output device. DPI expresses the number of dots a printer can print per inch, or that a monitor can display, both horizontally and vertically.

DSS (Decision support system):

A system that collects data analyzes models and presents the results in a manner to help managers make decisions. From a database perspective, the demands that analysis and presentation place on the system are different from those of a transaction processing system.

DTD (Document Type Definition):

Documents are regarded as having types, just as other objects processed by computers do. The type of a document is defined by its constituent parts and structure. A DTD defines the structure of an SGML (Standard Generalized Markup Language) document.

Dual-key encryption:

An encryption technique that uses two different keys: one private and one public. The public key is published so anyone can retrieve it. To send an encrypted message to someone, you use the person's public key. At that point, only the person' s private key will decrypt the message. Encrypting a message first with your private key can also be used to verify that you wrote the message.

Dublin Core:

A metadata element set intended to facilitate discovery of electronic resources. Two features of the Dublin Core metadata element set are simplicity and extensibility. Dublin Core is intended to be usable by both non-catalogers and specialists alike, to provide an economic alternative to more elaborate descriptive models such as full MARC cataloging, and be flexible enough to encode the structure and semantics inherent in rich descriptive standards. The Dublin Core seeks to promote a commonly understood set of descriptors to help facilitate interoperability across disciplines. The Dublin Core can be mapped to the MARC record and a variety of output structures can be generated.

Dummy values:

False values you enter as placeholders or tests.

Dynamic Range (Bit-depth):

The number of colors or shades of gray that can be represented by a pixel. The smallest unit of data stored in a computer is called a bit. Dynamic range is a measurement of the number of bits used to represent each pixel in a digital image. 1-bit or bitonal means that a pixel can either be black or white. Bitonal imaging is good for black and white images, such as line drawings and text. However, scanning in grayscale rather than bitonal may produce a better looking image. 8-bit color or 8-bit grayscale means that each pixel can be one of 256 shades of color or one of 256 shades of gray. 24-bit color means that each pixel can be one of 16.8 million colors.

EAD:

The EAD(Encoded Archival Description) is an SGML (Standard Generalized Markup Language) DTD (Document Type Definition) intended to assist in the creation of electronic finding aids., it was developed at UC-Berkeley and is now maintained and supported as a standard by the Library of Congress and sponsored by the Society of American Archivists. The EAD can be used to represent complete archival structures, including hierarchies and associations. The kinds of functionality that EAD affords can also be implemented using Dublin Core, and it is also possible to migrate records from Dublin Core into the EAD format if necessary.

Entity integrity:

An integrity rule requiring that each row has a primary key and that no primary key allows nulls.

Entity:

A person, place or thing about which you want to store data; this can include people, places, events in time and concepts.

Expert system:

A system with a knowledge base consisting of data and rules that enable a novice to make decisions as effectively as an expert.

Expression:

A constant, column name, function, or any combination thereof connected by arithmetic (and sometimes bitwise) operators.

FAQ (Frequently Asked Questions):

An acronym that refers to a text file on the Internet that contains answers to frequently asked questions. FAQ's are a valuable resource for gaining knowledge on particular subjects of interest.

Feasibility study:

A quick examination of the problems, goals, and expected costs of a proposed system. The objective is to determine whether the problem can reasonably be solved with a computer system.

File Size:

The file size is the capacity of the information stored in the computer file. The file size of an image is proportional to its resolution. The higher the resolution, the bigger the file size. File size is different from image size.

File:

The separately named unit of storage for all data and programs on most computers. For example a relation or a whole database may be stored in one file.

Flatbed Scanner:

An image capture device much like a photocopier. The

object to be scanned is placed face-down on a glass plate. The CCD array passes beneath the glass.

Floppy Disk:

A flexible plastic disk coated with magnetic media and packaged in a stiff envelope.

Front End:

The client part of a program that contains the user interface.

FTP (File Transfer Protocol):

FTP is the most common way to transfer files from one computer to another over the Internet.

GIF (Graphics Interchange Format):

A file compression format used for transferring graphics files over the internet.

GIF Graphic Image File:

Format. A widely supported image storage format promoted by Compuserve for use on the web.

GIS (Geographic information system):

Designed to identify and display relationships among business data and locations.

GPRS (General Packet Radio Service):

A packet-linked technology that may enable high-speed (up to 115 kilobit per second) access to wireless Internet in a GSM network. GPRS is IP-based and may allow users to be online 24 hours.

GPS (Global Position System):

Based on US defense satellite system enables tracking of individuals. This technology may prove helpful when navigating a car in the city, or help emergency rescue-team to locate the person in need of help.

GQL (Graphical Query Language):

Graphical Query Language is a graphical query tool used to access information stored in an SQL database.

Gray Scale:

A range of shades of gray in an image. Gray scales of scanners are determined by the number of grays, or values between black and white, that they can recognize and reproduce.

GSM (Global System for Mobile Communications):

The world's most widely used mobile system. Used on the 900 MHz and 1800 MHz frequencies in Europe, Asia and Australia and the MHz 1900 frequency in America.

GUI:

Graphical User Interface.

Hard Disk Drive:

Commonly called rigid disk drives, or Winchester disk drives. An electromechanical device that can read rigid disks. Though similar to floppy disk drives, the hard disks have higher bit density and multiple read/write surfaces.

Hardware:

Computer equipment (as opposed to the computer programs and software).

Hashed key:

Direct access storage of a row of data, where the key value is converted to a physical storage location.

Head Crash:

A head landing occurs when the disk drive is turned on or off. This function normally does not damage the disk as the disk has a very thin lubricant on it. A head crash occurs when the head and disk damage each other during landing handling or because a contaminant particle gets between them. Head crash is a catastrophic failure condition and causes permanent damage and loss of data.

Head:

An electromagnetic device that can write (record), read (playback), or erase data on magnetic media.

HTML (Hypertext Markup Language):

An encoding format for linking and identifying electronic documents and used to deliver information on the World Wide Web. It is the lingua franca for publishing hypertext on the World Wide Web. It is a non-proprietary format based upon SGML, and can be created and processed by a wide range of tools, from simple plain text editors - you type it in from scratch to sophisticated WYSIWYG authoring tools.

Hyperlink:

A hyperlink is a logical link between two related pieces of information in the same document or between different documents. It will allow you to quickly jump from one document or location to another transparently.

Image Capture:

Using a scanner or other device to create a digital representation or electronic photograph of an image. The scanning process is often labor-intensive and costly, requiring a substantial investment in handling and processing original materials and their surrogate images. The current strategy is to capture an image at the highest resolution appropriate to the original, and store it off-line as an archival image on CD-ROM. Techniques such as lossy compression and subsampling can then be used to create derivative images for use online. In the future, as the ability to deliver high-quality archival scans, it will be possible to place the archival scan online without cost of recapture. Scanning can be done in-house or contracted out to a vendor. Whether scanning is done in-house or outsourced, quality of the images can vary widely.

Image Manipulation or Alteration:

Making changes (such as tonal adjustments, cropping, more

reduction, etc.) to an image using image processing software.

Image size:

Describes the actual physical dimensions of an image, not the size it appears on a given display device.

Input:

Data entered into the computer to be processed. 2. User commands or queries.

Integrity:

The assurance that the database data is accurate and correct. One type of integrity is Entity integrity, where the table in question has to be entirely consistent with the entity that it models. In this case the table must have a primary key.

IP address:

Every device on the Internet is assigned an address that is used for communicating from device to device.

ISAM (Indexed sequential access method):

A data storage method that relies on an index to search and retrieve data faster than a pure sequential search.

ISO:

International Standards Organization.

Java:

A programming language developed by Sun Microsystems that is supposed to be able to run unchanged on diverse computers.

JPEG (Joint Photographic Experts Group):

A compression algorithm for condensing the size of image files. JPEGs are helpful in allowing access to full screen image files on-line because they require less storage and are therefore quicker to download into a web page.

Key values:

Primary keys uniquely identify a row, while foreign keys

provide a way to refer to those unique values from another table.

Key:

A field in a record that uniquely identifies a particular instance of that record so that it can be retrieved, updated, deleted or sorted.

Logical operators:

AND (joins two or more conditions and returns results when all the conditions are true), OR (connects two or more conditions and returns results when any of the conditions is true), and NOT (negates a condition).

Logical security:

Determining which users should have access to which data. It deals with preventing three data problems: (1) unauthorized disclosure, (2) unauthorized modification, and (3) unauthorized withholding.

Main Memory:

Random-access memory used by the CPU for storing program instructions and data currently being processed by those instructions.

MARC (Machine Readable Cataloging):

The MARC formats are standards for the representation and communication of bibliographic and related information in machine readable form. The MARC formats contain an explicit set of rules for the structure of fields and the content values within those fields.

MathML:

Mathematical Markup Language (MathML) is a way of describing math syntax so mathematical ideas can be exchanged using the web. It provides for two sets of markup tags: a set that presents the mathematical notations and a set that relays the semantic meaning of expressions. MathML is not intended as user language; it is meant for use with software tools that translate mathematical equations into a human-readable format.

Memory:

Any device or storage system capable of storing and retrieving information.

Metadata:

Data about data, or information known about the image in order to provide access to the image. Usually includes information about the intellectual content of the image, digital representation data, and security or rights management information.

Migration:

Preserving the integrity of digital images by transferring them across hardware and software configurations and across subsequent generations of computer technology. Migration includes refreshment (copying digital files from one media to another) as a means of preservation and access. However, migration differs from refreshment in the sense that it is not always possible to make an exact copy of a database or even an image file as changes in hardware and software occur and still maintain compatibility with the new generation of technology.

Multiprocessor:

A computer containing two or more processors.

Multitasking:

The ability of a computer system to execute more than one program or program task at a time.

Multi-User:

The ability of a computer system to execute programs for more than one user at a time.

Network database:

An older DBMS type that expanded the hierarchical database by supporting multiple connections between entities.

A network database is characterized by the requirement that all connections had to be supported by an index.

Noise:

Data or unidentifiable marks picked up in the course of scanning or data transfer that do not correspond to the original.

Null:

A null represents a missing or inapplicable value in a column of a database table.

ODBC (Open database Connectivity):

A standard database access method developed by Microsoft Corporation. The goal of ODBC is to make it possible to access any data from any application regardless of which database management system (DBMS) is handling the data. ODBC manages this by inserting a middle layer called a database driver between an application and the DBMS.

OLAP (On-line application processing):

The use of a database for data analysis. The focus is on retrieval of the data. The primary goals are to provide acceptable response times maintain security and make it easy for users to find the data they need.

OLTP (On-line transaction processing):

The use of a database for transaction processing. It consists of many insert and update operations and supports hundreds of concurrent accesses. High-speed storage of data, reliability and data integrity are primary goals. Examples include airline reservations online banking and retail sales.

One-to-many:

A master-detail relationship in which one row in the first table may relate to many in the second but a row in the second table can relate to only one row in the first.

One-to-one relationship:

Exactly one tuple in one relation is related by a common join attribute to exactly one tuple in another relation. This implies that each value of the join attribute appears no more than once in each of the relations.

Operating System:

An operating system is a program, which acts as an interface between the user of a computer and the computer hardware. The purpose of the operating system is to provide an environment in which a user may run programs. The goal of the operating system is to enable the user to conveniently use the computer's resources such as the CPU, memory, storage devices and printers.

Output:

Processing data being transferred out of the computer system to peripherals (Le. disk. printer. etc.). This includes responses to user commands or queries.

PDA (Personal Digital Assistant):

Usually a hand-held device, such as the Palm Pilot or Psion.

PHS (Personal Handyphone System):

Digital mobile telephone system according to Japanese stMidard (1900Mhz).

Physical data independence:

The independence of the physical storage of data from a database's logical design.

Pixel:

Often referred to as dot, as in "dots per inch". "Pixel" is short for picture elements, which make up an image, similar to grains in a photograph or dots in a half-tone. Each pixel can represent a number of different shades or colors, depending on how much storage space is allocated for it. Pixels per inch (ppi) is sometimes the preferred term, as it more accurately describes the digital image.

Plug-in:

A software component that is downloaded from a Web server to a Web client, where it is integrated with the client's browser, providing additional functions.

Preservation:

Digitizing an original photograph, document, or three-dimensional object is only a method of preservation if the digital file becomes the access tool and the original is no longer available for use. Although high resolution scanning (i.e., scan at the highest resolution possible appropriate to the type of media you are scanning) is recommended for all materials in order to achieve the highest quality possible and to ensure that information held in the original is not lost in the scan. However, the digital file, as of yet, should not serve as a replacement of the original for preservation purposes.

Primary memory:

The internal memory of a computer, usually consisting of RAM chips, on which the data and programs currently being used must reside.

Protocol:

A set of conventions governing the format of messages to be exchanged within a communications system.

QBE (Query-by-Example):

Query-by-Example is a tabular language for expressing queries, in which a query is specified by sketching an abbreviated 'schema' of the output desired, along with any criteria which should be applied to the attributes desired.

Quality Control:

Techniques ensuring that high quality is maintained through various stages of a process. For example, quality control during image capture might include comparing the scanned image to the original and then adjusting colors or tonal values, or checking for artifacts.

Query:

A command. written in a query language, for the database to present a specified subset of the data in the database.

RAID (Redundant array of independent drives):

A disk drive system that consists of multiple drives with independent controllers. There are several levels of RAID offering different features. The goal is to split the data to provide faster access and automatic duplication for error recovery.

Random Access Memory (RAM):

Memory where any location can be read from or written to in a random order. Random access memory usually refers to volatile memory where the contents are lost when power is removed. The user addressable memory of a computer is random access memory.

Read Only Memory (ROM):

A chip that can be programmed once with bits of information. This chip retains this information even if the power is turned off. When this information is programmed into the ROM. it is called burning the ROM.

Record:

A set of related fields that describes a specific entity. Also called "tuple" or "row."

Refreshment:

The transfer of digital files to a new media on a regular basis. Technology is usually outdated by the time it hits the marketplace. The data we generate today must be retrievable five, fifty, and a hundred years from now. In order to ensure long-term access to the data, it must be transferred to the most recent and stable type of media storage. In a hundred years, it is very unlikely that any of the computers on our desks today will function. We must make sure that the data can be retrieved by future technology.

Relational Database:

A type of database management system (DBMS) that stores data in the form of related tables. Relational databases are powerful because they require few assumptions about how data is related or how it will be extracted from the database. As a result the same database can be viewed in many different ways. An important feature of relational system is that a single database can be spread across several tables. This differs from flat-file databases, in which each database is self-contained in a single table.

Resolution:

The number of pixels (in both height and width) making up an image. The more pixels in an image, the higher the resolution, and the higher the resolution of an image, the greater its clarity and definition (and the larger the file size). Resolution can also refer to the output device, such as a computer monitor or printer, used to display the image. Image file resolution is often expressed as a ratio (such as 640x480 pixels), as is monitor resolution; however, resolution is also expressed in terms of dots per inch (dpi). The asssumed universal monitor resolution for web users is 72 dpi. Image file resolution and output (print or display) resolution combine to influence the clarity of a digital image when it is viewed.

Scanner:

A device for capturing a digital image. There are many types of scanners, such as flatbed scanners, drum scanners, slide scanners, and microfilm scanners.

Scanning:

see Image Capture

Schema:

A description of a database. It specifies (among other things) the relations, their attributes and the domains of the attributes. In some database systems, the join attributes are also specified as part of the schema.

SCSI:

Small Computer Systems Interface.

Secondary memory:

The external storage of a computer. usually consisting of magnetic or optical disks. on which data and programs are stored in the intervals between the times when they are actually in use.

Sector:

A sector is a section of a track whose size is determined by formatting. When used as an address component, sector and location refer to the sequence number of the sector around the track. Typically, one sector stores one user record of data. Drives typically are formatted from 17 to 26 sectors per track. Determining how many sectors per track to use depends on the system type, the controller capabilities and the drive encoding method and interface.

Server:

A computer where the server software resides, Such services as filing mail communications and authentication are a few of the services that are available.

Servlet:

A small program that runs on a server. Unlike embedded programs such as those found in ActiveX, web pages or Java applets, these programs do no have to be downloaded to the user via the web page. This allows much faster loading of web pages, and much faster execution of scripts.

SGML:

Standard Generalized Markup Language is an international

standard for the definition of device-independent, system-independent methods of representing texts in electronic form. SGML emphasizes descriptive rather than procedural markup. While HTML is a markup language which deals primarily with the appearance of a document, SGML is a more complex system for describing structural divisions in a text, typographical elements, and other textual features. The "tags" in SGML preserve the structure of a text, enable the user to constrain searches to particular structural features of the text and aid in the navigation and use of the text.

SMIL:

Synchronized Multimedia Integration Language (SMIL, pronounced "smile") enables simple authoring of interactive audiovisual presentations. SMIL is typically used for "rich media"/multimedia presentations which integrate streaming audio and video with images, text or any other media type. SMIL is an easy-to-learn HTML-like language, and many SMIL presentations are written using a simple text-editor. SMIL permits multimedia streams to be played sequentially or in parallel, and for different elements to be placed in absolute positions on the screen. Its hotlinks can be embedded in video multimedia elements, as well as in text and images. This would allow SMIL presentations to offer full interactivity. It enables authors to bring television-like content to the Web, avoiding the limitations of traditional television and significantly lowering the bandwidth requirements for transmitting this type of content over the Internet.

SMS (Short Message Service):

A service for sending messages of up to 160 characters to mobile phones that use Global System for Mobile (GSM) communication.

Software:

Application programs, disk operating systems and other programs (as opposed to Hardware). The instructions or programs usually stored on floppy or hard disks, which are used to direct the operations of a computer or other hardware.

Storage Capacity:

Amount of data that can be stored in a memory usually specified in kilobytes (KB) for main memory and floppy disk drives and megabytes (MB) for hard disk and tape drives.

Subsampling:

Using an algorithm to derive a lower-resolution image from a higher-resolution image.

Surrogate image:

A representation of the original image, used for study.

SVG:

Scalable Vector Graphics (SVG) offers web developers a method to create and animate images through an XML programming language. Consequently, rather than being removed from their code as is often the case with proprietary technology, developers can gain finer degrees of control over the appearance of Web pages. Animation techniques can range from a simple linear movement to 3D double helix morphing effects. Web developers, once they are more aware of the possibilities, can find unprecedented levels of control. It is open source and offers seamless database integration, server-scripting compatibility, and efficient accessibility/localization workflow. SVG is a language for describing two-dimensional graphics in XML. SVG allows for three types of graphic objects: vector graphic shapes (e.g., paths consisting of straight lines and curves), images and text.

Synchronous Data:

Data sent, usually in serial mode with a clock pulse.

System administrator:

The person who has overall responsibility for the data in the database and for its consistency and integrity.

TCP/IP (Transmission Protocol/Internet Protocol):

The protocol used by the Internet, intranets.

TEI:

Text Encoding Initiative is an international project to develop guidelines for the preparation and exchange of electronic texts for scholarly research. The TEI has created a set of SGML DTDs for the encoding of humanities and social science-related texts.

TIFF (Tagged Image File Format):

Tagged Image File Format is a graphic file format used to transfer graphic images across the Internet. It is a file storage format implemented on a wide variety of computer systems, usually used for archival scans.

Tuple:

A set of related attributes that describes a specific entity. Also called "row" or "record."

URL (Uniform Resource Locator):

The URL is the path information in an HTML coded source file used to locate another document or Image. It is a standard addressing scheme used to locate or reference files on the Internet. Used in World Wide Web documents to locate files. A URL gives the type of resource being used and the path to the file.

URN (Universal Resource Name/Number):

A storage-independent scheme to name all resources on the Internet with a unique and fixed name. URNs are likely to supersede URLs for identification and referencing of networked resources.

VOIP (Voice Over Internet Protocol):

Describes the process of transmitting voice via data I P packages.

VSAM (Virtual sequential access method):

A data storage method that uses virtual addresses instead of physical locations in the index. A true VSAM technique also provides multilevel indexes and other storage features. It has largely been replaced by B+-tree indexes.

WAN (Wide area network):

A network that is spread across a larger geographic area. Parts of the network are outside the control of a single firm. Long-distance connections often use public carriers.

WAP Gateway:

A WAP gateway is two-way software. Its main function is to offload the WAP mobile device from a lot of computational layers.

WAP:

Wireless Application Protocol, which is a family of protocols allowing mobile devices to access wireless services.

WCDMA (Wideband Code Division Multiple Access):

A technology for wideband digital radio communications of Internet, multimedia, video and others.

Web Server:

A computer that delivers (serves up) web pages.

World Wide Web (WWW):

An interconnected network of electronic hypermedia documents available on the Internet. WWW documents are marked up in HTML. Cross references or hyperlinks between documents are recorded in the form of URLs.

World Wide Web Consortium (W3C):

It was created to lead the Web to its full potential by developing common protocols that promote its evolution and ensure its interoperability. It is an international industry consortium jointly run by the MIT Laboratory for Computer

Science (MIT LCS) in the USA, the National Institute for Research in Computer Science and Control (INRIA) in France and Keio University in Japan.

WYSIWYG:

What You See Is What You Get.

Xform:

XForms are comprised of separate sections that describe what the form does, and how the form looks. This allows for flexible presentation options, including classic XHTML forms, to be attached to an XML form definition.

XML (Extensible Markup Language):

W3Cs standard for Internet Markup Languages. XML is one of these languages.

XML Linking:

XML Linking Language (XLink) allows elements to be inserted into XML documents in order to create and describe links between resources. It uses XML syntax to create structures that can describe the simple unidirectional hyperlinks of today's HTML, as well as more sophisticated links.

XML (Extensible Markup Language):

Designed to enable the use of SGML on the World Wide Web. XML is a metalanguage (a way to define tag sets) that allows you to design your own customized markup language for many classes of documents. XML is designed for easy and straightforward use of SGML on the web, ease of use in authoring and managing SGML documents, and ease of transmission and sharing of electronic documents across the web. XML is intended to deliver infomration, not just pages. XML preserves the key ideas of SGML, only simplifies them.

Xpath:

The purpose of XPath is to address parts of an XML document. In support of this basic purpose, it also provides basic facilities for manipulation of strings, numbers and booleans. XPath uses a compact, non-XML syntax to facilitate use of XPath within URIs and XML attribute values. XPath operates on the abstract, logical structure of an XML document, rather than its surface syntax. XPath gets its name from its use of a path notation as in URLs for navigating through the hierarchical structure of an XML document. Besides these, XPath is also designed so that it has a natural subset that can be used for matching (testing whether or not a node matches a pattern).

Xpointer:

XML Pointer Language (XPointer) is the language to be used as a fragment identifier for any URI-reference that locates a resource of Internet media type.

XSL:

Extensible Style Language (XSL) can handle tree transformations as well as document transformations, it permits XML documents to be displayed in different ways in response to different user queries, and it can support many languages, including historical texts like ancient Greek and Aztec.

Zooming:

Enlarging a portion of a digital image in order to see it more clearly or make it easier to alter.

BIBLIOGRAPHY

1. AGARWAL (S N), KHAN (R R) and SATYANARAYANA (N R)*Ed*. Perspectives in library and information science (Vo l – 2) Print house, Lucknow. 1982.
2. BESEMER (H) and Veerman (I). "Agricultural information on the Internet: What is out their and how to find it ", Quarterly Bulletin of IAALD 40 (2-3) p 60-67, 1995
3. BONN (George S), *Ed*. Library education and training in developing countries. East – west center press, Honolulu. 1967.
4. BOWEN (JP). "The World Wide Web Virtual library of Museums", Information services & use 15 p317-324 1995
5. BROWN (S). "The European Collaborative Backcross Database MBz is now available on the World Wide Web" Mammalian Genome 6(4) p223 1995
6. CLOYES (Key). "The journal from vision to reality of a virtual library", Special Libraries 85(4) p253-257 Fall 1994
7. CONTE (E). "Database on pesticides accessed through the internet", Proceedings of the first workshop of the European Network for information Technology in Agriculture, Rome, Italy, 28-29 Nov 1996 p155-162 1997
8. DALE (Sheila). Adult independent learning project: Work with adult self directed learners in public libraries. Journal of Librarianship. 11(2), April, 1979.
9. DAVIS (GL); GILMAN (E.F) and DECK (HW). "An electronically based horticultural information retrieval system", HortTechnology 6(4) p332-336 1996
10. DEWAY (J). Democracy and education. Macmillan, New York, 1916.

11. FAURE (E)...et.al. Learning to be: The world of today and tomorrow. UNESCO, Paris. 1970.

12. FOWELL (S) and LEVY (P). Developing a new professional practice: A model for networked learner support in higher education. Journal of Documentation. 51, 3; 1995; 271– 280.

13. GEORGE (KM) *ed.,* Indian Libraries: Trends and perspectives. Calcutta, Orient Longman, 1985.

14. GOLDEN (BL), "The World Wide Web: HTML, CGI and Java application in animal Breeding", Proceedings of 6th world congress on Genetics Applied to live stocks production, Armidale, Australia, Jan 11 - 16, 1998 p409-414 1998

15. GUPTA (Pawan) and Usha, Education Policy and public libraries. ILA Bulletin. 21 (3-4), 1985-96 PP. 111 - 117.

16. HARBERS (GW); HOOGENBOON (G), " The use of real-time database applications to develop dynamic web content for information delivery in time of crisis", 2000 ASAE-Annual international meeting, Milwaualle, USA, 9-12 Jul 2000 p 1-10 2000

17. HARGER (C) et.al., "The Genome Sequence Database (GSDB) improving data quality and data access", Nucleic Acids Research 26(1) p21-26 1998

18. HARGER (C) et.al., "The Genome Sequence Database version 1.0 (GSDB): from the low pass sequence to complete genomes", Nuclic Acids Research 25(1) p18-23 1997

19. HENDRIK (Vandes Zee), The Public library as an opening centre. Journal of librarianship. 20 (1), Jan, 1988 PP. 1-15

20. HENEGHAN (PA) et.al., "Pond FX: An internet Tool for exploring invertebrate population recovery", Aspects of Applied Biology 53 p263-270 1999

21. HIGHAM (Norman). The library in the university: observations on a service. Andre Deutsch, London. 1980.

22. HUTCHINSON (B); HENZEL (J); RAM (S) and TIMMERMANN (B). "Managing information products for the Bioactive Agents from Dry land Biodiversity of Latin America Project", Quarterly BuHetin pf IAALD 44(3-4) P 163-172 1999

23. INDIA, Ministry of Human Resource and Development. National Policy on education. MHROD, New Delhi. 1986.

24. INDIA. Education commission (1964-66) (chairman: D.S. Kothari) Educational planning and the national policy. NCERT, Delhi. 1971.

25. INDIA. Government of India, "Report of III Planning Commission, 1960-1965" New Delhi

26. INDIA. Government of India, "Report of the Education Commission, 1964-1966", New Delhi, 1966

27. INDIA. U.G.C. Development of Library facilities in Universities and colleges. U.G.C. New Delhi.1968.

28. U.K. U.G.C. Committee on libraries (1963) Chairman: Thomas Parry) Report, HMSO, London. 1967.

29. INDIA. U.G.C. Committee on University and college libraries, (1957) (Chairman: S.R. Ranganathan). Report. U.G.C. New Delhi. 1965.

30. KENT (Allen) and LANCUR (Harold), *Ed.* Encyclopedia of Library and Information science. Marcel Decker, New York. 1972.

31. KOLASKAR (AS) and NAIK (PS). "Online identification of viruses" Journal of Microbiology, Immunology and infection 33(2) p69-78 2000

32. LAFONTAINE (DA); MERCURE (S); PASSION (V) and PARREAULT (JP). "The viriod liked RNA database", Nucleic Acids Research 26(1) p190-191 1998

33. LENGRAND (P). An introduction to life long education. UNESCO, Paris. 1970.

34. LEX, J. "Virtual agriculture: Agriculture in the information in the information society", Zeitschrift fur Agrainfomatik 3(6) p125-130 1995

35. LIN (Nan) et.al. "Decision information systems for citrus: software implementation and testing", Proceedings of the Florida State Horticultural Society, 1999 112 p40-43 2000

36. LOWRY (CB). "Putting the pieces together: Essential Technologies for the virtual library" Journal of Academic Librarionship, p297 -300 Jul 1995

37. MCKIERMAN (G). "Give them what they want: participatory development of a WWW agricultural database collection", Quarterly Bulletin oflAALD 42(3-4) p270-277 1997

38. MINCIONE (A); PUZONE (L) and HAZEKAMP (TH). "Internet and internet technologies applied to germplasm databases", Characterization and documentation of genetic resources utilizing multimedia databases proceedings p 17-21 1998

39. MISRA (BL). Universities without walls: The case of India, *Univ. News.* 26 (3) 1988; p. 3 - 5.

40. MITHCELL (S) and BALDWIN (CM). "INFOMINE; a unique virtual library of scholarly and educational resources in the agricultural and related sciences", Quarterly Bulletin oflAALD 42(3-4) p230-233. 1997

41. MOHAN RAJAN (PA). The relevance of second and third laws of library science on the role of public libraries in comrnunity information and distance education. *ILA Bulletin.23* (1-2) 1987. PP. 31 - 37.

42. MOHANTY (J). Educational broadcasting: Radio and television in education. Sterling publications, New Delhi.

43. MOORE (M). Learner autonomy: The second dimension of independent learning. *Convergence*.5, 1; 1972; p76-88.

44. NIMONIY (S); KIURA (T); ETO (K); NANSEKI (T) and UEDA (M). "Field image acquisition system on WWW", Journal of Society of High Technology in Agriculture 9(1) 1997; p12-19

45. OJALA (Marydee). "What will they call us in the future?", Special liabraries 84(4) Fall 1993; p 226

46. POWELL (A)."Management Models and measurement in the virtual library", Special Libraries 85 (4) Fall 1994; p260-263

47. RAFFEL (JA) and SHISKO (Robert). Systematic analysis of university Libraries. MIT Press, Cambridge. 1969.

48. RANGANATHAN (SR). Academic library system: Fourth plan period. *LSD.* 2; 1965; p.293-347.

49. ROWNTREE (D). Education technology in curriculum development. Harper and Raw, London.

50. SAHI (SS) and GUPTA (VK). Open lJniversity library. A conceptual analysis. ILA Bulletin. 21 (3-4) 1986; p.96-99.

51. SAHI (SS). Distance education system and library science.*University News* 25(11), March 1987; p. 6 - 8.

52. SCHMID (H); ZIEGLER (W) and POWELL (AP). "AGRIS and the internet", Quarterly bulletin of IAALD 41(1) 1996; p130-136

53. SEAGER (Daniel A). To maintain quality. Journal of education for librarianship. 4, 1; summer 1963; p.27 – 39.

54. SEATON (WJ). "Computer mediated communication and student self directed learning", Open learning 8(2) June 1993; p49-54

55. SHERA (Jesse H.). The foundations of education for librarianship. Wiley Becker and Hayes publication, New York. 1972.

56. SPRAGUE (J); DOERRY (E); DOUGLAS (S) and WESTERFIELD (M). "The Zebrafish Infonnation Network

(ZFIN): A resource for genetic, genomic and developmental research", Nucleic Acids Research 29(1) 2001; p.87-90

57. TAYLOR (Robert S). Making of a library: The academic library in transition Wiley, New York. 1972.

58. TSUKIBOSHI (T) and SHIMANUKI (T). "WWW image database system: Encyclopedias of forage crop diseases", Grassland Science 45(2) 1999; p.193-197

59. Universities handbook of India. Association of Indian Universities, New Delhi. 1999.

60. VASHISHT (CP) *ed.,.* New Education policy Vis-a-Vis library development. Delhi, ILA, 1986.

61. VERMA (SC). New education policy and libraries. ILA Bulletin. 21 (3-4), 1985–86; p.100-106.

62. WALLDE (BV) and SCHILLER (N). "Creating the virtual Library: Strategic issues in the virtual library: Vision and realities" , West Port: CT:Mekler, 1993; p15-46

63. WHEELER (DL) et.al.. "Databases resources of the National Center for Biotechnology Information" , Nucleic Acids Research 29(1) 2001; p.11-16

64. ZIGERELL (J). Distance education: An information age approach to adult education. Ohio, National Centre for Research in Vocational Education, 1984.

REFERENCES

1. http://www.w3.org/2002/08/02-DOM-Disclosures.html
2. http://www.w3.org/2003/06/09-dom-core-issues/issues.html
3. http://www.w3.org/2002/10/DOM-Level-3-Val-issues
4. http://www.w3.org/2002/07/DOM-Level-3-Events-issues
5. http://www.w3.org/TR/2001/WD-DOM-Requirements-20010419/
6. http://lists.w3.org/Archives/Public/www-html-editor/
7. http://www.w3.org/MarkUp/Test/
8. http://lists.w3.org/Archives/Public/www-html-editor/
9. http://cgi.w3.org/MemberAccess/
10. http://www.rfc-editor.org/rfc/rfc2854.txt
11. http://lists.w3.org/Archives/Public/www-html/
12. http://www.w3.org/Talks/1999/05/www8-html/slide1.html
13. http://www.w3.org/Talks/1999/12/XHTML-XML99/slide1.html
14. http://www.gca.org/attend/1999_conferences/xml_99/
15. http://www.w3.org/2001/09/21-orf/xhtml-family/
16. http://www.kri.sfc.keio.ac.jp/ORF/2001/
17. http://www.w3.org/Talks/2002/04/11-pemberton
18. http://www.w3.org/Consortium/Offices/Germany/Events/Cross-Media-Publishing
19. http://www.w3.org/2002/Talks/www2002-xhtml/
20. http://www2002.org/> W3C Track http://www2002.org/w3ctrack.html
21. http://www.w3.org/2002/Talks/www2002-xhtml/Overview.xhtml

22. http://www.w3.org/2002/Talks/www2002-xhtml/Overview.html
23. http://www2003.org/> W3C Track http://www.w3.org/2003/03/w3c-track03.html
24. http://www.w3.org/2003/Talks/www2003-steven-horizontal/
25. http://www.w3.org/TR/WCAG10
26. http://www.w3.org/MarkUp/Guide/Style
27. http://www.boutell.com/faq/
28. http://lists.w3.org/Archives/Public/www-html/
29. http://lists.w3.org/Archives/Public/www-html-editor/
30. http://www.w3.org/2002/09/aa/
31. http://cgi.w3.org/MemberAccess/AccessRequest
32. http://lists.w3.org/Archives/Public/w3c-translators/
33. http://www.rfc-editor.org/rfc/rfc2557.txt
34. http://www.w3.org/MarkUp/HTML-WG
35. http://www2003.org/
36. http://tidy.sourceforge.net/
37. http://lists.w3.org/Archives/Public/html-tidy/
38. http://www.webreview.com/2000/06_16/webauthors/06_16_00_3.shtml
39. http://cgi.w3.org/cgi-bin/tidy
40. http://check.theinfo.org/html/tidy
41. http://valet.htmlhelp.com/tidy/
42. http://www.w3.org/People/Raggett/dtdgen/Docs/
43. http://www.w3.org/People/Raggett/tidy
44. http://www.w3.org/Talks/1999/03/24-stockholm-xhtml/
45. http://lists.w3.org/Archives/Public/www-math
46. http://camel.math.ca/mail/webmath/
47. http://www.dessci.com/en/support/tutorials/mathml/default.htm

48. http://www.charlesriver.com/titles/mathml.html
49. http://www.w3.org/People/maxf/papers/iamc.ps
50. http://www.mathtype.com/en/reference/webmath/status/status_Sep_02.htm
51. http://www.mathweb.org
52. http://www.ams.org/mathweb
53. http://www.mathmlcentral.com/
54. http://www.dessci.com/en/reference/webmath/tech/mathml.htm
55. http://www.oasis-open.org/cover/topics.html
56. http://www.zvon.org/HowTo/Output/index.html
57. http://pear.math.pitt.edu/mathzilla/
58. http://www.activemath.org/
59. http://mathforum.org/
60. http://www.joma.org/
61. http://www.w3.org/TR/2003/WD-MathML2-20030411/
62. http://www.w3.org/Consortium/Process-20010719/tr.html
63. http://www.w3c.or.kr/Translation/Math/XSL/Overview-Korean.html
64. http://www.soft4science.com
65. http://www.charlesriver.com/titles/mathml.html
66. http://www-dft.ts.infn.it/mathml/
67. http://mathosphere.net/editeurml/doc_english.html
68. http://mathosphere.net/editeurml/WeM.html
69. http://mathosphere.net/outils/index.html
70. http://www.w3.org/Math/testsuite
71. http://www.dessci.com/webmath/mathplayer
72. http://www.w3.org/Math/XSL/Overview-Chinese.html
73. http://eenk.new21.org/Math/XSL/Overview-Korean.html
74. http://www.w3.org/Math/XSL/pmathml2.xml

75. http://www.w3.org/Math/XSL/csmall2.xml
76. http://www.w3.org/TR/MathML2/chapter3.html
77. http://www.w3.org/Math/charter.HTML
78. http://www.w3.org/TR/REC-MathML/chapter2.HTML
79. http://www.w3.org/Math/Group/needs/MathMLRequ.html
80. http://www.w3.org/MarkUp/CoordGroup
81. http://www.w3.org/Math/Group/needs/MathMLRequ.html
82. http://www.adobe.com/
83. http://www.ams.org/
84. http://www.mathtype.com/mathtype/
85. http://www.elsevier.nl/
86. http://www.webeq.com/
87. http://www.ics.raleigh.ibm.com/ics/techexp.htm
88. http://www.mathsoft.com
89. http://www.uwaterloo.ca/
90. http://www.inria.fr/Equipes/SAFIR-eng.HTML
91. http://www.stilo.com
92. http://www.sq.com/
93. http://www.csd.uwo.ca/
94. http://www.maplesoft.com/
95. http://www.wri.com/
96. http://www.mathtype.com
97. http://www.w3.org/MarkUp/CoordGroup/9802/xml-in-html
98. http://www.w3.org/MarkUp/future/
99. http://www.w3.org/TR/WD-math/
100. http://www.dessci.com/webmath/mathplayer
101. http://www.nag.co.uk/projects/OpenMath/mml-files/
102. http://www.w3.org/People/Raggett/EzMath/
103. http://www.mathcad.com

104. http://www.wolfram.com

105. http://www.newmexico.mackichan.com/mathml/mathmled.htm

106. http://www.mathmlconference.org/2002/tutorials.html

107. http://www.w3.org/Math

108. http://www.mathmlconference.org/2002

109. http://www.adobe.com/acrofamily/main.html

110. http://www.dessci.com/en/reference/webmath/status/ </en/reference/webmath/status/

111. http://www.w3.org

112. http://www.dessci.com/en/products/mathplayer/ </en/products/mathplayer/

113. http://www.microsoft.com/windows/ie/default.asp

114. http://www.dessci.com/en/products/webeq/ </en/products/webeq/

115. http://www.mozilla.org

116. http://channels.netscape.com/ns/browsers/7/default.jsp

117. http://www.w3.org/Style/XSL/

118. http://www.w3.org/Math/XSL/

119. http://www.dessci.com/en/reference/webmath/strategies.htm

120. http://www.mathmlconference.org/2002/tutorials.html

121. http://www.w3.org/TR/MathML2/chapter2.html#fund_overview

122. http://cnx.rice.edu/

123. http://www.ams.org/msc/

124. http://www.openmath.org/

125. http://www.wolfram.com

126. http://www.maplesoft.com

127. http://www.mowgli.cs.unibo.it

128. http://www-2.cs.cmu.edu/~ccaps/

129. http://www.dessci.com/en/products/mathtype/ </en/ products/mathtype/
130. http://www.mathmlcentral.com/
131. http://www.ecollege.com/stories/press_08_14_02.html
132. http://www.ecollege.com/stories/press_05_15_02.html
133. http://jigsaw.w3.org/new.html
134. http://lists.w3.org/Archives/Public/www-jigsaw/
135. http://jigsaw.w3.org/
136. http://www.latoserver.it/jigsaw/
137. http://www.w3.org/pub/WWW/COPYRIGHT.html
138. http://dev.w3.org/cvsweb/~checkout~/java/classes/org/ w3c/jigsaw/https/readme.txt?rev=1.1&content-type=text/ plain
139. http://jigsaw.w3.org/Winie/
140. http://www.w3.org/1999/04/Editing/
141. http://www.webdav.org/
142. http://lists.w3.org/Archives/Public/www-jigsaw/
143. http://jigsaw.w3.org/Doc/JigsawDoc.pdf
144. http://jigsaw.w3.org/Doc/JigsawDoc.ps.gz
145. http://jigsaw.w3.org/Distrib/jigsaw_2.2.2.zip
146. http://jigsaw.w3.org/Distrib/jigsaw_2.2.2.tar.gz
147. http://jigsaw.w3.org/Distrib/jigsaw_2.2.2.tar.bz2
148. http://jigsaw.w3.org/Devel/Mirror/jigsaw_2.0.5.zip
149. http://jigsaw.w3.org/Devel/Mirror/jigsaw_2.0.5.tar.gz
150. http://jigsaw.w3.org/Devel/Mirror/jigsaw_2.0.5.tar.bz2
151. http://jigsaw.w3.org/Devel/Mirror/ jigsaw_webdav_2.1.2.zip
152. http://jigsaw.w3.org/Devel/Mirror/ jigsaw_webdav_2.1.2.tar.gz
153. http://jigsaw.w3.org/Devel/Mirror/ jigsaw_webdav_2.1.2.tar.bz2

154. ftp://ftp.w3.org/pub/jigsaw/jigsaw.zip
155. ftp://ftp.w3.org/pub/jigsaw/jigsaw.tar.gz
156. http://www.w3.org/TR/2002/NOTE-photo-rdf-20020419
157. http://www.w3.org/TR/photo-rdf
158. http://www.w3.org/TR/2000/NOTE-photo-rdf-20000928/
159. http://www.w3.org/Consortium/Legal/ipr-notice-20000612
160. http://www.w3.org/Consortium/Legal/ipr-notice-20000612
161. http://www.w3.org/Consortium/Legal/ipr-notice-20000612
162. http://dublincore.org/documents/2000/07/11/dcmi-type-vocabulary/
163. http://lists.w3.org/Archives/Public/www-smil/
164. http://www.roxia.co.kr
165. http://www.alphaworks.ibm.com/tech/tk4mpeg4
166. http://www.psych.uiuc.edu/~kmiller/dvguide/analysis_tools.htm
167. http://www.psych.uiuc.edu/~kmiller/smil/smil_umbrella.htm
168. http://www.smilmedia.com/
169. http://k-tai.impress.co.jp/cda/article/news_toppage/13103.html
170. http://developer.openwave.com/technotes/client_mms_capabilities.html
171. http://www.w3.org/TR/smil20
172. http://www.smilmedia.com/spec/spec1~7.htm
173. http://www.w3.org/TR/XHTMLplusSMIL/
174. http://www.w3.org/2001/SMIL20/testsuite/
175. http://www.w3.org/2001/05/23/SMIL-Implementation-result.html

176. http://www.mobilemms.com/mmsfaq.asp

177. http://lightning.prohosting.com/~qqiu/smil/trans/REC-smil-19980615-cn.html

178. http://www.sunshine-company.de/w3c/REC-smil-19980615-DE.html

179. http://www.w3c.cnr.it/office/traduzioni/REC-smil-it.html

180. http://www.doraneko.org/misc/smil10/smil10.html

181. http://www.mentallink.com/resource/smil/smil10-kr.html

182. http://www.utad.pt/~leonelm/w3ctranslations/smil/

183. http://smil.nist.gov/Testcase.html

184. http://smil.nist.gov/Feature.html

185. http://service.real.com/help/library/guides/production/realpgd.htm

186. http://developer.apple.com/techpubs/quicktime/qtdevdocs/PDF/insideqt_intmov.pdf

187. http://www.computer.org/multimedia/mu2001/pdf/u4082.pdf

188. http://www.xml.com/pub/a/2002/05/29/smil.html

189. http://www.allhtml.com/smil/index.php

190. http://www.smilbook.com/

191. http://www.w3.org/Talks/2001/06CSMIL/slide1-0.html

192. http://developer.openwave.com/technotes/client_mms_capabilities.html

193. http://www.webtechniques.com/archives/1998/09/bouthillier/

194. http://www.cwi.nl/~media/SMIL/Tutorial/

195. http://www.helio.org/products/smil/tutorial/

196. http://www.empirenet.com/~joseram/index.html

197. http://webreview.com/wr/pub/1999/03/12/feature/index.html

198. http://www.kevlindev.com/basics/index.htm

199. http://www.kevlindev.com/

200. http://www.empirenet.com/~joseram/universal/universal.html

201. http://aristote1.aristote.asso.fr/Presentations/Smil/Courtaud/SMIL-Presentation-fr.smi

202. http://www.euroclid.fr/Cours_SMIL_W3C/

203. http://v.hbi-stuttgart.de/~keitz/skripte/SMILStart.htm

204. http://lists.w3.org/Archives/Public/www-smil/

205. http://realforum.real.com/cgi-bin/realforum/postlist.pl?Cat=&Board=ccsmil

206. http://www.real.com

207. http://www.html.it/smil/index.html

208. http://www.realnetworks.com/solutions/ecosystem/realone.html?src=rnhmfs

209. http://www.oratrix.com/GRiNS/SMIL-2.0/

210. http://www.inobject.com/mmplay.htm

211. http://www.inobject.com/InterObjectSMILPlayerSpecification.htm

212. http://www.microsoft.com/windows/ie/preview/default.asp

213. http://www.w3.org/TR/2001/WD-XHTMLplusSMIL-20010807/

214. http://www.microsoft.com/windows/ie/default.htm

215. http://msdn.microsoft.com/workshop/Author/behaviors/htmltime.asp

216. http://k-tai.impress.co.jp/cda/article/news_toppage/13103.html

217. http://wam.inrialpes.fr/software/pocketsmil/

218. http://www.roxia.co.kr

219. http://lists.w3.org/Archives/Public/www-mobile/2002Aug/0007.html

220. http://www.oratrix.com/GRiNS/index.html
221. http://www.research.digital.com/SRC/HPAS
222. http://www.prodworks.com/
223. http://www.apple.com/quicktime/authoring/qtsmil.html
224. http://www.real.com/
225. http://www.helio.org
226. http://smil.nist.gov/player
227. http://www.salzburgresearch.at/suntrec/schmunzel/
228. http://www.xsmiles.org/
229. http://www.smilmedia.com
230. http://www.confluenttechnologies.com
231. http://www.oratrix.com/GRiNS/index.html
232. http://www.adobe.com/products/golive/overview.html
233. http://www.allaire.com/products/homesite/index.cfm
234. http://ncam.wgbh.org/webaccess/magpie
235. http://www.libpng.org/pub/png/
236. http://www.libpng.org/pub/png/pngdocs.html
237. http://www.w3.org/Graphics/PNG/
238. http://www.libpng.org/pub/png/pngapps.html
239. http://www.jpeg.org/
240. http://www.iso.ch/
241. http://www.jpeg.org/CDs15444.html
242. http://www.lizardtech.com/solutions/geospatial/
243. http://www.lizardtech.com/solutions/document/
244. http://www.djvu.com/solutions/document/whitepaper/
245. http://www.djvuzone.org/
246. http://www.planetdjvu.com/
247. http://djvu.sourceforge.net/
248. http://www.lizardtech.com/

249. http://www.celartem.com/

250. http://www.extensis.com/pxlsmartscale/

251. http://www.hisoftware.com/hmcc/acc4mcc.html

252. http://www.simple.co.jp/products/10MovieBorad.htm

253. http://lists.w3.org/Archives/Public/www-mobile/2002Aug/0007.html

254. http://www.webiphany.com/perlysmil/

255. http://forms.real.com/rnforms/products/tools/slideshowbasic/index.html?key=868E21032182964

256. http://autodownload.sausage.com

257. http://smibase.com/

258. http://www.docomo-sys.co.jp/prod/soft/smil2.html

259. http://www.smilgen.org

260. http://www.smilme.com

261. http://w3-mcgav.lab.kdd.co.jp/sc/indexe.html

262. http://tag.digital-ren.com

263. http://www.tagfree.com/english/product/product02.asp?menu=2

264. http://www.psych.uiuc.edu/~kmiller/dvguide/analysis_tools.htm

265. http://www.veon.com/

266. http://www.cwi.nl/~media/symm/validator/

267. http://www.smilmedia.com.

268. http://www.alphaworks.ibm.com/tech/tk4mpeg4

269. http://www.justsmil.com

270. http://www.wgbh.org/wgbh/pages/ncam/webaccess/captionedmovies.html

271. http://www.w3.org/TR/SVG/

272. http://www.w3.org/TR/1999/WD-SVG-19990211

273. http://www.oreilly.com/catalog/learnxml/index.html?CMP=IL7015

274. http://www.oreilly.com/catalog/learnxml/index.html?CMP=IL7015

275. http://www.oreillynet.com/cs/catalog/view/au/752?x-t=book.view&CMP=IL7015

276. http://www.oreilly.com/catalog/learnxml/toc.html?CMP=IL7015

277. http://www.oreilly.com/catalog/learnxml/inx.html?CMP=IL7015

278. http://www.oreilly.com/catalog/learnxml/chapter/index.html?CMP=IL7015

279. http://xml.oreilly.com/news/learningxml_0101.html?CMP=IL7015

280. http://safari.oreilly.com/0596000464

281. http://www.adobe.com/svg/viewer/install/

282. http://www.adobe.com/svg/

283. http://www.croczilla.com/SVG

284. http://www.xmlspy.com/

285. http://www.w3.org/TR/SVG11/

286. http://www.w3.org/TR/SVG/

287. http://www.w3.org/TR/SVGMobile/

288. http://www.w3.org/TR/SVG12

289. http://www.w3.org/Graphics/SVG/

290. http://www.w3.org/Graphics/SVG/Test/

291. http://www.peoplesnetwork.gov.uk/nof/technicalstandards.html/

292. http://heds.herts.ac.uk/resources/costing.html/

293. http://heds.herts.ac.uk/resources/matrix.html/

294. http://www.rlg.ac.uk/preserv/diginews/diginews3-5.html/

295. http://www.leeds.ac.uk/cedars/

296. http://www.bl.uk/services/preservation/digcult.html/

297. http://heds.herts.ac.uk/resources/papers/jidi_fs.html/

298. http://www.tasi.ac.uk/framework/capture/image.html/
299. http://www.epi-centre.com/basics/basics2.html/
300. http://www.image-acquire.com/scanner/
301. http://www.rlg.org/preserv/diginews/diginews3.html#hardware&software
302. http://www.rlg.org/preserv/diginews/diginews3.html
303. http://www.imaging-resource.com/
304. http://www.epi-centre.com/reports/reports.html/
305. http://www.tasi.ac.uk/framework/capture/camera.html/
306. http://www.cimtech.co.uk/cimtech/pub/p1.htm/
307. http://www.jstor.org/
308. http://imago.library.mcgill.ca/osler
309. http://www.xerox.com/scansoft/pagis
310. http://antonio.emeraldinsight.com/rpsv/cgi-bin/linker?ext=y&ref=23817bb1-3
311. http://computer.org/ computer/dli/index.html/
312. http://www.nlc-bnc.ca/cidl/cidle.html/
313. http://www.dlib.org/dlib/july97/07chesnutt.tml
314. http://antonio.emeraldinsight.com/rpsv/cgi-bin/linker?ext=y&ref=23817bb1-7
315. http://www.gii. getty.du/index/imaginit.html
316. http://www.mellon.org/jsback.tm
317. http://www.jstor.org/about/production.html
318. http://www.princeton.edu/cit/campus_com/jstorsep
319. http://www.nlc-bnc.ca/pubs/netnotes/notes14
320. http://www.princeton.edu/cit/campus_com/jstor2.tml
321. http://www.rlg.org/preserv/
322. http://www.geom.umn.du/docs/cecm/steinberger/talk.html
323. http://www.orbeon.com/oxf/doc/processors-xforms
324. http://www.alphaworks.ibm.com/tech/xmlforms

325. http://www.xmlform.org

326. http://www.formsplayer.com/

327. http://www.xsmiles.org/features_xforms.html

328. http://www.novell.com/xforms

329. http://www.w3.org/TR/2002/CR-xforms-20021112/

330. http://www.w3.org/2002/11/xforms-pressrelease

331. http://www.w3.org/2002/11/xforms-cr-testimonial.html

332. http://www.w3.org/TR/2002/CR-xforms-20021112/http://lists.w3.org/Archives/Public/www-forms-editor/

333. http://www.FormsPlayer.com/

334. http://www.novell.com/xforms

335. http://trustform.comsquare.co.kr

336. http://www.achieveforms.com

337. http://jxforms.cybernd.at/

338. http://www.handwise.com/Products/XFUI.html

339. http://www.holosofx.com/x_form.htm

340. http://sourceforge.net/projects/xserverforms

341. http://www.alphaworks.ibm.com/tech/xmlforms

342. http://www.orbeon.com/oxf/doc/processors-xforms

343. http://www.formfaces.com/

344. http://www.nforms.net/

345. http://www.w3.org/TR/xforms

346. http://www.cardiff.com/XForms

347. http://www.w3.org/TR/1999/REC-xpath-19991116

348. http://www.w3.org/TR/1999/REC-xpath-19991116.xml

349. http://www.w3.org/TR/1999/REC-xpath-19991116.html

350. http://www.w3.org/TR/xpath

351. http://www.w3.org/TR/1999/PR-xpath-19991008

352. http://www.w3.org/1999/08/WD-xpath-19990813

353. http://www.w3.org/1999/07/WD-xpath-19990709

354. http://www.w3.org/TR/1999/WD-xslt-19990421

355. http://www.w3.org/1999/11/REC-xpath-19991116-erratahttp://lists.w3.org/Archives/Public/www-xpath-comments

356. http://validator.w3.org

357. http://validator.w3.org/about.html

358. http://validator.w3.org/source/

359. http://validator.w3.org/checklink

360. http://www.w3.org/2000/07/checklink

361. http://dev.w3.org/cvsweb/validator/httpd/cgi-bin/checklink.pl

362. http://jigsaw.w3.org/css-validator/

363. http://jigsaw.w3.org/css-validator/README

364. http://jigsaw.w3.org/css-validator/DOWNLOAD.html

365. http://www.w3.org/RDF/Validator/>

366. http://www.w3.org/P3P/validator

367. http://dev.w3.org/cvsweb/p3p-validator/20020128/

368. http://www.w3.org/QA/Tools/LogValidator/

369. http://www.w3.org/QA/Tools/MUTAT/

370. http://www.w3.org/Protocols/HTTP/Forum/

371. http://lists.w3.org/Archives/Public/www-html/1994Jul/0015

372. http://www.w3.org/QA/Tools/LogValidator/Manual

373. http://www.w3.org/P3P/compliant_sites

374. http://www.w3.org/P3P/validator/20000510/

375. http://www.w3.org/P3P/validator/20020128/p3p.xml

376. http://www.w3.org/P3P/validator/20020128/base.xml

377. http://dev.w3.org/cvsweb/p3p-validator/20020128/

378. http://www.w3.org/TR/REC-CSS2/

379. http://lists.w3.org/Archives/Member/w3c-voice-wg/2003Feb/0084.html

380. http://cgi.w3.org/MemberAccess/AccessRequest
381. http://lists.w3.org/Archives/Public/www-voice/
382. http://www.voicexml.org/
383. http://www.speechtechmag.com/
384. http://www.kenrehor.com/voicexml/
385. http://www.speech.cs.cmu.edu/openvxi/
386. http://www.heyanita.com/
387. http://www-3.ibm.com/software/pervasive/products/voice/voice_technologies.shtml
388. http://www.intervoice.com/
389. http://www.loquendo.com/
390. http://www.loquendocafe.com/
391. http://fife.speech.cs.cmu.edu/openvxi/
392. http://www.speechworks.com/
393. http://www.pipebeach.com
394. http://www.publicvoicexml.org/
395. http://sourceforge.net/projects/publicvoicexml/
396. http://www.speechworks.com/
397. http://www.voicegenie.com/
398. http://developer.voicegenie.com
399. http://www.voxpilot.com/
400. http://ode.voxpilot.com/
401. http://www.microsoft.com/speech/
402. http://www.w3.org/WAI/GL/2003/07/f2f-agenda.html
403. http://www.w3.org/WAI/UA/impl-pr2/
404. http://www.w3.org/WAI/UA/TS/
405. http://www.w3.org/WAI/UA/2002/08/eval
406. http://www.w3.org/WAI/events.html
407. http://www.w3.org/WAI/events.html
408. http://www.w3.org/WAI/about.html

409. http://www.w3.org/WAI/about.html
410. http://www.w3.org/WAI/about.html
411. http://www.w3.org/WAI/contacts.html
412. http://www.cgmopen.org/
413. http://www.cgmopen.org/webcgmintro/paper.htm
414. http://www.cgmopen.org/
415. http://www.w3.org/2001/12/xmlbp/xml-linking-wg-charter.html
416. http://www.w3.org/TR/xlink/
417. http://www.w3.org/TR/xmlbase/
418. http://www.w3.org/2001/06/link-base-pressrelease
419. http://www.sun.com/software/xml/developers/xlink.html
420. http://www.xmlsoftware.com/xlink/
421. http://www.simonstl.com/projects/xlinkfilter/resources.html
422. http://www.zvon.org/xxl/xlink/Output/xlink_refs.html
423. http://www.zvon.org/xxl/xlink/xlink_extend/OutputExamples/frame_xlinkextend_html.html
424. http://www.w3.org/TR/2003/REC-xptr-framework-20030325/
425. http://www.cs.unibo.it/~fabio/XPointer/
426. http://www.google.com/search?q=XML+Conferences
427. http://www.google.com/search?q=XML+books
428. http://www.google.com/search?q=XML+training+courses
429. http://www.google.com/search?q=XML+online+tutorials
430. http://www.google.com/search?q=XML+bibliography
431. http://www.google.com/search?q=XML+parser
432. http://www.google.com/search?q=XML+magazines
433. http://www.google.com/search?q=%22XML+movie%22
434. http://www.w3.org/TR/2001/REC-xmlbase-20010627/

435. http://www.w3.org/TR/2001/REC-xmlbase-20010627/Overview.html
436. http://www.w3.org/TR/2001/REC-xmlbase-20010627/Overview.xml
437. http://www.w3.org/TR/xmlbase/
438. http://www.w3.org/TR/2000/PR-xmlbase-20001220/
439. http://www.w3.org/XML/Activity
440. http://www.w3.org/2001/06/xmlbase-translations
441. http://lists.w3.org/Archives/Public/xml-encryption/
442. http://www.w3.org/TR/xml-encryption-req
443. http://www.w3.org/TR/xmlenc-decrypt
444. http://lists.w3.org/Archives/Public/xml-encryption/
445. http://www.w3.org/2000/09/XML-Encryption-Workshop.html
446. http://www.w3.org/Signature/2001/04/05-xmldsig-interop.html
447. http://www.w3.org/TR/xmldsig-core/
448. http://jcewww.iaik.tu-graz.ac.at/products/ixsil/index.php
449. http://www.ubisecure.com/index.php?page=ubisignature
450. http://www.xmltrustcenter.org/xmlsig/developer/verisign/index.htm
451. http://www.wedgetail.com/xmlsecurity/
452. http://www.w3.org/TR/xmldsig-requirements
453. http://www.w3.org/TR/1999/REC-xpath-19991116.xml
454. http://www.w3.org/TR/1999/REC-xpath-19991116.html
455. http://www.w3.org/TR/xpath
456. http://www.w3.org/TR/1999/PR-xpath-19991008
457. http://www.w3.org/1999/08/WD-xpath-19990813
458. http://www.w3.org/1999/07/WD-xpath-19990709 http://www.w3.org/TR/1999/WD-xslt-19990421

INDEX